HEROES OF THE REFORMATION

HEROES
OF THE
REFORMATION

GIDEON DAVID HAGSTOTZ, PH.D.
&
HILDA BOETTCHER HAGSTOTZ, PH.D.

Published and Distributed by
Hartland Publications
PO Box 1
Rapidan, Virginia 22733, USA

Cover design:
Richard Ramont

Cover photo:
Janet Evert

ISBN 0-923309-48-9

To
Our Twin Nieces
Beatrice and Bernice

PREFACE

BEFORE reading a book some persons turn to the last page to determine the length; others leaf through it to see the illustrations, if any; still others without preliminaries begin at the beginning and start reading; but a few, a very few, wanting to know why or how the book ever came to be written, as well as a few things about the author, turn to the preface, if perchance there they may find the answer to their query. To such inquiring readers we wish to say that this book grew up somewhat after the nature of Topsy: it began without any inclinations or aspirations to become a book.

The first impetus to writing about any of these heroes began more than four years ago in the request for a series of articles for the *Signs of the Times*. Inspired by the words of John Ruskin, who said that if he wanted to learn about a subject he wrote a book on it, we proceeded to write the articles, G. D. as researcher and author, and H. B. as amanuensis and typist. Each wrote some essays in their entirety, but more often the two of us did research and collaboration, writing, and rewriting each other's work, until now it is often difficult to tell where the labor of one ends and that of the other begins.

In the process of gathering material on many of the lesser known, yet equally important, heroes for this volume, it became H. B.'s privilege to study at the Huntington Library, San Marino, California, as well as at other leading libraries in the West.

Thus Topsy has grown into a full-fledged book. Not only that, but there are plans on foot for more on the heroes of the Reformation in the nations of Southern Europe, a somewhat neglected field, and on the still more ignored subject of heroines of the Reformation —those women, of whom there were scores, who stood shoulder to shoulder with the men in the promulgation of the gospel.

Should the reader desire to know anything about us personally, we refer you to the hundreds of students who have passed through our college classroom doors and who have given us the inspiration to carry on. If their opinion of us is a tithe as great as ours is of them, the heroes and heroines of our modern day, then our reputation rests in safe hands.   G. D. H. and H. B. H.

CONTENTS

Italy

Poland

Scandinavia

Spain

Switzerland

INTRODUCTION

THE twentieth century should be impressed by the legacy of human freedom bequeathed by the Protestant Reformation. Without question Western man was directly and indirectly emancipated by the spirit of the mighty leaders of reform. The Bible, so long closed from the laymen by the clergy, was opened for all men to read. The feudal remnants, which clung like chains to civilization, were shattered by the blows of freedom-loving men. The freedom of the believer to be his own "priest," the freedom from burdensome and hollow sacramentalism, and the freedom of conscience and worship —all of these stem from the Reformation's influence on the human mind.

The authors of this volume have brought together a comprehensive picture of the leaders of the Reformation who arose in every part of Europe. Here were heroes of the cross, who were willing to suffer persecution and death in order that the faith they held dear might be kindled in a thousand other lives. Their basic faith has come down to modern Protestantism from the church of the apostles. It is well for us to remember, too, that "when Protestantism is true to Him who was crucified and risen, it is strong; when it diverts from His word and spirit, it becomes decadent and disintegrates."

The faith and freedom bequeathed to us must be preserved in our day. We must know of the sacrifices and aims, the beliefs and hopes of the Reformation leaders who blazed the way out of the darkness of the Middle Ages. The authors of this volume are to be congratulated on their sincere endeavor to make the men of Protestantism live anew in the hearts of this generation.

MERLIN L. NEFF.

PROTESTANT REFORMATION

What Was It?

W HAT is meant by the term, Prot-
estant Reformation? To some people it denotes a religious fascination bordering on the miraculous. To others it is synonymous with
the name of Martin Luther. Some think of it as a series of changes
in religious ideas which developed out of the controversies engendered by the Ninety-Five Theses. And to still others the name con-
jures up a sudden and phenomenal emergence of most of Western
Europe from the despotic control of the church, a burst of freedom
created by the intellectual and religious impact of a new set of values
never known or thought of before.

Actually the Reformation came not as the result of any one
idea or any single overt act; many factors aided the rise of this
mighty movement, but it took many years to arrive. It came not
as a miracle or as the work of one or more brave souls, but as the
result of different factors, working many times apparently at cross-
purposes. Neither did reform activities spring exclusively from
religious leaders: The princes of Germany, the nobles of France,
the citizens of Switzerland, and the kings of England and Sweden
—all interested in prevailing conditions—played stellar parts in this
moving sixteenth-century drama.

The various developments in the dual status of the church as
an ecclesiastic and temporal power, as well as the varied views
supported by the reigning monarchs and princes of the period, at
times hindered as well as advanced the arrival of the Reformation.
The work of the Humanists, too, contributed to the unrest of the
time and added impetus to the movement as it increased its objections to the religious status quo.

But through all, the hand of God guided the development of

conditions which ushered in the turbulent period of the Reformation.

> God moves in a mysterious way
> His wonders to perform.

To understand how freedom came to the individual from the universal dominance of papal authority, as well as surcease to temporal powers from the taxing prowess of the church and its interference in the legal processes of government, one needs to trace the development of various lines of human aspirations preceding the decades of the Reformation. By the term "freedom," as here used, is meant the right to formulate one's own religious conclusions, unhampered by dogma. Such a procedure constituted a first approach during the eras of both the Renaissance and the Reformation. It implied the acceptance of sound reasoning as applied to Scriptural interpretations as a whole, the relegating of tradition to nothing more than subtle presentations of circumstantial evidence.

Causes of the Reformation

Historians, both ecclesiastical and secular, agree substantially on the causes which combined to give the setting for this period. As has already been stated, there was no one reason, nor should it be supposed that the causes can be rigidly listed in sequence of importance. Yet from the time shortly following the Crusades to the time of the Reformation there developed an increased popular feeling that changes in religious matters were greatly needed. Commonly listed causes for the appearance of the Reformation include the following:

1. The growth of national states.
2. Printing and its impetus to learning.
3. The activity of the Humanists.
4. Changes in the economic outlook.
5. Troubles in the Holy Roman Empire.
6. Decentralized government in Germany.
7. A growing spirit of religious enthusiasm.
8. The abuses in the church.

Only a brief view may be taken of each of these topics; yet sufficient material will be presented to enable the reader to catch a glimpse of the meshing conditions and factors which show that the Reformation resulted from many situations rather than from any one specific cause.

1. Prior to the marked development of centralized monarchies in Western Europe the church held undisputed sway. Taxation and appeals to the higher courts were the prerogatives of the church. The feudal system left in the control of the papacy large areas of land from which the state received no revenue. In Sweden the church held two thirds of the land and in England between a third and two fifths, and the proportion in favor of the papacy in Hungary and Germany showed a still more deplorable ratio. Such vast holdings enriched the church, but resulted in a depletion of national revenues.

As monarchies developed, clashes of other interests were bound to arise, for both the government and the church needed money. Who was to be supreme? When a matter of taxation failed to be satisfactorily settled in a governmental court, appeal was possible to a papal court. Yet the church was under the control of a foreign power which had its seat in Rome.

As the states grew stronger, more and more power disappeared from the church to find lodgment in the state. Repeated frictions of this type often led to open warfare, with the power of the state growing ever stronger at the expense of the church. The result was a growing antagonism by the people toward a church which sought for temporal power without giving much in return.

2. The development of printing brought with it possibilities of enlightening the rank and file of the middle and upper classes. It razed the walls of medieval ignorance, and the people suddenly learned more than the church had taught; many fields of knowledge became common property. Printing as an art and a profession expanded apace. Before 1500 more than 30,000 separate publications had been issued, and fifteen editions of the Bible appeared in Germany before the open revolt against the papal power occurred.

As general information became available, many persons refused to stay in blind submission to the papacy, with its claims of divine origin. Printing fostered an upsurge of intellectual pursuits; men chose to follow reason in preference to the supposed authority of the clergy.

3. Playing very effectively into this awakened intellectual growth came a group of individuals knows as Humanists. They called attention to the Bible as the source of faith for a Christian. These men also maintained that the veneration of saints was useless, pilgrimages they derided, and religious consideration of relics they called stupid. The idea of temporal power for the church they pointed out as being foreign to apostolic Christianity.

Only a few of the early Humanists felt the deep desire for the spiritual satisfaction they awoke in the hearts of the people, but they did show that the church withheld truth from the masses. Basically they wanted reform within the church; but once their idea that the hierarchy was not infallible struck root, an irresistible force was unleashed against the church.

4. As the feudal period began to recede and omens of modern history began to appear, new ideas of economics arose. Formerly, to be poor was accepted as a religious virtue; but as wealth began to accumulate, poverty began to be looked upon as a social evil. These changing conditions soon resulted in cash payments for peasants' services. Guilds, with exclusive control over business and prices, lost their pre-eminence to the growing system of bargaining. The period of exploration, with its consequent change from barter to sale, made people realize that land did not compose the basic source of wealth.

The expansion of Europe during the age of discoveries transferred people's minds from things religious to things secular. A class of people since known as capitalists came into existence, and they, too, provided a rift in the armor of the formerly all-powerful church. As the middle class rose in importance in the social strata, the church lost still more of its support.

5. For years the Holy Roman Empire posed as the protector of the church, and more than once the emperor's forces supported the papacy against those Italian rulers who aimed at a consolidation of the various areas.

Many high governmental officials also held offices in the church. But the time came when the empire became so absorbed in attempting to keep its sprawling territories from disintegrating and in working to maintain sufficient men under arms to assure a measure of safety from the threatening Turks, that it had no time nor power to safeguard the church from the dangers of ambitious and incensed lay rulers. This was the condition before the monk of Wittenberg had his open break with the church, and it continued until some time after the Reformation had become so well established that its progress could not be retarded.

6. In Western Europe strong centralized governments worked to curtail the power of the church and help make a religious revolt possible. The decentralized governmental status in Germany added fuel to the fire which destroyed the former universal structure of the church. At first the church gained ground because no strong central government existed, but in so doing she aroused the ire of the secular feudal lords who stood to lose whenever the church took funds out of their domain. Soon these rulers began to apply the rule of "Might makes right," and thus they hindered the papal representatives from making further financial and jurisdictional gains. The lack of any effective central government also made it impossible to prevent any groups from uniting to thwart the financial exactions of Rome. The princes developed a system whereby they enriched themselves by confiscating lands held by the church.

7. As a result of wars, famines, plagues, fears of Turkish invasion, general social unrest, the activity of the Humanists and their call to literal Bible study, a growing objection to the secular activity of the papacy, wrongs suffered at the hands of the clergy, and a desire to find a spiritual experience and satisfaction which the church never seemed to supply, there arose a religious fervor and a longing for a return to apostolic simplicity.

The teachings of the Brethren of the Common Life, and of the forerunners to the Reformers, stressed a need for Bible study and personal religion without recourse to the clergy. Soon people began to look for spiritual uplift outside the church, a situation which belittled the older accepted ideas of strict conformity to the authority of the church.

8. Perhaps the foremost reason for the coming of the Reformation is that there were abuses in the church itself, abuses that had existed for nearly two centuries, with only occasional efforts at their elimination.

As the church became more and more enmeshed in secular affairs, more money was needed to carry on all phases of governmental and other activities. Furthermore, the ecclesiastics, not satisfied with the exalted dignity afforded them by their doctrine of transubstantiation, or their vantage point which gave them access to the secret thoughts and acts of others by means of auricular confession, they coveted political eminence and preferred governmental status, and they possessed an insatiable greed for material gains.

This need for more finances led to increased taxation, already odious, and to the collection of various fees, including the sale of indulgences. This was carried to such unbelievable lengths that it finally crushed blind fealty. When the church, despite her claim as the sole way of salvation, deteriorated to the status of a temporal power, controlled by worldlings for secular gains, the moral sense of the people suffered a fatal blow.

Even more noxious than the taxing system was the inveterate immorality of the clergy. Their sharp appetite for luxury caused their moral standards to decline. Even the popes contributed to their own hurt when they claimed exemption from obedience to the laws of man and heaven. In general their conduct did not engender personal respect, and several of their number during the Renaissance led dissolute lives.

Furthermore, the creeds of the church had evolved into such subtleties that few tried to grasp their meaning. The supreme power of the papacy, verging on totalitarianism, gradually became so unbearable that many people, though remaining nominally in the church, refused to be awed by it or to be kept in subjection to it.

CHARACTERISTICS OF THE REFORMATION

The Protestant Reformation possessed definite characteristics, many of which set it apart from any other revolution in history.

One of the distinguishing features was its territorial scope. It began simultaneously and independently in various European countries. About the time that Martin Luther posted his ninety-five theses on the church door in Wittenberg in 1517, John Colet, dean of St. Paul's in England, was denouncing the abuses of the Catholic Church and upholding the supremacy of the Bible as the rule of faith. Lefèvre in France and Zwingli in Switzerland were at the same time preaching against the evils of the church and pointing to Christ as the door of salvation. Although Luther is called the originator of the Reformation, the other Reformers discovered and preached the same message that he did, without having received knowledge of it from him.

There was a power, however, that brought the Reformation into existence and made its progress possible—and that was the Holy Scriptures. The Greek New Testament prepared by Erasmus was a help to scholars all over Europe in learning the way of truth and life.

After the Reformation once got under way, there existed a great friendship and fraternization among the Reformers. There was frequent interchange of ideas, and hospitality was freely extended. One of the surprising features of the Reformation was this extent of contact and co-operation among the Reformers as they encouraged each other in their efforts.

The Reformation spread with great rapidity. Of course, consolidations, refinements, and extensions needed to be made; but that so tremendous a revolution, on such a vast scale, could be executed in so short a time, bringing with it a complete change in thought and habit, still remains one of the amazing events of history.

The Protestant Reformation actually began in Europe's citadels of learning, her universities. There were scholars, such as Luther and Melanchthon at Wittenberg; Erasmus, Colet, and More at Oxford; Bilney, Latimer, and Cartwright at Cambridge; and Lefèvre and Farel at Paris. Almost without exception the leaders of the Reformation were highly trained men of that generation. In some instances, as Beza and Tyndale, they ranked high as men of letters. Others, like Cranmer and Valdés, carried responsibilities at court.

Wycliffe, Huss, and Savonarola each ranked high in his country; all three were eminent in literary circles.

Why was this so necessary at that time, when in other ages men of lesser abilities and education have been used effectively to preach the gospel with power? At least two answers can be given: Only the educated knew the Hebrew, Latin, and Greek necessary to read the Bible as it then existed. Then, too, it was essential that the Bible be translated into the vernacular of each country so that the common people could have the privilege of reading the Scriptures in their own tongue. This task demanded scholarship.

All the preaching of many Luthers, Latimers, Zwinglis, Knoxes, and Wisharts would have failed to accomplish the Reformation if, at the same time, the Bible in the vernacular had not been provided for the common people. If at the moment Latimer was preaching at Cambridge it had not happened that Tyndale, who had fled to the Continent, was smuggling back thousands of copies of the English New Testament so that every Englishman could read the way of salvation for himself, there would have been no Reformation in England. A similar situation obtained in Germany, France, and other countries.

With these two phases must be combined the indispensable third —the invention of printing, which had made possible the publication of the translations of the Bible and had brought the price within range of the common man's purse.

Within a ten-year period many of the nations of Europe had received translations of the Bible in their own tongue. Luther had translated it for Germany in 1522, Lefèvre for France in 1523, Tyndale for England in 1525, Bruccioli for Italy in 1532. Within the next ten years Francisco Enzinas had translated the Bible into Spanish, and Petri had translated it into Swedish. Shortly after, Karoli, one of the most energetic of Magyar preachers, had done the same in the Magyar tongue.

Another noteworthy characteristic of the Reformers was the basic agreement on important doctrines. The tenet upon which all Reformers agreed was justification by faith. They believed that salvation is not obtained by works, fasting, money, or penance, but that it is God's free gift. This doctrine formed the cornerstone of the Reformation. Agreement also existed on the supreme and sufficient authority of the Scriptures, Communion in both kinds, and the disavowal of saint worship, images, relics, purgatory, mass, celibacy, and the pope as head of the church.

The major Reformers gave little attention to the form of baptism, religious liberty, the state of the dead, the Decalogue, the Trinity, and other doctrines, except as they agreed or disagreed with what they termed the heretical sects, like the Anabaptists and the Libertines. Once or twice arguments on baptism flared briefly. Disagreement also existed on predestination and the definition of original sin.

But the topic that brought the cleavage between the Lutherans and the Calvinists, or the Reformed Church, was the eucharist. Was or was not the bread the body of Christ? Numerous conferences and colloquies restored neither unity nor good will between the two factions. In England the vestment and ritual controversy brought a rift between the developing Church of England and the Puritans.

Bigotry and intolerance, shortcomings for which the Reformers bitterly upbraided the Catholic Church, raised their hydra heads repeatedly in Protestant circles. Many Reformers sought to curb opposition and to stop the infiltration of contrary beliefs by the use of force. Freedom of conscience was not one of their principles.

The executions by strangling, burning, and drowning, and the wars to eradicate those of different faiths, are a sorry chapter in the annals of the Reformation. It may be observed that such destruction failed to bring expressions of disapprobation. On the contrary, these executions were frequently applauded as indicative of the advancement of God's cause upon earth.

Critics who point to these defects as a reason for disbelief in the authenticity of the Reformation are shooting beside the mark. In not all things did the Reformation immediately release men from the prejudices and false thinking of their times, and this was one instance. The Reformation proper, the break with Roman Catholic authority, was accomplished in a relatively short time; but not all the papal teachings were abruptly terminated.

Furthermore, the Reformers were human. They had faults. Perhaps it was part of God's plan to allow their weaknesses to be revealed to the public, lest the people's affection be transferred from the truth to the leaders. God intended that the people focus their attention upon the truth in the Bible.

Of Protestant Reformers there were many, some clearing the highway so that others could march further along toward the goal; some began where others ended. Some laid the foundation, others built the walls, and still others put on the coping stone. Who shall say which were the greatest among them? Historians extol some as eminent—those Reformers, perhaps, who by the times and the influences at work were brought into greater prominence.

The Reformation was a continuous, all-enveloping movement of action and reaction, accruing more glory by the addition of more light. It was a glorious spiritual awakening, a state of mind that gave the world the mighty heritage of Protestantism.

JOHN HUSS

Preacher and Patriot

"THREE mighty currents were running through the life of Prague. The first, a moral movement, involved the moral improvement and efficiency of the clergy; the second, a movement of doctrinal reform, centering in the views of Wycliffe; the third, a patriotic movement, in which the Czech population were seeking supremacy over the German element and the management of all Bohemian affairs.

"In all three, as a preacher of righteousness, as a religious reformer and as a patriot, Huss was the acknowledged leader. He had the elements of popularity and leadership. His sincerity of purpose was evident, his devotion constant, his energy unflagging, his courage fearless, his daily life lifted above reproach."—David S. Schaff, D.D., *John Huss, His Life, Teachings and Death*, page 58.

This brief sketch outlines the trend of the times and gives a glimpse of the man who by the age of thirty stood as the most famous preacher of his era and the most important churchman in Bohemia. John Huss was born about 1373 of peasant parents at Husinec, near the Bavarian frontier. His father died while John was still in his boyhood.

Early in her son's life, John's mother recognized an exceptional devotion to study. She had no funds to support him in school, but nonetheless she encouraged him to obtain an education. Although a charity student, he determinedly entered the University of Prague, earning part of his way by singing. His main interest centered in the study of theology. Early in his college career he became an able debater. It was said of him that during all his growth as a scholar he remained humble and moderate in his relationships with others.

In 1393 he received the bachelor of arts degree, the next year he became a bachelor of theology, and two years later the University of Prague conferred the master of arts degree upon him. He did not take any studies toward the doctor of theology degree, but turned to active participation in national and university affairs. His ordination to the priesthood came in 1400, after which he became attached to the court in the capacity of chaplain to Queen Sophia.

By 1401 he accepted the deanship of the philosophical faculty, and the following year he rose to be rector of the university. With this recognition of ability also came the appointment as preacher of Bethlehem Chapel. This house of worship had been built and dedicated to the specific purpose of preaching to the citizens of Prague in their native tongue.

During all his life, Huss distinguished himself by constant application to duty and tireless devotion to preaching according to the Scriptures. His conduct has been termed exemplary, his life blameless, and his personality winning. Apparently this estimation of the man agrees with his life, for even his enemies did not attack his character during his life nor after his death.

What was it that led Huss into religious paths which diverged at first but slightly, then gradually further and still further from the then universally accepted authority of the church? The answer cannot be found in one word, nor even in one statement. W. T. Selley and A. C. Krey present the following reason. "He criticized the church in Bohemia as Wycliffe had criticized it in England. His views found all the more favor among his fellow Bohemians because the higher ecclesiastical offices in Bohemia were held by Germans. The books of Huss show clear evidence of the influence of Wycliffe, whom Huss respected highly, though it is quite possible that he arrived at his opinions independently."—*Medieval Foundations of Western Civilization*, page 316.

While still a student at the University of Prague, Huss knew of Wycliffe's writings and opinions. He did not agree with all the religious ideas promoted by Wycliffe, but the two men's unity of thought regarding the authority of the church as it related itself to the teachings of the Scriptures made them enemies of papal authority.

Up to 1405 Huss seemed unconscious of any violent opposition by the church, but by 1408 this "pale, thin man in mean attire" was being accused by the clergy to the archbishop for using stinging remarks in describing prevalent moral and other abuses among the priests.

What were the objections that Huss had to the church and its teachings? Possibly one of the greatest reasons for his dissatisfaction was the moral corruption of the clergy. This situation kept the spiritual indignation of Huss at a fever pitch. His eloquent preaching and his whiplash remarks concerning the failure of the clergy to live godly lives, combined with his ability to show fallacies in the church, led to more than one excommunication and finally to death at the stake.

Among the opinions he espoused and preached were the following: Christ, not Peter, is the Rock upon which the church was built; the Scriptures comprise the all-sufficient rule in matters of religion; priestly intervention for salvation is unnecessary; and masses for the dead and the use of most religious relics are useless. He also attacked the worldly attitude of papal monarchy, particularly as it affected secular matters. The rights of the individual's conscience were to him higher than all church and papal authority.

It seems, however, that he placed much more stress on the need for organizational reform than he did on particular theological points. Had he lived longer, it is possible that his views might have been summarized into a creed. But, above all, he preached with the purpose of calling the people to stop sinning and to seek after God. He constantly challenged his fellow clergymen to bring their lives into harmony with the life of Christ.

Twice during 1411 the papacy issued bulls proclaiming indulgences to all who would supply funds for a campaign against the king of Naples. Hardly had these bulls of indulgences reached Bohemia before Huss attacked the whole corrupt system.

His opposition raised such a tumult in Prague that upon the advice of friends he withdrew from the city and went to his native village, where he remained two years to study and write. But it could not be gainsaid that he had stepped out openly and defiantly against the papal hierarchy, for as A. H. Wratislaw states, "Hus's uprising against the papal indulgences was such an assault upon the simoniacal system of the day that it could not but raise a storm against him in the highest ecclesiastical quarter, the court of Rome."
—*John Hus,* page 181.

From this time on all events pointed to an ultimate trial of Huss in which the control of the entire proceedings centered in the hands of the church. News of the Hussite opposition to the indulgences, with a consequent loss of money to the papal treasury, and other anticlerical disturbances, reached Rome and resulted in a summons for Huss to appear there. The pope's first efforts to subdue and silence Huss fell fruitless because Huss had too many influential friends, among whom he counted the queen and many nobles. Consequently, upon the refusal of Huss to respect the papal summons and go to Rome, the city of Prague soon felt the weight of an interdict. This act caused a great deal of disturbance, for to have a city placed under an interdict meant that all religious services were suspended, sacraments were not administered, and burials were halted. In short, an interdict deprived all people of the comforts of religion. It was because of this disturbance, and not because of cowardice, that Huss left the city temporarily upon the advice of his friends.

Huss did not entirely ignore the summons to Rome, but because of ill health he sent three personal representatives. When their efforts proved unsuccessful, Huss was again excommunicated. But upon the receipt of a safe conduct granted by Sigismund, emperor of the Holy Roman Empire, and by the king of Bohemia, Huss, in the company of three nobles and others, started for the Council of Constance in October, 1414, and arrived there November 3.

The Council of Constance convened to the call of Pope John XXIII, one of the three rival popes, upon the urging of Sigismund, the emperor. Based on the number of church and other dignitaries present and the areas represented, this council has the distinction of being one of the most colorful gatherings known in European history. The purposes of this council have always been listed as three; namely, (1) to suppress heresy, (2) to heal the papal schism, and (3) to reform the church.

It has been said that the emperor attempted to keep the safe-conduct assurance to Huss in effect, but that powerful enemies of Huss maliciously determined to appeal to the emperor's prejudices. As a consequence the emperor finally let them have their way against Huss. It is, however, true that upon Huss's arrival at Constance the Reformer received full liberty, and Pope John added his personal word that Huss was not to be harmed. But in spite of all these promises of security, by December 6 Huss was placed under arrest by the joint order of Pope John and the cardinals.

Huss soon found himself in a filthy dungeon in a Dominican convent, where he remained chained day and night with insufficient food. Upon his complaints concerning the condition in the dungeon, he was first transferred for safekeeping to the castle of Gottlieben, and by June, 1415, he was under guard in a local Franciscan convent.

As was to be expected, his arrest and imprisonment created a great deal of fruitless indignation among the Bohemians. Furthermore, his confinement under poor sanitary conditions and improper care brought on an illness which nearly resulted in death. When he finally appeared in the council before the emperor he stood in chains as a common criminal.

It is a widely accepted opinion among scholars that what has been called the trial of Huss was nothing but a mockery and a violation of all principles of justice and honor. At the public hearings of June 5, 7, 8, 1415, he was repeatedly shouted down when he tried to speak. He maintained that he was not conscious of any errors, but that if shown to be in error according to the Scriptures he would gladly lay his offenses aside.

During the long, tiring days of the hearing, misnamed a trial, Huss consistently upheld the Scriptures as the sole guide for the salvation of sinners, and protested against the corruption of the hierarchy. When the news of his conviction reached Bohemia, not less than two hundred fifty lords affixed their seals to a letter addressed to the council requesting leniency for Huss. The letter caused some delay in his execution, but it could not save him.

Briefly the charges preferred against Huss may be summarized by stating that he had disregarded the discipline of the church and that he had rejected some of its doctrines. It seems that the council did not propose to give instruction and correction to Huss, which he repeatedly requested, as much as it endeavored to make a final condemnation of him and his teachings.

If Huss would have been willing to make a full retraction without any question of all charges laid to his account, he might have been set free. But he unwaveringly maintained the position that he could not abjure errors he had never held. He repeatedly expressed his willingness to be instructed and to submit to the decision of the Council, but he stated that he could not make a denial of principles he had never taught. Throughout the hearings many witnesses appeared against him, but not one person was permitted to speak in favor of Huss.

On July 6, 1415, the farce came to an end, and Huss was condemned as a heretic. Then in a prepared ritual Huss was deposed, degraded, commended by the priests to Satan, and delivered to the secular government, which was to carry out the death sentence imposed by the church upon one who believed that a person had a right to have a conscience.

A week before his death he wrote a letter to the university authorities at Prague assuring them in the following words of his steadfastness, "Be confident I have not revoked nor abjured a single article. I refuse to renounce unless what the council charged against me shall be proved false from the Scriptures."—Schaff, *John Huss*, page 264. It was reported that he walked to his death with a steady, firm tread, singing or praying as he went. He showed neither fear nor regret for his actions.

When his executioners led him to the stake in a meadow outside the city, huge crowds followed. At the stake he was divested of all clothing except his boots. Chains held him securely to the stake. A mixture of wood and straw was piled around him until it reached his face. While the fire licked around his body he sang and prayed until the flames stilled his voice. After his body had been consumed, his ashes and the soil upon which they lay were gathered and thrown into the Rhine River.

His death came as a result of the system of the Roman Catholic Church and the sentiment of the time. Fire was only a medium. John Huss was dead, but the ideals for which he stood and the principles he advocated will never die. By his death he gave the church more trouble than he could have given had he lived.

An almost immediate result of his martyrdom was the growth of international conditions which culminated in a series of wars in Bohemia. These wars, called the Hussite Wars, lasted about fourteen years and were aimed at the papacy, the Council of Constance, the emperor, and all efforts to invade Bohemia and suppress the teachings of Huss. Finally the rebelling Bohemians were brought under control; the Hussite teachings and their influence, however, spread all over Europe.

In evaluating the life of Huss, one needs to remember that he was a patriot as well as a preacher. He loved his people and did all he could to set their language and culture on a high level. His writings, in the Bohemian language, are considered the richest and most stimulating in all Bohemian literature. As an outstanding preacher and intellectual leader he holds an eminence never reached by anyone else in the life of the University of Prague.

He was also honored at the court and was deeply loved by the common people. He has been characterized as a true scholar, the bravest of martyrs, and an eloquent preacher of a democratic religion. Yet his chief glory consists not in his patriotism, nor in his deep learning, but in the beauty and simplicity of his spiritual teaching. So long as the work of the Council of Constance will be studied, the name of Huss and his work will be discussed. The Council of Constance, under the control of the church, intended to silence Huss and eradicate his teachings; but it made of Huss an international hero and spread his spirit and teaching over all the civilized world.

"It is doubtful," says Schaff, "if we except the sufferings and death of Jesus Christ, whether the forward movement of religious enlightenment and human freedom have been advanced as much by the sufferings and death of any single man as by the death of Huss."—*John Huss*, page 2.

JEROME OF PRAGUE

A Noble Layman

ACCORDING to historical data, the gospel found its way into Bohemia about the ninth century. Shortly after this the people were having the Bible propounded to them in their own language; but as the power of the papacy increased, preaching to the people in the Bohemian tongue decreased, and the use of Latin became more and more prevalent. In spite of this situation, however, the use of the native tongue in private and in some public worship never ceased entirely.

From its earliest history Bohemia had been a pawn among ruling houses and political-minded factions. The papacy, as a political-religious power, was ever mindful of the importance of holding its gains as strongly as that of any other power, and in a religious way the papacy gradually increased its strength until it was the dominant influence in the lives of both the people and the government.

Nevertheless, some men here and there dared to raise their voices against the evils in the Roman Catholic Church. Their messages called for a return to the religion of the Bible and drew attention to the gross sins of the clergy. The church was aroused to drastic action against those who pointed out the flaws in the lives of the clergy and errors in points of doctrine.

Although John Huss was the outstanding clergyman of the day to oppose the Catholic hierarchy, the most important layman to fight against the weakness of the church and the moral degeneracy of the priesthood was Jerome of Prague, born sometime between 1365 and 1379. He was a close friend of Huss and with only slight lapses of time aided him in his work and followed him in death. He came of a well-to-do noble family. In personal appearance he is said to have been a large man. In character he has been described as leading a blameless life. Since he was a man of means, he traveled widely and appears to have delighted in attending various universities, among them the one at Prague, where he received his bachelor's degree in 1398; the one at Oxford, where he fell under the influence of the writings of Wycliffe; the one in Paris, where he gained the enmity of Gerson, the chancellor; the one at Cologne; and the one at Heidelberg. He obtained the master's degree from the universities of Paris, Cologne, and Heidelberg. Upon his second visit to Oxford he was expelled because of his open opposition to the papacy and his adherence to the Wycliffian ideas.

In scholarly ability he outranks his contemporary, John Huss. He was a Humanist with anticlerical trends derived in part from his studies at Oxford and in part from his keen analytical sense, which soon determined for him the distinction between priestly claims and priestly lives.

Jerome's noble birth made it comparatively easy for him to enter the courts of Europe. This background naturally assured a gentlemanly bearing, his means made it possible for him to dress well, and his ability as a scholar and a forceful debater gained him popularity and fame. As he grew bolder in his denunciation of the existing evils in the church he soon assumed a place in the minds of students as a hero, whether he was lecturing or leading a mob.

Usually anyone in the guise of a reformer has difficulty in co-ordinating his activities and interests with various social and political groups, but Jerome was able to effect a close affinity between those who were working for reform on the one hand and the more or less fashionable world on the other. His masterful eloquence, together with his magnetic Latin style, and his ability to speak Bohemian, made him a strong foe of priestly corruption as well as of those who sought to destroy Bohemia as a nation.

He was deeply attached to the Roman Church. As others before him, he strove for a devoted clergy, and in pointing out the wickedness of the priesthood he felt that he was upholding the purity of the church. He supported the views of the church on the Lord's Supper as against the position of Wycliffe. But he openly and boldly opposed the church in the sale of indulgences, and consequently received the disapproval of the entire hierarchy.

Jerome's entire experience seems to have been one of repeated and consecutive mental clashes with church officials and doctrines. He took pleasure in slyly opening discussions on debatable points of theology in the universities he visited or attended. He was found in Prague sponsoring nationalism for the Czechs. He appeared in Vienna, where he was arrested for supporting the writings of Wycliffe. From there he escaped into Moravia, and this won him an excommunication from the bishop of Cracow. Then he was found at the court of King Sigismund of Hungary, to whom he preached and stigmatized the covetousness and unchastity of the priests. Because of this sermon, the archbishop of Prague accused Jerome to Sigismund, and this led to the Reformer's arrest. He was freed on parole, which he broke, and he soon made his way into Bohemia. His impetuous spirit led him to ridicule the Austrian bishop in a letter, and this act was preferred against him at his trial. Later he arrived at the courts of Poland and Lithuania, where his learning, his wit, and his eloquence made him an honored guest.

Gradually the hatred of church officials against Jerome grew to the point where means were sought to apprehend him and bring him to trial. Again his hastiness played into the hands of the church officers, for contrary to Huss's desire that he not appear at the Council of Constance, Jerome arrived there April 4, 1415. Upon his arrival he attempted to obtain a safe conduct from Emperor Sigismund. When he failed to obtain such assurance, he fled toward the border of Moravia. Before he could make good his escape, he was arrested and returned to Constance on May 23, 1415, where he immediately faced the charge of attempting to flee a citation.

His trial, if it may be dignified as such, began almost immediately. The hearing granted him was as biased as that granted Huss. Jerome had written no tracts or treatises, yet the council was able to gather 107 charges against him based on reports of witnesses.

Worn and starved into serious illness while in prison and recoiling from the death of a heretic, he requested permission to recant. This he did on September 10 or 11, and again on September 23, 1415. But if Jerome felt that recantation would win him his freedom, he was sorely disappointed, for he was placed in prison, where he remained through the autumn and winter of 1415-16.

It seems that the Italian members of the Council of Constance wished to set Jerome free after his recantation, whereas the German delegation, nursed on centuries of antipathy toward all that was Bohemian, insisted that Jerome's recantation was untrustworthy and that the case called for further investigation. In their zeal they overreached themselves and made of Jerome a hero.

On May 23, 1416, he again appeared before the council. At this time he renounced his recantation and could not be cajoled or threatened into weakening. The work of Wycliffe, Huss, and his own position were brilliantly defended. His criticism of the degeneracy of the church of his day was mingled with deep learning, wit, and sarcasm. Repeatedly he came out the winner in all the evidence arrayed against him.

Finally the farce ended, and Jerome was committed to the secular government to be executed. He marched to the stake with a soldierly step and with the face of one who had conquered fear. He died not because he differed basically from the beliefs of the church, but because he respected and upheld the ideals of Wycliffe and Huss and was violent in his criticisms of a corrupt clergy.

No finer evaluation of Jerome's ability and character during his trial and death can be presented than that written by the pen of Poggio Bracciolini, the papal representative at the Council of Constance. He was no friend of Jerome nor of Jerome's view, yet he said:

"I must confess that I never saw one who in eloquence of his defense came as near to the eloquence of the ancients, whom we admire so much. His voice was sweet, clear, and resounding. The dignity of the orator's jests now expressed indignation, now moved to compassion, which, however, he neither claimed nor wished to obtain. He stood before his judges undaunted and intrepid. Not only not fearing, but even seeking death, he appeared as another Cato. He was indeed a man worthy of eternal memory in men's minds.

"With joyful brow, cheerful countenance, and elated face he went to his doom. He feared not the flames, not the torments, not death. None of the Stoics ever suffered death with so constant and brave a mind, and he indeed seemed to desire it. When he had reached the spot where he was to die, he divested himself of his garments, and knelt down in prayer. Logs of wood were then piled about his body, which they covered up to the breast. When they were lighted, he began to sing a hymn, which was interrupted by the smoke and the flames. This, however, is the greatest proof of the constancy of his mind, that when the official wished to light the stake behind his back, that he might not see it, he said, 'Come here and light the stake before my eyes, for if I had feared it I should never have come to this spot, as it was in my power to fly.'

"Thus perished a man eminent beyond belief. I saw his end, I contemplated every one of his acts. Be it that he acted thus from faithlessness or from obstinacy, you could perceive that it was a man of the philosophic school who had perished. . . . Socrates did not drink the poison as willingly as this man submitted himself to the flames."–Quoted by Will S. Monroe in *Bohemia and the Czechs*, pages 227-229.

THOMAS BILNEY

Winner of Men for God

ALTHOUGH not listed among the great in Reformation circles, Thomas Bilney was, nonetheless, an important link in the progress of that movement in England. "Little Bilney," as he was affectionately named because of his diminutive stature, is sometimes called "The father of the English Reformation," for two reasons: He was the first to be converted by the reading of Erasmus's New Testament, and he converted more great men among the English Reformers than did anyone else.

He was born at or near Norwich in 1495 and lived in Cambridge from childhood. He attended Trinity College and attained the degree of doctor of laws. He was ordained a priest in 1519.

Of a serious turn of mind and abstemious, he attempted early in life to fulfill the commandments of God; and he strove by fasting, long vigils, masses, and the purchase of indulgences to win peace of mind. Like Luther, Bilney discovered that good works alone were not enough to secure him the relief he sought.

Many of Bilney's acquaintances were talking about a new book, the Greek New Testament. But the priests had forbidden Bilney to read it, and, being a good Catholic who desired to fulfill all obligations, and especially ecclesiastical commands, he desisted. Finally, unable to resist his curiosity any longer, he decided to read it in secret, for he was greatly attracted to its reported beauty of style.

With considerable fear he purchased a copy from a house that was secretly selling it, against the law. Locking himself in his room, he allowed the book to fall open, and he read, "This is a faithful saying, and worthy of all acceptation, that Christ Jesus came into the world to save sinners; of whom I am chief." 1 Timothy 1:15.

Bilney grasped the idea readily that if Paul thought himself the chief of sinners and yet was saved, then he, Bilney, even a greater sinner in his own estimation, could be saved, too. What a revelation! What a relief! Instead of despair, a great inward peace now came into his soul.

Merle d'Aubigné, who writes the account, quotes Bilney's words: "I see it all; my vigils, my fasts, my pilgrimages, my purchase of masses and indulgences, were destroying instead of saving me. All these efforts were, as St. Augustine says, a hasty running out of the right way."

From then on Bilney became a devotee of the Bible; he never grew weary of reading it. More than that, he had a great urge to share his new-found faith with others. He desired nothing more than to be able to show his associates God's great love.

Since he was of a shy and bashful nature, he did not at first with boldness preach to the world. It is written that his vocation was prayer. He made it his business to call upon God day and night, pleading for souls; and God answered him. Any evangelist would be proud to count among his converts those that Bilney made, names that stand high in the Reformation's hall of fame, persons without whom the English Reformation would perhaps not have been accomplished. Of Cambridge's eminent professors, Arthur, Thistle, and Stafford were the first to respond to him. Latimer, Barnes, Lambert, Warner, Fooke, and Soude were also among those he converted. All were men who played foremost roles in the English Reformation.

After Bilney converted Latimer, the students flocked to hear Bilney preach. "Bilney, whom we continually meet with when any secret work, a work of irresistible charity, is in hand," knew how to approach these men. "The pious man often succeeds better, even with the great ones of this world, than the ambitious and the intriguing."

He had the secret power gained by long hours on his knees in his closet. He prayed, "O Thou who art the truth, give me strength that I may teach it; and convert the ungodly by means of one who has been ungodly himself."

Bilney always attempted to fit his method to the individual he wished to convert. In the case of Latimer, a Catholic who disdained the evangelicals at the university, he won by confessing to him the story of his own conversion. In the case of Barnes, "the Goliath of the university," he first prayed long and earnestly. Then he held many conversations and prayers with Barnes, and urged him to declare his faith openly without fear of reproach. At other times he assembled his friends together and pointed his finger at the text that had converted him. By this means he converted large numbers.

For a time the little Reformer joined his efforts with those of John Frith and William Tyndale. Together they preached repentance and conversion, denying that anyone could get his sins forgiven by any priest or by doing any good work.

Bilney had little regard for the popes. He declared, "These five hundred years there hath been no good pope; and in all the times past we can find but fifty: for they have neither preached nor lived well, nor conformably to their dignity; wherefore, unto this day, they have borne the keys of simony." (As an example of the men of whom he spoke, who held low moral standards, we may consider Rodrigo Borgia, who succeded Innocent VIII to the papal chair in 1492 as Alexander VI. He lived illicitly with a Roman woman and one of her daughters, having some four children by the latter, all of whom he acknowledged openly and provided with high positions. He bribed all of the cardinals, and gave at least one of them large amounts of silver, to obtain the papal chair. His manner of life and his procedure in obtaining the papal crown were characteristic of other popes of that period.) At another time Bilney said, "The cowl of St. Francis wrapped round a dead body hath no power to take away sins."

Bilney was the leader of the Protestant group at Cambridge, and he preached simply and directly that Jesus Christ delivered from sin. As matter-of-fact as this statement may sound to present-day Christendom, it was nearly as startling as an atomic bomb to the people living in sixteenth-century Europe. They knew but one route to heaven; namely, good works, fasting, indulgences, purgatory, and the mass.

Mainly as the result of Bilney's work at Cambridge "seven colleges at least were in full ferment: Pembroke, St John's, Queens', King's, Caius, Benet's and Peterhouse. The gospel was preached at the Augustine's, at St. Mary's, (the university church,) and in other places."

Thus the Reformation received impetus in England. Eventually overcoming his shyness, Bilney began preaching with the vigor of an evangel. In 1525 he secured a license to preach in the diocese of Ely. He left the university and in the company of Arthur went many places. In Suffolk, at the town of Hadleigh, many were converted. Here he performed such faithful work in teaching the people that they became great Bible students, so much so "that the whole town seemed rather a university of the learned than a town of clothmaking or laboring people."—John Foxe, *Book of Martyrs,* page 176. They read their Bibles through many times, memorizing whole portions.

It was not long, however, before opposition to his preaching developed. Twice monks forcibly drew him out of the pulpit. His denunciation of saint and relic worship, of monkish conduct, and of pilgrimages drew the attention of Cardinal Wolsey. When cited to appear before him in 1527, Bilney denied holding any Lutheran views. Since Wolsey was too engrossed with the tasks of the kingdom, he left the trial in the hands of Cuthbert Tunstall, bishop of London.

Bilney was convicted of heresy, but Tunstall, who sympathized with his victim, could not bring himself to pronounce the sentence. Bilney wanted to go to the stake, but the arguments of his friends not to cast his life away, and Tunstall's continuous putting off the evil day, finally wore down the little man so that he recanted. Knowing that the bishop was a friend of Erasmus, Bilney, during the days of waiting, wrote letters to Tunstall about the Greek New Testament. Tunstall apparently was impressed, but not enough to relent. Wolsey had commanded that Bilney either abjure or die.

The day following his recantation he bore his fagot to Paul's Cross, the accepted procedure to indicate to the world that he had abjured his heresy. After this he was placed back in prison.

Now Bilney's real torment began compared to which his soul struggle before conversion was nothing. After he spent a year in the Tower he returned to Cambridge, but he was so tortured by remorse that he had denied his Christ, that he could not bear to have anyone, not even his old friend Latimer, read or mention the Scriptures to him. "His mind wandered, the blood froze in his veins, he sank under his terrors; he lost all sense, and almost his life, and lay motionless in the arms of his astonished friends." He could obtain no consolation.

Yet the Holy Spirit did not entirely forsake him. Finally when peace was once more restored in his heart, he resolved to rectify the great wrong he had done. He determined never again to renounce the truth of God's word.

One night at ten o'clock, in 1531, he bade his friends at Cambridge good-by, saying that he was going to Jerusalem. (He referred to Christ's words, when He went to Jerusalem to suffer the crucifixion.) His destination was Norfolk, where he had first preached. Since his license had been revoked, he went from house to house, and he also spoke in the fields. There he openly confessed that he had denied the truth. From Norfolk he went to Norwich, where he was apprehended and placed in prison. Here the sheriff, a special friend of his, who wanted to do something for him, treated him well.

The night before the execution, friends who came to comfort reminded him, "Though the fire would be hot, God's spirit would cool it." To show them his lack of fear he put his finger in the candle flame, leaving it there until it was burned off to the first joint. He told them, "I feel by experience, and have known it long by philosophy, that fire by God's ordinance is naturally hot; but yet I am persuaded by God's Holy Word, and by the experience of some mentioned in that word, that in the flame they felt no heat, and in the fire they felt no consumption; and I can constantly believe, however the stubble of this my body shall be wasted by it, yet my soul and spirit shall be purged thereby, a pain for the time, whereon, notwithstanding, followeth joy unspeakable." He referred them to Isaiah 43:2: "When thou walkest through the fire, thou shalt not be burned; neither shall the flame kindle upon thee."

Bilney was executed at Lollard's Pit, in a low valley surrounded by hills. This spot was chosen, says Foxe, so that people might have the comfort of sitting quietly to see the executions. A "vast concourse of spectators" came to see "little Bilney" burn. People living in sixteenth-century England were apparently as enthusiastic for these burnings as were those of pagan Rome to see the early Christians thrown into the arena to be devoured by wild beasts.

Of Bilney's last moments Foxe writes, "Then the officers put reeds and fagots about his body, and set fire to them, which made a very great flame, and deformed his face, he holding up his hands, and knocking upon his breast, crying sometimes, 'Jesus,' sometimes, 'I believe.' The flame was blown away from him by the violence of the wind, which was that day, and two or three days before, very great; and so for a little pause he stood without flame; but soon the wood again took the flame, and then he gave up the ghost, and his body, being withered, bowed downward against the chain. Then one of the officers with his halbert smote out the staple in the stake behind him, and suffered his body to fall into the bottom of the fire, laying wood on it; and so he was consumed."

ROBERT BROWNE

He Lighted the Candle of Freedom

THE most important event of the English Reformation in its relation to America, according to some church historians, was the rise of the Brownist sect in the latter half of the sixteenth century.

The Brownists, who were also called Separatists and Independents, were the forerunners of modern-day Congregationalism. They were the peculiar people of the English Reformation, as the Anabaptists were of the Continental Reformation. Robert Browne was the founder and "the first Englishman to express the Anabaptist doctrine of complete separation of church and state."

Although at first of the Cartwright school of Puritanism, he soon took his place to the left of the Puritan party, the difference between the two being that in Cartwright's case the keys, the power of the church, belonged in the hands of the ministry; whereas according to Browne's view, they lay in the hands of the brotherhood, the entire church.

He maintained that the Established Church still contained many "filthy traditions and inventions of men;" therefore separate congregations of true Christians should be organized, omitting those who were Christians in name only. His views on doctrine differed but little from those of the Church of England; he contended primarily for measures of polity. He believed that there was as little Biblical evidence for presbyterianism as for episcopacy.

According to the Scriptures, he said, groups of worthy believers should be formed into local congregations, or churches, each separate and independent of the other. A pure democracy should prevail, with all members having the same rights and privileges. With them there was to be no distinct order of priesthood; all were brethren, with Christ alone accorded the headship. The ministry should be chosen from the brethren by the brethren, who likewise were to have the power to relieve the ministry from their office, in case of necessity. The right of fellowshiping also rested with the members, as well as decisions on all affairs of the church.

Born into "a family of consequence" at Tolethorpe Hall, three miles from Stamford, in Rutlandshire, near 1550, Browne attended Corpus Christi College, Cambridge, where he attained the A.B. degree in 1572. Here he subscribed to the views of those who "were there known and counted forward in religion." At that time Thomas Cartwright, the founder of Puritanism, served as Lady Margaret professor of divinity at Cambridge.

For three years following his graduation Browne engaged in teaching, in Northamptonshire. Here he taught religion, along with other subjects. Perturbed that the church offered so little help in maintaining Christian standards among its members, he delved into the study of ecclesiastical government with the view of discovering its shortcomings and abuses.

With true missionary zeal he imparted his findings, not only to his pupils but to the townsmen as well. Consequently he was not slow in making enemies, and shortly thereafter he received his dismissal as a teacher.

He remained in the town, however, teaching what pupils were sent him, until the plague forced him to return to his home. His biographer maintains that Browne could have lived the life of a country gentlemen, but that his restlessness, his ever seeking for an ideal, led him to return to Cambridge, where Richard Greenham, a thoroughgoing Puritan preacher at Dry Drayton, invited him to preach in his parish.

This he proceeded to do. He disdained the use of a bishop's license, even when his brother later procured one for him. His preaching brought him fame in Cambridge circles, so much so that he was invited to preach there, with the consent of the mayor and the vice-chancellor of the university.

His views had crystallized by this time, in 1579, at least on two points. He believed that the headship of the church belongs to Christ alone, and that next under Him in authority was, not the bishops, nor any other individual, but the church collectively.

Feeling himself rejected at Cambridge, he went to Norwich, accompanied by Robert Harrison. He had met Harrison at Cambridge and had persuaded him not to accept ordination at the hands of a bishop, but to join him in his mission of reform. They lived in the same house, as Browne took the lead in their crusade against the legalized churches. Here their preaching found fertile soil among the Lollards, who had resided there since Wycliffe's day, and among the Mennonites from the Low Countries, who had been invited to settle there by the duke of Norfolk.

They condemned the "popish power" of the Established Church, the ministers who took their orders from that church, and the parishes guided by those ministers. Browne called the Church of England "a Jericho partially pulled down at the Reformation, but since rebuilt on the old foundations (probably referring to the Acts of Supremacy and Uniformity under Elizabeth), and so inheriting Joshua's curse."—Frederick H. Powicke, *Robert Browne, Pioneer of Modern Congregationalism*, pages 69, 70.

Browne's preaching gained listeners—a hundred at a time crowded into private houses to hear him. He extended his labors to other parts of the country, constantly remonstrating "against bishops, ecclesiastical courts, ceremonies, and ordinations of ministers."—Thomas Fuller, *The Church History of Britain*, vol. 3, p. 65. The bishops complained that Browne's "corrupt and contentious doctrine" was likely to mislead "the vulgar sort of people," with the result that Browne was thrown into prison.

When he was released, his parishioners, now tried as by fire, organized themselves into a church. But when Browne was imprisoned the second time and taken to London, there to be released at the intercession of his relative, the Lord Treasurer Burghley, and when many of his members were likewise persecuted and imprisoned, they decided to leave England and go to Middelburg in Zeeland, which, like Holland, was under the direction of William of Orange, a friend of Protestantism.

For two miserable years they remained there trying out their experiment of a pure democracy in a local church, a corporate self-government. Doubtless Browne, with his tyrannous temperament, impulsiveness, lack of patience, and arrogant spirit, was at fault for the lack of unity and the breach that resulted; but Powicke con-

cludes, "The main root of bitterness lay in the jealousy and insta-
bility of his colleague Robert Harrison."—*Ibid.*, pp. 32, 33.

During this period Browne published several books upholding
his views. One of the most important is *A Treatise of the Reformation Without Tarrying for Any, and the Wickedness of Those
Preachers, Which Will Not Reform Till the Magistrate Command
or Compel Them.* He wrote at least twenty-five different works before he was forty years old.

Browne had waited in vain for action on the part of the civil
magistrates, whose duty he believed it to be to reform the existing
ecclesiastical system. According to him, Elizabeth had failed to do
her duty. Now necessity demanded that the true and faithful
Christians separate themselves from the existing corruption of the
Established Church "without tarrying for any," not even the queen.
"The kingdom of God . . . is not to be begun by whole parishes,
but rather of the worthiest, were they never so few."

Originally of the opinion that magistrates should make proper
provision for right religious practices, to see that the clergy and
the church members performed their duty, Browne grew weary of
waiting for these reforms to take place. Consequently he affirmed,
"The magistrates have no ecclesiastical authority at all, but only as
any other Christian if so they be Christians."

It is thought by some historians that after having produced a
clean, pure church, he would have turned it back to civil authority
to have it run properly. Of course this view weakens his position
on true religious liberty; nonetheless, this idea is perhaps the most
logical one to accept if one wishes to trace a thread of consistency
through what otherwise, in the light of his later actions, appears to
be a deplorably vacillating life.

After quarreling with Harrison, Browne took four or five families with him and crossed over to Edinburgh, Scotland, where he
obtained a letter of introduction from Andrew Melville. Immediately Browne started preaching his peculiar doctrines, setting the
teeth of the Scottish kirk on edge. He forthrightly pronounced,
his biographer, Powicke, says, that "the whole discipline of Scotland
was amiss and that he and his company were not subject to it."—
Powicke, *op. cit.*, pp. 36, 37.

Again Browne found himself in custody, from which the king

(James VI of Scotland, later James I of England) released him, not because he liked Browne, but because he wished to embarrass the kirk, with which he was at odds at the moment.

In his earnestness and zeal to present his message, Browne never stopped traveling and preaching while free to do so. He endured much hardship and many imprisonments, as often as thirty-two times, he stated, until he returned to his wife and family at Tolethorpe sometime in 1584, as a marked man. Because of his doctrines, which implied subversiveness to existing government, and the books he had published, he remained in constant danger of imprisonment.

In 1583 Elizabeth had sent out a proclamation against these "sundry seditious, scismaticall, and erronious printed Bookes and libelles, tending to the depraving of the Ecclesiastical government established within this Realme." Two men had already been executed on the charge of helping spread his books.

About this time a printed form of a letter Browne had written concerning "joining with the English church," an answer to Cartwright's charges against Harrison, fell into the hands of Whitgift, prime minister of England and archenemy of all that differed from the episcopal order of things.

Again Lord Burghley came to his kinsman's assistance, and it seems that Browne, after promising to conform, was turned over to his father for safekeeping. This was a task his father little relished, because of his son's continual aberrations. Browne was excommunicated on October 7, 1585, and he placed his name to a long list of articles signifying his conformity to the Established Church.

But neither Browne nor his wife went to church as they had promised. Browne, contrary to his word, met with his followers in London in conventicles, and bade his listeners not to attend the churches of England.

Browne took an inconsistent course of action, promising the church authorities he would obey their demands, when he had no intention of doing so. He yielded, outwardly at least, to the commands of the Church of England, all the while preserving his faith under a cloak of submission. Perhaps he silenced his conscience by reasoning that since it was a wicked church and a child of Satan, a promise to comply with its requests was a mere external, that God looked upon the heart; and if his heart was right, if he believed the true doctrine, it made little difference what he told the bishops.

This attitude of counterfeiting conformity brought down many anathemas upon his head from many biographers, particularly those of the Anglican and Presbyterian extraction, and even caused some of his followers to deny him the primacy of starting the Separatist movement. Few other Protestant Reformers have been so much maligned or received so much ill will from their fellow Protestants as did Browne, as the result of his not remaining stanch to the cause he espoused. Henry M. Dexter calls him "an elaborately slandered man."—*The Congregationalism of the Last Three Hundred Years,* page xxii.

A number of biographers have attempted to account for his actions, and have assigned reasons for his dissembling and subsequent return to the Established Church; among them are insanity (a theory which has gained wide acceptance); fear of the stake, or at least of further imprisonments and consequent removal from his wife and family; ill-health and broken spirits, to which his Middelburg experiment may have contributed; and his reasoning that it was useless to kick against the pricks, to beat one's head against a stone wall; therefore, why should he not spend the rest of his days in peace and return to the church ruled by the magistrates? for, after all, he had originally been of that opinion.

In 1586 Browne became master of a grammar school in Southwark, after signing another series of articles to conform to the Established Church. Again he promised to abstain from preaching his Separatist doctrines and to attend the duly authorized church.

In 1591 he gave up his school and asked that he be given a "living," to which Lord Burghley helped him. The rectory of Achurch-cum-Thorpe in Northamptonshire was supplied him, and shortly afterward he was ordained a priest.

During the forty years he served at Achurch he continued at heart to be a rebel from the Established order, although conforming frequently enough to save himself. It cannot be denied that he deserved the appellation of a spiritual and moral coward. But it is to be doubted that he changed his opinions on the separation of church and state, regardless of what his outward conformity might have been; for in 1587 he still wrote on the old themes as he had before 1583. The church continued to irk him. A letter to an uncle, written about 1588, contended that elders should be selected by the church, by a group of true believers.

At Achurch he repeatedly wandered from the path of Established rectitude and openly flaunted its discipline. He refused to wear the surplice, to use the cross in baptism, and to follow portions of the *Book of Common Prayer.*

For such acts of nonconformity he was suspended from his office. He had succeeded in winning some to his way of thinking, and for them he built a chapel house to which they resorted at times for counsel and worship. There is some question whether he was ever reinstated in Achurch as its pastor.

Toward the end of his life he was imprisoned once more, this time for striking a constable who attempted to collect taxes. A feeble, aged man, without means of transportation, he was carried to the jail on a cart cushioned by a feather bed. He was released after a short time and lived for a few years longer. He died in 1633, more than eighty years of age, and was buried in the St. Giles churchyard.

Browne was married twice, the first time to Alice Allen at Middelburg. She died in 1610, and two years later he married Elizabeth Warrener, of Stamford. It is recorded that a scandal which she incurred drove them apart.

To appraise Browne's worth by the results of his work would mean to accord him a foremost place among Reformers, for in this case "the harvest was better than the sower." He lighted a candle which caused the gleams of religious liberty to shine throughout the earth. After he made the beginning, other men, all acclaimed for their scholarship and deep consecration as Nonconformists— Henry Barrow, John Greenwood, and John Penry—bore the same message of religious freedom and laid down their lives for the truth as they saw it.

Firm in their opposition to both Anglicanism and Presbyterianism, the Separatists were persecuted largely by the ecclesiastical courts until they literally had "no place to hide."

They took refuge in the Low Countries; but there, too, oppression became so severe that they sought means to liberate themselves, lest they be completely destroyed. Departure for New England proved to be the solution.

Their arrival at Plymouth, Massachusetts, in 1620, represented the first step in the development of religious and civil liberty in the United States. This was to be the outgrowth of the principle which had had its inception in the mind of Robert Browne in England.

Oliver Wendell Holmes expressed their plight and their contribution to humanity in his "Robinson of Leyden":

> No home for these!—too well they knew
>   The mitered king behind the throne;—
> The sails were set, the pennons flew,
>   And westward ho! for worlds unknown.
>
> And these were they who gave us birth,
>   The Pilgrims of the sunset wave,
> Who won for us this virgin earth,
>   And freedom with the soil they gave.

THOMAS CARTWRIGHT

Leader of the Puritans

THE Reformation, as embodied in the Anglican Church in England, had scarcely taken root when the Puritan party arose. Or perhaps it would be more accurate to say that they had existed side by side from the inception of the Reformation. The Puritan party was not content with the existing state of affairs in the Church of England; they were anxious to carry the Protestant Reformation to further lengths, to make the break with the Catholic Church more nearly complete.

In the 1520's Cambridge University was a seething caldron of religious fervor and unrest, seeking after the "new" doctrine of salvation by grace—by faith in Christ. Fifty years later, in the 1570's, it was again the center of disturbing ideas as Thomas Cartwright, the founder of Puritanism, preached against the existing church government, the liturgy of the service, and the gorgeous vestments of the bishops, all of which he esteemed a part of popery.

The Act of Supremacy, which had made Elizabeth the head of the church, and the Act of Uniformity, standardizing the form of worship, which made it unlawful to conduct religious services except according to the prescribed Anglican form, left little room after 1559 for dissenters to deviate. In conjunction with the Act of Uniformity came the decision to use the Prayer Book of 1552, changing, however, the rule that denied "the real and essential presence" and adding the one on the wearing of priestly ceremonial garments, which had been removed in 1553.

The penalties for disobedience were heavy. The third offense for failure to wear the vestments entailed life imprisonment, and absenteeism from church service on the part of the laity meant the payment of a fine.

The Puritans, believing as they did that nothing should be introduced into religious worship that was not prescribed in Scripture, rejected the wearing of the vestments. The controversy which had raged during the time of Hooper was now resumed. Puritans regarded these garments as symbols of the church order which they had set aside.

Elizabeth remained adamant; it was her wish that these rules be enforced. The battle of the vestments became heated; the universities, the bishops, and the court all engaged in the controversy. Preachers were prohibited from preaching because they refused to wear the square cap, the gown, the tippet, or the linen surplice.

In March, 1566, the clergy of London were compelled to decide whether they would wear the enforced garb. Of 110 ministers, 37 refused, thereby leaving many of the parishes vacant; and the laity who disliked worshiping in the presence of what they termed "idolatrous gear" assembled themselves in private houses, in woods, and in secret chambers, where they could praise God without offending their consciences.

To the vestment question was now added the one concerning the entire hierarchical system of the church, whose form of government was patterned after that of Roman Catholicism.

Into this turbulence stepped the leader of the Puritan movement, Thomas Cartwright of Cambridge, "a man of genius and one who would have been prominent in any age," "an eloquent preacher and a rising theological scholar," "the first one to introduce extemporary prayer into the service."

In 1569 he was assigned the Lady Margaret chair of divinity at Cambridge. In the course of fulfilling his duties, while he attained his doctor of divinity degree, he preached against the popish form of church government existing in England, including the title and office of archbishop, archdeacon, and lord bishop.

He averred that bishops should preach, deacons should look after the poor, and only ministers who knew how to preach should be selected to govern their own churches; that it was the right of the churches, rather than of the state or of the bishops, to elect their own pastors; and that only what the Scriptures taught should be sanctioned in a church.

Furthermore, all parts of the Scripture, he maintained, were equally entitled to reverence; hence there was no point to kneeling at some words and standing at others, a practice followed by the Church of England. The Lord's Supper, he stated, might be celebrated either kneeling or standing. And other evidences that the church had not yet expelled all papal customs from her veins were: the making of the sign of the cross at baptism, keeping saints' days, forbidding marriage at certain times of the year, the use of "with my body I thee worship" in the marriage service, observance of Lent, and fasting on Friday. The presbyterian system, which he advocated, was ordained of God, he said; whereas prelacy was contrary to Scriptures.

Such opinions, spoken from the university pulpit, created a tremendous stir. Dr. John Whitgift, then master of Trinity and later the archbishop of Canterbury, of whom it has been said, "No ecclesiastic since Wolsey had departed so far from Puritan simplicity of life," assumed the role of representative for the opposition. Although William Cecil (Baron Burghley), Elizabeth's chancellor, defended Cartwright by saying that the professor was merely comparing the ministers of apostolic times with that of England, Whitgift lost no time in reporting Cartwright's lecture to the chancellor of the university. He succeeded in getting Cartwright dismissed from his professorship in December, 1570; from his fellowship in September, 1571; and then from the university.

Cartwright was born in Hertfordshire in 1535. As a lad, probably fifteen years old, he came to Cambridge. He was granted a scholarship at St. John's College, where the doctrines of the Reformation received great emphasis.

When Mary came to the throne, Cartwright, along with others, left the university to avoid joining the Catholic Church, only to return when Elizabeth became the reigning monarch. He attained the master of arts degree at Trinity, and in 1562 he was appointed the junior dean and major fellow at St. John's College.

It was about this time that Cartwright's fame as an eloquent speaker and a thorough scholar gained momentum. One biographer called him a "pure Latinist, accurate Grecian, exact Hebraist." Another biographer called him "the head and most learned of that sect of dissenters then called Puritans."

As one of those selected to debate on theology in Elizabeth's presence when she visited Cambridge in 1564, he is said to have drawn such a crowd that the windows of St. Mary's Cathedral were removed to permit those outside to hear him.

Perhaps weary of incessant controversy over church polity, he went to Ireland in 1565 to become chaplain of the archbishop of Armagh. Upon his return to England he received the appointment as Lady Margaret professor at Cambridge, and from then on he began to take a definite position against the organization of the Church of England.

When he found himself expelled from the university because of his views, he journeyed to the Continent, where he visited Beza, who at that time had already succeeded to Calvin's command over Geneva.

But for his approval of the ideas expressed in the First Admonition to Parliament he might have been made professor of Hebrew at Cambridge when he came back in 1572 at his friend's request. This admonition had been written by John Field and Thomas Wilcox as an appeal from the Puritans to Parliament, rather than to the queen. They had given up all hopes of winning her to their cause.

Of Parliament, the Puritans had asked: "Your wisdoms have to remove advowsons, patronages, impropriations and bishops' authority and bring to the old and true election which was accustomed to be made by the congregation. Remove homilies, articles, injunctions, and that prescript order of service made out of the mass book; take away the lordship, the loitering, the pomp, the idleness and livings of bishops, but yet employ them to such ends as they were in the old church appointed for."—John Brown, *The English Puritans*, page 59.

This pamphlet was circulated throughout the realm and went through four editions. It created a great sensation. The authors were imprisoned, and Dr. Whitgift was selected to make the reply to the Puritan request. His argument, learned and scholarly, expressed the view that it was unnecessary to maintain the same form of church government as did the apostles, and, furthermore, it was illogical to suppose it sin to retain a ritual or church policy simply because it prevailed in the Catholic Church.

To this the Puritans replied with a Second Admonition, this

time with Cartwright as the author. In it he set forth methods by
which the changes called for in the First Admonition should be
effected. These included a properly paid clergy, so that every parish
might be supplied with a pastor; the equalization in rights and functions of all ministers; and the institution of conventions for the
edification—both spiritually and doctrinally—and the discipline of
the ministry.

He also suggested the establishment of synods to which problems
too difficult for local solution could be referred. Above the provincial synod should be a national one, and a general synod should be
over all. In addition he recommended the formation of a local con-
sistory, a church board as it were, to enable every congregation to
have jurisdiction over church discipline, even excommunication if
need be, and over the relief of the poor, and in general to assume
the obligation of looking after the welfare of the local church.

These admonitions were directly opposed to Elizabeth's position
as head of the church, as the one who frocked and unfrocked the
clergy; and, naturally, her temper was aroused. She rebuked the
bishops for their negligence in not imprisoning these men. Whitgift
and Cartwright exchanged one more round of written argument,
and then Cartwright, to avoid arrest, went back to the Continent.

Other Puritans now lent their pens to the strife. Walter Travers,
an associate of Cartwright's, wrote *Ecclesiastica Disciplina*, the most
important treatise printed on the Puritan side. As a reply to it from
the Anglican point of view, Richard Hooker brought forth his work,
The Laws of Ecclesiastical Polity, "a finely tempered work," and
a classic in English literature.

Upon Cartwright's arrival on the Continent, he visited Heidelberg, and subsequently he became pastor of the church at Antwerp, and later of Middelburg in Zeeland. In 1575 he assisted the
Huguenots, who had fled to the Channel Islands after the Paris
massacre in 1572, in bringing uniformity into their church organization. He also exerted a guiding hand at the Synod of Guernsey
the following year, and at Jersey in 1577. Puritan representatives
from England were present at both places. In 1577 Cartwright
married a sister of John Stubbe. About this time he was offered
the chair of theology at St. Andrews, which he refused.

Because the lowlands did not agree with his health, he made a plea to the queen to permit him to return to England. This she denied; but nonetheless, he returned in 1585 to London. Here he was imprisoned, but Elizabeth released him because the bishop of London had acted before getting her consent. In 1590 the earl of Leicester procured the appointment of the master of the hospital in Warwich for him, and gave him a life annuity of £50.

In 1583 Elizabeth charged Whitgift, who had become the archbishop of Canterbury, to enforce the Act of Uniformity and thereby to restore in the church the discipline which she said the Puritans had destroyed.

Then ensued in England a tightening of church regulations by the crown, to the exclusion of all parliamentary proceedings that might be contrary, so as to cause Hume the historian to declare, "So absolute indeed was the authority of the Crown that the precious spark of liberty had been *kindled* and was *preserved* by the Puritans *alone;* and it was to this sect that the English owe the whole freedom of their constitution."

A system of "metropolitan visitation" was carried out to see that the rules made by Whitgift and aimed against the Puritans were enforced. In December, 1583, Whitgift established the court of high commission, whereby a man was made to tell what he knew of himself or anyone else. This oath, called *ex officio,* could be administered to anyone without a charge accompanying it.

The commons, somewhat at variance with the queen, persisted in considering bills bringing about changes in ecclesiastical laws. These efforts she stamped out vigorously.

The Puritans, having lost hopes of getting any help from the queen, began to set up their own organization, a "presbytery in episcopacy." At no time did Cartwright wish to break with the church. Along with their private assemblies and their attempts at establishing church synods, they resorted to another means of propaganda, namely, pamphleteering.

The many hundreds of Nonconformist ministers who had been driven underground and denied the right of preaching began to send forth tracts and brochures, some with satire and bitter invective laying bare the evils of the Church of England.

Whitgift retaliated by gagging the press; no printing establishment could operate except under strict censorship. Undaunted, the press, too, went underground, and a greater flow of pamphlets ensued.

Foremost among the Puritan scribes was John Udall, who died in prison for his defiance of the church. His *Diotrephes,* the fore-runner of the famous Martin Marprelate series, made conversation everywhere.

Attack after attack upon the church followed in quick succession. When one press was seized, another in a distant place rolled off copies of another diatribe. Ridicule, banter, and satire, mingled with some sound theology, were the means Martin (a pen name) used to expose the abuses of the church. So well were these harangues written that, as one writer puts it, "Martin now sits among the classics."

But the crown was determined to extirpate this heresy. Since Cartwright was under suspicion as having a part in the pamphlet-eering, the long arm of the law took him from his hospital at War-wick and in 1570 put him in Fleet prison in London. Here he, with his companions, including Udall, remained for two years because of their refusal to take the oath *ex officio.* But since he was a man of great influence he was finally released under bond to appear before the high commission when summoned, and under promise that he would conduct himself quietly and peaceably. Some of his companions ultimately yielded and revealed the names of others, a few remained in prison for many years before release came, and some were executed.

Thus ended the Puritan attempt at establishing a church organ-ization within the Church of England. But as every child who has ever heard of Plymouth Rock and the Pilgrims knows, it did not end their labors to obtain the right to worship according to the pristine pattern, freed from all frippery of Catholicism.

Cartwright returned to the Island of Guernsey and remained there from 1595 to 1598. He died at his home in Warwick in 1603, where he spent his last years regarded "as a patriarch by many."

JOHN COLET

Bible Scholar and Christian Educator

N EARLY a century had passed since Wycliffe's death and Huss's martyrdom at the stake. The spiritual revolution instigated by these men and their followers had been crushed, and in England, particularly at its universities, lectures upon Biblical subjects, if conducted at all, were greatly restricted.

Frederic Seebohm, in his book *The Oxford Reformers,* says, "The Bible, both in theory and practice, had almost ceased to be a record of real events and the lives and teachings of living men. It had become an arsenal of texts; and these texts were regarded as detached invincible weapons to be legitimately seized and wielded in theological warfare, for any purpose to which their words might be made to apply, without reference to their original meaning or context." —Page 17.

So it must have been with some degree of uneasiness, if not actual dismay, that the Oxford dons and those duly authorized to discourse upon the Scriptures heard that John Colet, a late student, recently returned from Italy, was about to deliver, without benefit of ordination, a series of lectures upon Paul's epistles.

This set of gratuitous sermons was the initial blow of the Oxford Reformers to break the chains of ignorance concerning spiritual subjects. These Reformers were More, Erasmus, and Colet, a trio of non-Protestants who wished to cleanse the church from within by peaceful, moderate methods rather than by violent revolution; to change the life and practice of the clergy rather than to change the doctrines. All Christendom was heaving like an ocean in a storm from the impact of the New Learning, a revival of classical literature, and its effect upon the Christianity of the age; and England could not remain unaffected.

John Colet was the first-born child in a family of twenty-one children, and all of these, except John, died in childhood. His father, Sir Henry Colet, was the lord mayor of London and a rich dealer in fabrics. Thus John, born in 1466, had all the opportunities which wealth and position could assure him.

He began his education at St. Anthony's, which rated as one of London's famous schools of that period. When he was seventeen he entered Oxford, where he remained until he attained the M.A. degree in 1494. Following this he spent two years in Italy for further study.

Although it is not definitely known whether he became acquainted personally with Savonarola or ever heard this fiery, flaming preacher, it seems probable that he did, for by some biographers he has been termed Savonarola's spiritual disciple. A comparison of the principles of the two men reveals that they were identical. Both wished to reform the church without a revolution, without breaking with the church, yet all the while both preached the Scriptures with clarity and devotion as they waged unrelenting warfare against the worldliness of monks and priests.

His two years in Italy made him an excellent Greek scholar and gave him a deep insight into the writings of the New Testament. In 1496 he was back in Oxford, where he began the series of lectures based on Paul's letter to the Romans. His singular approach to this subject brought him hearers, not only from the ranks of the students, but also from among the Oxford abbots and lecturers in the various faculties. Instead of using the method of exposition followed by the schoolmen when explaining Biblical texts, namely that of drawing out a "thread nine days long from an antitheme of half an inch," Colet considered each epistle as a real letter from a living man addressed to his fellow men.

In his presentation he showed deep earnestness and an anxious endeavor to make the epistles alive to his hearers. This type of lecturing was something distinctly new, and needless to say did not bring him into favor with the schoolmen, for his views were too far advanced for them. But his procedure elevated him in the minds of the students and made him dearly beloved by the common people, while leaving him without preferment by the officials of Oxford university.

When Erasmus came to England in 1498, Colet took him to his bosom as a friend and companion. He perhaps loved Erasmus as he never loved anyone else, or anyone else ever loved Erasmus. For parts of two years the two men talked and argued, Colet all the while hoping to win Erasmus to complete conversion in order to make of him a colaborer in the cause of England's reformation. But this Colet did not succeed in doing; nonetheless Erasmus received his greatest impetus toward Christianity from Colet. In much of this comradeship, Sir Thomas More, a young lawyer and author of *Utopia*, was a trusted and sympathetic partner.

After having the doctor's degree conferred upon him in 1505, Colet was installed as dean of St. Paul's Cathedral by order of Henry VII. Here he expounded and preached in much the same manner as he had at Oxford, never taking an isolated text and preaching upon it, but carrying forward a series of sermons upon some book of the Bible, preferably the epistles. Here Sir Thomas More came to hear him and received much comfort and spiritual enlightenment.

Shortly after his appointment to this highly influential position, Colet began to propound his ideas of reform, in which purpose he was repeatedly opposed by the clergymen who functioned as counselors to the bishop of London, Colet's immediate superior. Colet found little to commend in church tradition, he rejected the teachings of scholastic divines, he cast aside the writings of such men as Thomas Aquinas, and went back to the words and life of Christ.

Fearlessness, frankness, and freedom characterized all his preaching. He ably promoted the ideals of Christian education, personal religion, and piety marked by simplicity. Wherever worldliness and corruption raised its head, even among the order of which he was a member, he exposed it without fear or favor. W. Hudson Shaw stated in *The Oxford Reformers*, "No such preaching as Colet's, it may be safely asserted, had been heard in England for a hundred years."

But in spite of his influential position as dean of St. Paul's he exhibited no sign of vanity. It is said of him that during a period of nearly universal debauchery he lived a life of blameless purity. In his expenditures on himself he was very frugal. For years he abstained from supper, yet he set an acceptable table which was neither expensive nor excessive. He had many guests of whom it was said that they always left better than they came. This doubtless referred to Colet's ability to enliven the meal by challenging conversation in which he deftly drew out many of the more reticent.

In 1510 Colet founded his famous St. Paul's School and thereby instituted educational as well as ecclesiastical reforms. He started a revolution in secondary middle-class education which has beneficially influenced education in England down to the present time. More than one hundred fifty boys in his school each year studied Christian authors who wrote chastely in Latin and Greek. Colet remarked, "My intent is by this school specially to increase knowledge, and worshiping of God and our Jesus Christ, and good Christian life and manners in the children."—Samuel Knight, *Life of Colet,* page 364.

To secure the best, most capable teachers for his school, Colet went to great lengths, even providing proper remuneration for their services, a well-nigh unheard of procedure in those days. As evidence of his estimation of Christian teachers, he asserted that he considered "the education of youth the most honorable of all callings, and that there could be no labor more pleasing to God than the Christian training of boys." New textbooks also needed to be written, for the old ones contained too much contaminating material, and in this project his friend Erasmus lent a helping hand.

Before his death, Colet made explicit provision that the control and management of the school not fall into the hands of the church. It is said that he expended approximately $200,000 of his private fortune on this institution.

At this time Lollardism, which had perhaps never been completely stamped out since Wycliffe's day, was again in the ascendency, possibly because of Colet's preaching; at least the Lollards came in droves to hear him preach. As their numbers grew, martyr fires became common occurrences, until in 1512 the archbishop of Canterbury summoned a convocation of clergymen to meet in St. Paul's Cathedral, primarily for the purpose of eradicating heresy. Colet was invited by the archbishop to present the opening address.

Colet's initial remarks are worthy of quoting since they show the fearlessness of the man and his intense desire for a basic reform, especially in the lives of the clergy. He said, "You are come together today, fathers and right wise men, to hold a council. I wish that,

mindful of your name and profession, ye would consider the reformation of ecclesiastical affairs; for never was it more necessary, and
never did the state of the church more need your endeavors. For
the church, the spouse of Christ, which He wished to be without
spot or wrinkle, is become foul and deformed."—Shaw, *The Oxford
Reformers*, pages 21, 22. Throughout the sermon he inveighed
against the pride of life, the covetousness, the lust of the flesh, and
the numerous worldly occupations which beset the clergy.

This address had not the slighest effect in bringing about the
reform he desired; on the contrary, it earned him the enmity of
some of the most influential churchmen and made him a marked
man. The bishop of London preferred charges of heresy against
him, but these were promptly and angrily rejected by the archbishop
of Canterbury. For a short time only was Colet denied the privilege
of preaching in St. Paul's, and this because he had translated the
Pater Noster into English.

But his life was spared from the burning pyre or the axman, and
he once more preached with all boldness and straightforwardness
from his pulpit in St. Paul's.

At this time Henry VIII was relentlessly waging war on the
Continent. Colet took up verbal cudgels against the king's foreign
policy, for it blasted his vision of an approaching age of spiritual
rejuvenation. Colet's enemies thought that surely now they would
have their chance to get their quarry. But when summoned to the
royal court, Colet by discretion and moderation satisfied the mind
of the king that there could be a just war lawful to Christians. He
gained the king's favor to the extent that no one could touch Colet
from thenceforward, although the bishop of London did not cease
to harass him until the day of his death, which came in 1519.

Colet is listed among the great of earth because of his far-reaching influence upon the lives of others. His power over a large
number of people was nowhere more apparent than during his
deanship of St. Paul's, when the pulpit of the cathedral literally
became the focal point for men of every class of life—the merchant,
the courtier, the beggar, the highest of earth, and the humblest
classes. It was Colet who influenced More and Erasmus, the
other two of the Oxford Reformers. More owed his convictions
to Colet; and Erasmus, who received from Colet whatever spiritual

tone his studies acquired, called Colet, "My best-beloved teacher."

Colet was the originator of the Oxford Reformers, the leader of the English Renaissance, the founder of St. Paul's School, and the father of rational Christianity. His high moral character and his never-flagging interest in promoting a higher level of Christian practice and thought in the church gives him the exalted status accorded him.

Colet died before the Reformation under the direction of Luther burst upon Europe in all its political, economic, and religious fury. Luther had not yet broken with the pope. It seems that Colet sympathized with Luther's views and his attack on indulgences. He had read Luther's pamphlet, which had reached England. Conjecture as to what position he would have taken on Luther's Reformation had he lived must remain in the realm of pure speculation, although some assert he would have remained with the church.

Upon hearing of Colet's death, his colleague, Sir Thomas More, said: "For generations we have not had amongst us any one man more learned or holy!" And Erasmus, Colet's close friend, remarked tearfully: "What a man has England and what a friend have I lost!" —Frederic Seebohm, *The Oxford Reformers*, page 16.

MILES COVERDALE

Lover of the Scriptures

To MILES COVERDALE goes the credit for translating and editing the first complete Bible to be printed in the English language. He enjoyed the patronage of Thomas Cromwell, who, as vicar-general (1536-40), had power of jurisdiction over the affairs of the church in England.

In a letter to Cromwell he appealed for assistance in his work, "Now I begin to taste Holy Scriptures; now, honor be to God! I am set to the most sweet smell of holy letters, with the godly savor of ancient and holy doctors, unto whose knowledge I cannot attain without a diversity of books, as is not unknown to your most excellent wisdom. Nothing in the world I desire but books as concerning my learning: they once had, I do not doubt; but Almighty God shall perform that in me which He of His plentiful favor and grace hath begun."

Coverdale dedicated his Bible to Henry VIII. Toward the end of his inscription he remarked, "I have neither wrested nor altered so moch as one worde for the mayntenance of any maner of secte: but haue with a cleare conscience purely and faythfully translated this out of fyue sundry interpreters, hauing onely the manyfest trueth of the scripture before myne eyes." And near the beginning of his prologue he wrote, "And to helpe me herein, I haue had sundrye translacions, not onely in Latyn, but also of the Douche [German] interpreters: whom (because of theyre syngular gyftes & speciall diligence in the Bible) I haue ben the more glad to folowe for the most parte."

In other words, it was a translation of other translations, and not one out of the original Greek or Hebrew. The "fyue sundry interpreters" seem to have been the German-Swiss version of Zwingli and Leo Judä, the Latin version of Pagninus, Luther's German version, the Latin Vulgate, and Tyndale's Pentateuch and New Testament.

Although Coverdale's work does not rank as the true primary version of the English Bible (that honor is reserved for William Tyndale, as the translator of the Thomas Matthew Bible, published in 1537), yet "its importance in the history of the English Bible is great." Three fourths of the Old Testament was for the first time printed in English.

Neither Coverdale's Bible nor Tyndale's Matthew Bible, which came off the press the same year, was satisfactory to the officials. Thus Coverdale, still under Cromwell's patronage, set to work on yet another version intended to be free from the faults of the two already translated. As a result, he produced a revised edition of the Matthew Bible.

It is true that the Matthew Bible received royal acclaim, and during the next few years 24,000 copies were sold in London alone. But the Catholic clergy bitterly opposed it, for they saw in it the instrument which would deal the death blow to popedom in England. In 1542 this book of "Thomas Matthew's doings" received particular prominence on the prohibited list.

Since a better quality of type and paper could be obtained in France than in England, Henry VIII of England and Francis I of France permitted an English subject to do the work in Paris. But scarcely had 2,500 copies been printed when they were seized by the Inquisition and sent to be burned. One of the officers, wishing to make some money, sold much of the consignment for wrapping paper to a haberdasher. From this haberdasher a portion was later repurchased, and these copies, along with the presses, type, and some of the workmen, were transported at Cranmer's request to London. This enabled Grafton and Whitchurch, the famous printers of the time, to publish the *Great Bible* in 1539.

Because the first edition had been hurriedly printed, on account of the forced exodus from France, a revised edition appeared the following year, this time called *Cranmer's Bible,* because a preface written by the vicar-general appeared in it. In 1540 and 1541 six editions were distributed to the people.

Coverdale wrote a great deal, his works numbering approximately twenty-eight in all, most of them translations. Nearly all of them have been edited by the Parker Society.

Besides being famous for his writings, Coverdale deserves considerable praise as a preacher and a Reformer. He was born in 1488, probably in the district called Cover-dale, in North Riding, of Yorkshire. As a zealous papist he entered the Augustinian monastery early in life, became a priest in Norwich in 1514, and later joined the Augustinian friars in their convent at Cambridge, where Dr. Robert Barnes, its prior, influenced him to reject popery.

As the doctrines of the Reformation began to circulate around that university about 1526, a group of like-minded persons gathered in a house called White Horse. The papists nicknamed it "Germany" because its visitors discussed the beliefs advocated by the German Reformers.

When Barnes was arrested for heresy in 1526 and sent to London for examination, Coverdale, who had escaped a like charge, went up to help Barnes with his defense. After that event Coverdale left the monastery, dressed in the garb of a secular priest, and began to preach the reformed doctrines. In 1528 he went to Steeple-Bumstead in Essex and spoke against the worship of images and the celebration of the mass. He likewise asserted that confession to God, rather than to a priest, was the proper procedure to follow in order to have one's sins forgiven. In 1531 Cambridge granted to Coverdale the degree of bachelor of canon law.

When Cromwell and Barnes were executed in 1540 by Henry VIII, Coverdale fled to the Continent and remained in exile for eight years under the name of Michael Anglus. At Tübingen he attained the doctor of divinity degree. At Bergzabern, in Bavaria, he served as Lutheran pastor and schoolmaster. Here he spent his leisure hours translating various religious works, "of great service in promoting the Scriptural benefit of those persons in the lower ranks of life."

Shortly before he left England he married an excellent, godly woman, Elizabeth Macheson, sister-in-law of Dr. John Alpine, who helped translate the first Danish Bible. This matrimonial move served as an open protest against the doctrine of priestly celibacy and allied Coverdale more firmly with the Protestant group.

When he returned to England in 1548 at the accession of Edward VI he was well received at court, largely because of Cranmer's influence. He became the king's chaplain, and repeatedly served as funeral orator at burials of high dignitaries, such as Lord Wentworth, Sir James Welford, and Dowager Queen Catherine Parr, whom he had served as almoner. He also gave assistance to the civil arm by helping Lord Russell at Devon and Cornwall to put down the western rebels. Coverdale preached a thanksgiving sermon after the victory.

Upon Mary's accession he was deprived of his bishopric and thrown into prison, along with other leading Reformers. Seemingly his offense was that of his marriage, although when Coverdale's brother-in-law, who was then chaplain to Christian III of Denmark, influenced the king of Denmark to intercede in Coverdale's behalf, Queen Mary said that all she had against the prisoner was his failure to pay a debt due her treasury.

Coverdale was permitted to leave the country at the moment when Rogers, Hooper, and others were going to the stake. It is probable that Coverdale escaped martyrdom because his translation of the Bible was not considered dangerous, "for he appears to have carefully avoided attacking many of their chief doctrines, and to have so construed certain passages as to retain the spirit, and often an exact literal translation, of the language of the Vulgate. Where the word 'repentance' now appears in the Authorized Version, he almost uniformly inserted 'penance,' and in such a way as to convey no other meaning than the corporeal suffering enjoined by the Romish Church, instead of the sorrow of heart and penitence of soul required by the gospel. He yielded to demands of papists and withdrew most obnoxious features of the Matthew Bible when revised for the second edition."—John L. Chester, *John Rogers*, page 45.

Coverdale was "a pious, conscientious, laborious, generous, and a thoroughly honest and good man," but also "somewhat weak and timorous," leaning on those of stronger nature. He did not shout his defiance of the papacy from the housetop, as did Rogers at Paul's Cross the Sunday following Mary's accession; he preferred rather to withdraw meekly into obscurity when the storm signals of persecution were hoisted.

Upon his arrival in Denmark, Coverdale was offered a benefice, which he did not accept because of his inability to preach in Danish.

He settled in Wesel in Westphalia, where he preached to the many English refugees. Then the duke of Zweibrücken asked him to come to Bergzabern once more to become the pastor of the congregation at that place.

In 1558 he was in Geneva, and it is supposed by some that he had a part in the preparation of the *Geneva Bible*, which was published in 1560. Coverdale returned to England in 1559, after Elizabeth ascended to the throne.

During the years his power to preach had not diminished, and he was called upon repeatedly to address large congregations at Paul's Cross. Here, nine years before, he had spoken with such vigor and earnestness that, immediately following his sermon, the people pulled down "the sacrament of the high altar." But his stay in Geneva had inclined him more toward Puritan ideas, and he became more of a militant Protestant.

Archbishop Grindal, who was greatly concerned over the neglect shown the aged Coverdale, who, he said, "was in Christ before them all," obtained for him the rectory of St. Magnus, London Bridge, in 1564. Coverdale's poverty was so great that the queen was called upon to forgive him the first fruits (that is, the customary payment to the crown of a sum equal to the first year's wages) before he could enter upon his position.

Because of the stricter enforcement of the observance of the liturgy, Coverdale resigned in 1566; but he kept on preaching in secret, and many came to his house to find out where he would preach next.

In spite of his being deprived of a bishopric, he officiated at the famous consecration of Archbishop Parker in 1559, his objection to the wearing of vestments glaringly apparent by his appearing in a plain black gown. In 1563 the University of Cambridge granted him the degree of doctor of divinity, and in the same year he was given power by the vice-chancellor to admit Grindal as a doctor of divinity. In 1564 he published his last book, *Letters of Saints and Martyrs*.

According to the parish register of St. Bartholomew, Coverdale died February 19, 1568, at the age of eighty-one. He was buried inside the church.

THOMAS CRANMER

Archbishop and Martyr

"WHERE is Dr. Cranmer? Send and fetch him immediately. . . . This man has the right sow by the ear. If this had only been suggested to me two years ago, what expense and trouble I should have been spared."

Thus spoke Henry VIII in 1529, but only reluctantly did Cranmer allow himself to be brought before the king. Following a short conversation between the two, Cranmer was begged, then commanded as the king's subject, to lay aside all his present employment and devote his time wholly to giving a written opinion concerning the king's proposed divorce from Catherine, so that his majesty's conscience might find rest. Thus Cranmer made his entrance into the ecclesiastical and political affairs of this period of England.

Because of the wishes of his father, Henry VII, and because of diplomatic considerations with Spain, Henry VIII had married his brother's widow. Canon law did not sanction such a union, but a dispensation from the pope permitted it. Varied opinions still exist as to the reason why Henry VIII felt guilty over the matter, but whatever it may have been, Henry wanted a divorce. Negotiations appeared fruitless, for neither the pope nor Emperor Charles V displayed a willingness to yield. Then seemingly by chance a way for Henry's escape appeared.

An epidemic raged at Cambridge. A certain Thomas Cranmer, private tutor, left the city with his pupils to escape the ravages. At Waltham he met Gardiner, the king's secretary, and Foxe, the king's almoner. Since the king's proposed divorce had become the central theme of the realm, even overshadowing the prevalent question of the Reformation, these men soon began to discuss the issue.

Cranmer, a renowned scholar and clergyman, versed in the Scriptures, expressed the opinion that the answer to the question of the canonical legality of the marriage should not be sought at Rome, but from the Bible. It could be ascertained through the investigation of university theologians in England and on the Continent.

To Gardiner and Foxe, Cranmer said, "The true question is this, *What says the word of God?* If God has declared a marriage *bad* the pope cannot make it *good*. Discontinue these interminable Roman negotiations. When God has spoken, man must obey. . . . Consult the universities, they will discern it more surely than Rome." Cranmer's opinion reached the king the next day directly through Foxe and Gardiner. When he heard it he expressed himself in the opening words of this chapter.

Cranmer was born in Aslacton, in Nottinghamshire, July 2, 1489. He came from a family that traced its beginnings to the period of the Conquest. He was the second son of Thomas Cranmer and Ann Hatfield. Since the father's chief interest consisted in military sports, the chase, and racing, his sons came to excel in sports and horsemanship, too. Thomas particularly was a skilled horseman, and he was known to ride with grace the most unruly steeds during the time he served as archbishop.

His pleasing manner, modesty, and nobility of bearing made it easy for him to win friends. Such a man perhaps would have been more at home as a preacher or a schoolman, but it was Cranmer's fate to step suddenly into outstanding national and international prominence when he was forty-four years of age.

Early in life he went to school to "a marvelously severe and cruel schoolmaster." At the age of fourteen he entered Cambridge, to remain eight years studying logic, philosophy, the classics, and the opinions of Erasmus. In 1510 he was elected a fellow of Jesus College, but his marriage forced his resignation.

The following year he taught at Buckingham and afterward at Magdalen College. Upon the death of his wife, about a year later, popularity again won him a place as a fellow of Jesus College. By 1515 he had earned both bachelor and master of arts degrees, and his thoroughness in intellectual pursuits brought him both friends and foes.

At the appearance of Luther's writings he decided to know the truth of the disputed questions, and therefore he directed himself to three years of Bible study unhampered by commentaries. It is this period of learning that dates his gradual separation from the Roman Church.

After his ordination in 1523 Cranmer took the degree of doctor of divinity. Subsequently, he received in turn the appointments of university preacher, professor, and examiner. In the last position he had the opportunity, which he did not neglect, of insisting that candidates for graduation from the theological course know the Scriptures as well as the classics and the church fathers. Irksome and arduous as this procedure was to some, it did produce men who had studied the word of God.

Not long after his meeting with the king at Waltham he received appointment as archdeacon of Taunton and also became one of the king's chaplains. In January, 1530, he went to Italy as a member of the royal commission to confer with the pope and Charles V regarding the status of the king's case for divorce.

He remained on the Continent until September of the same year. When he returned to England other honors came to him at the hand of Henry VIII. In the summer of 1531 he called on Charles V as sole ambassador from England, with the hope of improving trade relations and of obtaining a closer political affiliation with the German princes.

He was in Europe again in January, 1532, to confer with the emperor. During this trip he married a niece of Osiander, a Lutheran theologian, some time before the death of Warham, the archbishop of Canterbury, in August of that year. Almost immediately Henry VIII appointed Cranmer as Warham's successor.

Hoping for a change in the king's intention, Cranmer delayed his return to England for weeks. It may be said, however, that even before Warham's death, Cranmer had virtually become the pope of England, so much had Henry honored him with power and influence.

There still remained the formality of obtaining the pope's permission for Cranmer's elevation to the archbishopric of Canterbury. On March 30, 1533, when Cranmer was consecrated in Westminster, he took the oath of obedience to the pope, a procedure which he later claimed to be a mere formality. He had no intention of permitting that oath to keep him from making corrections in anything he considered wrong in church doctrine or organization. From that time forward he ruled that the bishops and archbishops in England would be appointed without papal sanction.

Because he believed that royal power superseded papal power in the realm in all matters, Cranmer held court on the divorce case and summoned Catherine to appear. When she disregarded the order, he declared her action a contempt of court and forthwith, on May 23, 1533, declared her marriage with Henry illegal from the beginning.

Henry had won his case! Five days later the archbishop pronounced valid the marriage of Ann Boleyn and Henry VIII, which had been secretely celebrated on January 25. On June 1, Henry's second spouse received her diadem. Paradoxically, almost three years later, on May 17, 1536, Cranmer ruled that this marriage with Ann Boleyn had never been legal. "The grounds for both decisions were never made public."

As the gulf between royalty and papacy widened, and continual changes developed in the order of service, Cranmer was the first to make a denial of allegiance to the papal power, after which the bishops made their abjurations singly.

When the Reformation was permitted to grow in England after the papal rule had been cast off, it was Cranmer, as archbishop of Canterbury, who determined which of the many religious views clamoring for recognition should be accepted or rejected. He was "perhaps the only fit man in the whole kingdom, for superintending the ecclestiastical affairs at a crisis so peculiar."

A Lutheran at heart, he naturally leaned toward fitting that doctrine into the circumstances and environment of English law. He followed the middle of the road, rejecting the tenets of Catholicism as well as those of Puritanism. He took the position that whatever the Bible did not specifically forbid should remain; and remain it has, even to this day, in the Church of England.

One of Cranmer's most far-reaching acts for the cause of the Reformation was the encouragement he gave to the translation and sale of the Bible. To this project he gave unstintingly of his time. In 1538 he obtained a parliamentary order that every church should have a copy of the English Bible, placed so as to be easily accessible for those who desired to read it.

In spite of this action the papal party still had great powers, and it must be remembered that Henry VIII was not a Protestant. The papal partisans promoted a bill, partially against Cranmer, which passed and became known as the Act of the Six Articles. Cranmer, like another Luther before the Diet of Worms, had opposed the bill almost singlehanded for three days. All the articles of the bill counteracted the ideals of the Reformation. They re-established the Catholic view concerning the eucharist, the manner of giving the Communion, celibacy, the doctrine of purgatory, and auricular confession.

Cranmer particularly felt the blow, for he had married a second time, and now he would have to put away his wife. The penalties for ignoring these acts were severe in the extreme. Denying transubstantiation branded one as a heretic and paved the way to fagot and stake; ignoring any of the rest meant confiscation of all lands and goods, and death on the gallows, as well as being stigmatized as a traitor.

The archbishop escaped only because the king protected him constantly, regardless of the articles or the intent of his enemies. In fact, Cranmer was one of the few individuals to whom Henry was known to remain consistently loyal.

On January 6, 1540, Cranmer officiated at the marriage of Henry VIII and Anne of Cleves, and less than a year later the primate's official position called him to declare another divorce. Between 1540 and 1543 he directed a royal commission to revise and produce various works relating to church affairs. His litany, written in a beautiful, rhythmical style, and published in 1545, is practically the same as the one in use at the present time.

The death of Henry VIII on January 28, 1547, cleared the way for further expansion of Protestant ideas. Cranmer had been instrumental in winning the young Edward to Protestantism, and became, by the will of the king, a member of the council which governed during the nonage of Edward VI.

Now came Cranmer's high day. During Edward's kingship, he invited outstanding scholars and clergymen from all over the Continent to help clear the church of the practices and beliefs of Rome. Among these were Pietro Virmigli (Peter Martyr) to teach theology at Cambridge; Bernardino Ochino, who wrote and preached in

London; John Laski, a Polish nobleman, who preached to Italian, French, and German congregations in London; Emmanuel Tremellius, a Jew of Ferrara, who taught Hebrew; and Martin Bucer, Paul Fagius, and John Knox to preach and teach.

In the course of time Cranmer's influence gained strength among political and church leaders, and they looked to him to work out the details of ecclesiastical development. Before the end of the year 1547 he published the *Book of Homilies* and Erasmus's *Paraphrase* of the New Testament, translated into English. From the convocation, a group of religious leaders dealing with ecclesiastical problems, he obtained a vote favoring marriage by the clergy, and thus made it possible for his wife to return from Germany. The first Parliament of Edward VI repealed the laws against heresy, set aside the Act of the Six Articles, reinstated Communion in both kinds, promoted Bible reading and preaching, and instituted other measures to free the church from political and papal bondage.

By November the *First Book of Common Prayer* appeared, possibly without the approval of the convocation. Cranmer's *Catechism*, a translation out of the German of Justas Jonas, reached the public in 1548; and in 1550 he published his views on the sacraments under the title of *Defense of the True and Catholic Doctrine of the Sacrament*. The Forty-Two Articles, a constitution and ritual for the Anglican Church, drawn up by Cranmer in 1552, were based on an earlier work of English and Continental churchmen. These articles were distinctly conciliatory in tone, but basically Lutheran in sentiment.

The accession of Mary to the throne, however, meant a reversion to Catholicism, and perilous times to the friends of the Reformation.

In September, 1553, Cranmer was committed to the Tower. He could have escaped, but he did not feel that flight would be fair to the cause he represented. In November came his trial for treason, at Guildhall, where he was condemned, but the queen saved him to stand trial for heresy on the charge that he had written against the mass. In March, 1554, his place of imprisonment was changed from the Tower to the common jail at Oxford.

Because he was an archbishop, a special procedure obtained in his case. He received a technical summons to come to Rome; but when he did not appear there, the pope pronounced him guilty of contempt of court, excommunicated him, and appointed a commission to degrade him.

He went on trial for heresy, and received his sentence September 12, 1555. His degradation, a ritual by which the accused successively loses all the offices held in the church, occurred February 14 of the following year, after which he was remanded to the secular power.

For some time he parried all efforts aimed at obtaining his renunciation of Protestant views; but, once he had made his first recantation, he did not stop until he had abjured his heresy six or seven times. None of these recantations, however, saved him from the stake. Then, as the time of his execution neared, he made the bold assertion that he decried all his weaknesses, and took his position courageously for the Reformation and against the papal power.

He approached the stake calmly, clad only in a long shirt. When the flames rose, he held his right hand to the fire, saying that since that hand had signed the recantation it should be the first to suffer. He held it there until the flames consumed it. He died March 21, 1556, at Oxford, at the same spot where Ridley and Latimer had preceded him in martyrdom by five months.

"If the martyrdom of Ridley and Latimer lighted the torch, Cranmer's spread the conflagration which in the end burned up the Romanist reaction and made England a Protestant nation," historians have said.

Historians and biographers naturally vary in their estimate of a man of as many facets as Cranmer. Some maintain that his literary ability as demonstrated in his liturgical works overshadows him as a Reformer and a theologian. Blunt says that he had "an almost unspotted character." To arrive at an objective evaluation, one needs to weigh many of his acts in the light of the high favor he had obtained from Henry VIII. This pre-eminence does not excuse his vacillations, but it does indicate that, since he continually accepted royal favors, there was little left for him to do but to kiss the hem of Henry's garment. He made mistakes; but, withal, he lived in the main a praiseworthy life.

JOHN FOXE

He Wrote of the Martyrs

JOHN FOXE was not a great preacher. He took no part in the councils of kings and queens, nor in the conferences of the great, as they argued the merits of Protestantism versus Catholicism. Neither did he collaborate with other Reformers in producing confessions and beliefs. He did not translate the Bible, and he did not die a martyr's death.

His fame as a Reformer rests chiefly upon his having chronicled the events of the Reformation, particularly its martyrdoms. He occupies a unique place in the annals of reform because of his church history, *Acts and Monuments of the Church,* popularly named *Book of Martyrs,* the only work of its kind during this period in English history to give readers an insight into Protestant social habits and thinking.

During the past centuries in England and America the reading material supplied around many a hearthstone consisted mainly of the Bible, supplemented by the *Book of Martyrs.* And many a boy and girl, as well as older youth, from the sixteenth century down to the twentieth, have had their early thinking shaped by what they read in Foxe. Because of this considerable influence he is given a place as worthy of mention among the heroes of the Reformation.

Foxe was born in Boston, in Lincolnshire, one hundred miles north of London, in 1517, the same year that Luther nailed his ninety-five theses to the church door in Wittenberg. Foxe came of good stock. While he was still young his father died. His mother then married a Richard Melton, whom John evidently liked. Later on John was to dedicate one of his books to his stepfather.

His childhood was characterized by a great love for reading. Because his stepfather was poor, two friends sent John, at the age of sixteen, to Brasenose College, Oxford. Here he attained the A.B. and A.M. degrees; and at Magdalen College, in 1543, he was elected to a full fellowship.

He witnessed the discrepancies between the profession and the conduct of the Romish clergy, and began to study the Latin and Greek scholars, as well as the various disputations, acts, and decrees of the church. He also gained a thorough knowledge of the Bible in the original tongue, which "led him to discern the errors of popery and to seek the only way of salvation."

Frequently he spent whole nights in study. At times in the dead of night he walked in a pleasant grove near the college to confirm his mind upon the great Biblical truths, and to determine his course of action in the light of his new-found faith. To renounce popery in that period was no light matter; it frequently involved danger, loss of friends and preferment, and even death itself.

"From these nightly vigils," says a biographer, "sprang the first suspicion of his heresy. Some were employed to observe his words and actions. They questioned why he stayed away from church, shunned the company of his associates, and refused to recreate (take part in sports) as he had in the past."

By request of the college officials he resigned his fellowship in 1545 and returned to the home of his father-in-law, an ardent papist, who forthwith disowned him for his heresy.

Foxe then obtained temporary employment as tutor in the home of Sir Thomas Lucy, in Warwickshire. Here, in 1546, Foxe married Agnes Randall, a servant in the Lucy home.

Persecution drove him away, however, and, penniless and sick, he went to London, to Paul's Church. He became the tutor of the grandchildren of the duke of Norfolk.

Upon the accession of Mary Tudor, in 1553, Foxe wished to join his friends in exile, but the young duke of Norfolk, although a Catholic, felt honor bound to protect his tutor. However, Foxe, who had been ordained a deacon of St. Paul's Cathedral by Ridley in 1550, and who had been the first to preach Protestantism at Ryegate, had made some pointed remarks against the worship of images and other popish idolatry; and Gardiner, "the sleuthhound of the reaction," suspected heresy.

One day, as Gardiner was visiting in the duke's house, Foxe, whom the duke attempted to keep hidden, inadvertently walked into the room. When he saw Gardiner he immediately withdrew, and the duke explained that this was his young physician who, just coming from the university, had not yet learned the amenities of court life. Gardiner remarked that he liked the young man's looks and would doubtless sometime want to make use of him.

Realizing that his mentor's life was in danger, the young duke provided a boat at Ipswich and sent Foxe and his wife to a farmhouse near the seashore, to be out of harm's way until sailing time. A heavy storm caused the boat with the Foxes on board to return to port. Upon landing, Foxe learned that a messenger of Gardiner's had searched the farmer's house for him and had followed him to the port. The messenger had left when he discovered that the vessel had sailed.

Foxe decided to set sail again that night regardless of the rough sea, and in two days he and his wife landed in Flanders. For a time they lived in Frankfort, in the house of Anthony Gilby, a well-known Protestant. Because controversy in that city raged among the Protestants as to which ritual to use, Foxe left for Basel.

At Basel, then celebrated for its superior printing, Foxe became a "corrector of the press," as he worked for John Herbst (or Oporinus), an enthusiastic Protestant printer. He also continued his work on a church history which he had already begun in England. His labors were severe. In addition he "suffered want, sat up late, and kept a hard diet," but, accustomed to hardship from his youth, he did not seem to mind.

With his history he was assisted by Grindal, afterward archbishop of Canterbury, who was living in Strasbourg. Grindal kept up a constant correspondence with England and obtained many accounts of those who were burned at the stake, from the Reformers undergoing persecution and from their friends. These he gave to Foxe, who later also had access to the archives and the registers of the bishops.

In 1559 his *Acts and Monuments of the Church,* written in Latin and dedicated to the duke of Norfolk, his former pupil, appeared at Basel. In excellent Latin, Foxe congratulated Queen Elizabeth, in the name of the German people, upon her accession to the English throne.

Foxe returned to England the same year. Still in financial straits, he appealed to the duke of Norfolk, who provided him with a home. Foxe in turn encouraged his patron to read the Scriptures and stand manfully for Christ.

Foxe remained with the duke, then one of the most powerful noblemen in England, until the duke was executed in 1572 as a result of becoming involved in the intrigues of Mary, queen of Scots. Foxe accompanied the duke to the scaffold as his comforter, and heard him renounce the Romish doctrines and express his belief in Jesus Christ. The duke left Foxe an annuity of £20.

During the autumn of 1561 Foxe began to translate his *Acts and Monuments of the Church* into English. Every Monday he worked at the printing office of John Day, famous printer in Aldergate Street; and from this office the first complete English edition, dedicated to Queen Elizabeth, appeared in 1563.

The popularity of the volume was instantaneous. In the course of years it went through many editions—at least four editions within the first twenty years. By order of the canons of the convention of 1571, all high dignitaries were to receive a copy, as well as every college hall and university. A copy was ordered to be placed in every parish church, along with the *Great Bible*, that all people might read it. "Even now," said George Stokes, a historian, in 1841, "the well-worn remains are sometimes found in village churches." It is recorded that Nicholas Ferrar, pastor at Little Giddings, had a chapter of it read every Sunday along with the Bible. So great was its influence that "with Puritan clergy, and in almost all English households where Puritanism prevailed, the *Martyrs* was long the sole authority for church history, and an armory of arguments in defense of Protestantism against Catholicism."

Judged by twentieth-century standards Foxe's book can hardly be termed a critical work, but his supporters feel that it is unfair to accuse him of deliberate falsehood. In the years following its first printing he kept on revising wherever misrepresentations and new facts came to light. What he wrote, it is said, he wrote in good faith; and this is established by the internal evidence in the book. It possesses "a simplicity in the narrative, particularly in many of its minute details, which is beyond fiction; and homely pathos in the stories which art could not reach."

Because of his Nonconformist views, the extreme kind at that, Foxe never succeeded to special favor with Queen Elizabeth or her bishops, who had settled upon the Anglican form of church service. Consequently he did not advance in church office. For a time under Elizabeth's reign the Nonconformists were as greatly persecuted as were the Catholics.

He did, however, receive some consideration in the lower ranks. As a reward for his *Martyrs* he was made a prebendary in Salisbury Cathedral and vicar of Shipton. While holding these offices he had occasional conflicts with the ecclesiastical authorities, for he believed that too many of the fripperies of popery had been retained in church affairs. When Archbishop Parker asked him to conform, Foxe held up a copy of the New Testament and said, "To this I will subscribe."

He continued to preach, even at the famous Paul's Cross, the greatest outdoor religious meeting place of the time. Invited by Grindal in 1570, he preached his renowned sermon on the crucified Christ, and later amplified it for the press.

Foxe was a kind man, noted for his charity. Always poor himself, he shared what little he had with those less fortunate. Foxe also possessed tolerance. He hated the persecutions meted out to those of divergent faith. In 1575 he interceded valiantly with Elizabeth and other authorities to obtain a remission of the sentence to burn two Anabaptists. Although the queen called him "her father Foxe," she did not accede to his pleadings.

Shortly after 1570 to the time of his death, he probably lived on Grub Street. In 1586 his health began to fail rapidly, and after much suffering he died the following year. He was buried in the chancel of St. Giles Church, Cripplegate, London, where a monument inscribed by his son Samuel marks the spot.

JOHN FRITH

He Preached Bible Doctrine

JOHN FRITH, William Tyndale's "son in the gospel," was the first among English Reformers to expound the doctrine of the symbolic presence of Christ in the eucharist. He also believed that the church is the depository for all truth for all the earth, and not merely for an area or a nation. This conception gave birth to the missionary idea and caused the gospel to encircle the globe in later generations.

He was born in 1503 at Westerham, Kent. During his early childhood he and his parents removed to Sevenoaks, where his father became an innkeeper. At King's College, Cambridge, he attained the A.B. degree in 1525, and so great was his learning and ability that it was reputed that scarcely his equal existed anywhere. Even Cardinal Wolsey was greatly attracted to the young man, and invited him to be among the first to teach in his newly founded Christ's College at Oxford. Here Frith became junior canon. Henry VIII was so impressed with him that he wanted to place him among the leading theologians of the realm.

But neither academic achievements nor the king's preferments could turn him aside from a new pursuit, namely, to help Tyndale translate the New Testament. Although proficient in mathematics, he had discovered a new kind of learning, a type that comes from the study of the Holy Scriptures. "These things are not demonstrated like a proposition in Euclid," he said; "mere study is sufficient to impress the theories of mathematics on our minds; but this science of God meets with a resistance in man that necessitates the intervention of a divine power. Christianity is a regeneration."

His ardor in preaching the doctrines of the Reformation led him, along with some of his associates, to be imprisoned for some months in a deep cellar at Oxford. The damp dungeon, filled with the stench of salt fish, caused several to die. Wolsey released Frith upon the promise that he remain within a ten-mile radius of Oxford. Instead, the young Reformer escaped to the Continent, to the newly established Protestant university of Marburg. There he associated with many of the eminent Reformers, including Tyndale, who had preceded him, and Patrick Hamilton of Scotland. Frith's first publication was a translation of Hamilton's *Patrick's Places* from Latin into English. While abroad, Frith married and had several children.

In 1529 Tyndale and Frith left Marburg and went to Antwerp. The New Testament had been completed, and the learned Frith was now a great aid to Tyndale in translating the Old Testament. The king was ready to welcome Frith back to England any time he would renounce his heresies, but this he was not ready to do.

He returned to England without Henry's permission in 1532, perhaps to seek his friend, the prior at Reading. When he arrived in the city his disreputable appearance, for "exile had not used him well," caused him to be set in stocks for vagabondage. He remained there for some time because he refused to give his name, lest the king hear about it.

Finally, in desperation and in a semistarved condition, he sent for Leonard Coxe, the master of the grammar school, who was greatly astonished to hear a tramp clad in rags speak such eloquent Latin. With the schoolmaster, Frith conversed in both Latin and Greek concerning the universities, and he even quoted from the *Iliad* some lines which applied to his case. With great respect Coxe hastened to the mayor to obtain Frith's release, on the basis that a great wrong was being done a worthy man. Thus Homer was credited with saving a Reformer's life.

After he was set free from the stocks, Frith went to Bow Lane, London, and there he taught the Scriptures to those who wished to hear. For one of his listeners who desired an explanation of the eucharist he wrote a *Lytle Treatise on the Sacraments,* but without any intention of having it circulated. In it he expressed the following views:

"1.The doctrine of the sacrament is not an article of faith to be held under pain of damnation.

"2. The natural body of Christ had the same qualities as those of all men, except that it was free from sin, and it is therefore not ubiquitous.

"3. It is neither right nor necessary to take the word of Christ literally, for it should be construed according to the analogy of the Bible.

"4. The sacrament should be received according to the institution of Christ, and not according to the order in use."—Quoted in *The New Schaff-Herzog Encyclopedia of Religious Knowledge.*

A tailor named William Holt, under pretense of friendship, asked for a copy, and forthwith presented it to Sir Thomas More, then lord chancellor and successor to the ill-fated Cardinal Wolsey.

About this time Tyndale, back on the Continent, was becoming greatly alarmed lest his friend Frith should fall into enemy hands. He regarded Frith as "the great hope of the church in England," and he did not wish any evil to happen to him. He wrote:

"Beloved in my heart, there liveth not one in whom I have so great hope and trust, and in whom my heart rejoiceth, not so much for your learning and what other gifts else you may have, as because you walk in those things that the conscience may feel, and not in the imagination of the brain. Cleave fast to the rock of the help of God; and if aught be required of you contrary to the glory of God and His Christ, then stand fast and commit yourself to God. He is our God, and our redemption is nigh."

When More received Frith's statement on the Lord's Supper he was angered and wrote a tract in reply, characterizing Frith's doctrine "under the image of a cancer." Then he sought to have him imprisoned, and by all means available hunted him everywhere. He even offered a great reward for his capture. "There was no county or town or village where More did not look for him, no sheriff or justice of the peace to whom he did not apply, no harbor where he did not post some officer to catch him." Frith fled from place to place, changing his garb frequently to elude his pursuers.

Irked at the successes of the evangels, More gave vent to his feelings against them: "These diabolical people," he said, "print their books at great expense, notwithstanding the great danger; not looking for any gain, they give them away to everybody, and even scatter them abroad by night. They fear no labor, no journey, no expense, no pain, no danger, no blows, no injury."

As Frith made preparation to flee to Holland and rejoin Tyndale, More's agents were stationed at the wharf of a small seaport in Essex. They caught him as he attempted to board a ship, in spite of all his precautions.

From there he was transported to the Tower, where, for a time, he enjoyed considerable freedom, even going out on parole and conversing all night long with friends of the gospel. One such friend was Petit, a prosperous merchant and a member of Parliament, who later suffered imprisonment because of his Protestant views. With them Frith planned ways and means to promote the Reformation. He also wrote much, part of which constituted his debate with More and his associates about the Lord's Supper, and also about purgatory, which Frith termed an invention of the papists. His little tract "Bulwark" converted Rastell, More's brother-in-law, thereby creating such a sensation that many people came to visit the prisoner. This encouraged him to write still more, insomuch that with his pen he "enlightened many souls" and "contributed powerfully to the renovation of England."

During Lent of 1533, Dr. Curwin, a friend of the papists, preached a sermon against those who denied the physical presence of Christ in the eucharist; and he mentioned that it was not surprising that this pernicious doctrine was gaining such headway when "a man now in the Tower of London has the audacity to defend it, and no one thinks of punishing him."

Aroused by these remarks, Henry VIII commanded Cromwell and Cranmer to bring Frith to trial, and added, "If he does not retract, let him suffer the penalty he deserves."

Cranmer, who, twenty-three years later, was to go to the stake for the same belief, sympathized with Frith and wanted to save him; but he wrote to Archdeacon Hawkins, "Alas! he professes the doctrine of Oecolampadius." Cranmer believed with Luther and Osiander in consubstantiation or impanation, the doctrine of ubiquity, which teaches that Christ is present everywhere. But he still considered Frith a disciple of Jesus.

Four times, as one of a six-man board appointed by Henry VIII to try Frith, Cranmer privately attempted to influence him to change his mind. He even made provision whereby the prisoner could escape, by calling him to Croydon for a conference. As his escorts took him on the twelve-mile journey at night and on foot between Lambeth and Croydon they presented him with Cranmer's plans, so that he could flee. But he refused, going resolutely forward to his final trial and death.

On June 20, 1533, the Reformer appeared before a committee in his last formal trial, and again he refused to state that the doctrine of purgatory and transubstantiation were necessary articles of faith. The bishop of London condemned him to be burned at the stake.

Again Tyndale wrote from Antwerp: "Dearly beloved, fear not men that threat, nor trust men that speak fair. Your cause is Christ's gospel, a light that must be fed with the blood of faith. The lamp must be trimmed daily, that the light go not out. . . . See, you are not alone: follow the example of all your other dear brethren, who choose to suffer in hope of a better resurrection. Bear the image of Christ in your mortal body, and keep your conscience pure and undefiled. . . . The only safety of the conquered is to look for none. If you could but write and tell us how you are. . . . Your wife is well content with the will of God, and would not for her sake have the glory of God hindered."

Frith was now confined to a dark cell in Newgate prison, where he was chained in such a manner that he could neither lie down nor stand up. Yet by the light of a small candle he continued writing. The priests and the bishops visited him with the intent of getting him to recant. As they accused him of "having collected all the poison that could be found in the writings of Wycliffe, Luther, Oecolampadius, Tyndale, and Zwingli," he exclaimed, "No! Luther and his doctrine are not the mark I aim at, but the Scriptures of God." He prayed his judges to shed his blood the next day, if by his death the king's eyes might be opened.

Imprisoned with Frith was a young man, named Andrew Hewet, who also believed in the symbolic presence of Christ in the Lord's Supper. Back to back, they were tied to the stake at Smithfield, July 4, 1533. And thus at the age of thirty died Frith, who had "seemed destined to become one of the most influential Reformers of England." His interpretation of the Lord's Supper was some twenty-six years later adopted in the *Book of Common Prayer* and became "the publicly professed faith of the English nation."

PATRICK HAMILTON

Young Reformer of Scotland

AMONG the prominent men and women who devoted their lives to the cause of the Protestant Reformation, perhaps none was so youthful when his lifework was ended as Patrick Hamilton, the first preacher and martyr of the Scottish Reformation, and second only to John Knox in his influence on reform in Scotland. When he died for his faith at the stake he was probably not more than twenty-four years of age.

Of royal lineage, the great-grandson of a king, Hamilton is thought to have been born in 1504 of Sir Patrick Hamilton of Kincavel and Stonehouse, and Catherine Stewart, daughter of Alexander, duke of Albany, the second son of King James II. Two of his cousins attained eminent ecclesiastical rank, and other relatives gained high distinction.

He was surrounded from birth by an environment of courtesy and high breeding, rank and refinement; and early in life his parents dedicated him to the church. When he was twelve they procured for him the appointment of abbot to the abbey of Ferne in Ross-shire, the revenue of which furnished him with sufficient funds to pursue the advanced education he later sought on the Continent.

At this time Scotland was torn by strife for ecclesiastical power. Hamilton was nine years of age when on September 9, 1513, occurred the Battle of Flodden Field, a disaster which plunged the church and civil government into an unequal conquest for power, with the church gaining the ascendancy.

During the battle a large number of high church and government officials lost their lives, leaving their posts to be filled by youthful aspirants. Experienced statesmen were replaced by young noblemen who deferred to the prelates in matters of governmental

(71)

policy, thereby permitting the clergy to grasp the dominant places in politics.

The highest families in the realm resorted to force of arms as they rushed into the struggle to place their favorites on ecclesiastical thrones, and particularly that of the primacy of St. Andrews. Family influence and political intrigue determined the outcome. Hamilton's biographer, Lorimer, declared, "The church's patrimony suffers all the ignominy of a simoniacal partition in order to satisfy their covetousness and ambition; and a reconciliation of all parties is effected only when all parties are gorged with ecclesiastical booty."—Peter Lorimer, *Patrick Hamilton*, page 17.

The Hamiltons were in the midst of the strife, their affiliation divided by the contending parties. Young Patrick could hardly have escaped being impressed by the flagrant corruption of the church—for which his parents had destined him.

Hamilton left Scotland in 1517, if not earlier, to attend the University of Paris. He studied Greek and Hebrew, and read the Scriptures in their original languages, and he took his master's degree at the age of sixteen. It is true that obtaining a higher degree from a sixteenth-century university did not present the formidable academic hurdles that a similar achievement at the first-class university does today.

His stay in Paris proved to be the turning point of his life. He had passed from the middle ages of Scotland to the modern age of France, with its seething unrest and awakening to a new birth of religion. Here he came under the influence of Erasmus, who was an advocate of freedom of thought; it is even probable that he made the personal acquaintance of the man.

Of still greater importance to Hamilton was his reading of Luther's writings. Thus he learned about justification by faith, instead of by works, as he had been taught. A great many copies of Luther's account of the Leipzig disputation between himself and Eck were distributed in Paris and at the university in 1519. University officials purchased copies in order to evaluate and criticize Luther's orthodoxy. For more than a year the doctors of the Sorbonne deliberated, and on April 15, 1521, in the presence of the faculty and students they declared Luther a heretic, and they burned his writings.

After Luther's condemnation, Melanchthon took up his pen in defense of the great Reformer and the evangelical doctrines, and against the Sorbonne. His writings, too, were consigned to the flames. All this Hamilton saw. He could not have been more propitiously stationed to watch the ebb and flow of this theological war, to determine what was good and what was bad about Catholicism and Protestantism alike.

He spent six years in Paris; the three years following his graduation he studied probably at Louvain, where Erasmus resided in 1521, and it is possible that he also spent some time in Basel after Erasmus had moved to that city.

In 1523 Hamilton was back in Scotland as a student in St. Andrews University. The following year he was admitted to the faculty of arts in St. Leonard's College, where his proficiency in music led him to compose a mass arranged in parts for nine voices. This was presented in the Cathedral of St. Andrews, with himself as conductor.

At this time Hamilton's mind was probably still in a state of transition, a thoroughgoing Erasmian, but uncertain about Luther's theology.

In 1525 the Scottish clergy placed a ban on Luther's writings, which had been extensively circulated. Those who brought these works into Scotland were faced with imprisonment. Tyndale's Bible had also reached Scottish shores.

It was probably the following year that Hamilton first openly declared his new convictions, perhaps prematurely urged on because of his irritation at papists' actions against Luther's writings. But as soon as he began preaching he was faced with the proposition that either he cease doing so or die, for when Archbishop Beaton heard the rumor of Hamilton's defection from the Catholic faith he made investigation and found him "inflamed with heresy, disputing, holding and maintaining divers heresies of Martin Luther and his followers, repugnant to the faith."—*Ibid.*, p. 82.

Hamilton fled to Wittenberg, Germany, early in the spring of 1527, and associated himself with Luther and Melanchthon. He also met Tyndale and Frith, and for some time he studied under Francis Lambert, head of the theological faculty at the newly founded University of Marburg. Lambert praised his learning and spiritual insight, and said, "His learning was of no common kind for his years, and his judgment in divine truth was eminently clear and solid. His object in visiting the university was to confirm himself more abundantly in the truth; and I can truly say that I have seldom met with anyone who conversed on the word of God with greater spirituality and earnestness of feeling. He was often in conversation with me upon these subjects."—*Ibid.*, p. 93.

It was one thing to be converted to Protestantism through reading Luther's writings and to hear about the Reformation from afar; it was an altogether different matter to associate personally with some of "the most illustrious teachers and heroes of the reformed faith" and to witness at firsthand the progress of the Reformation with its sweeping social, religious, and political changes. For six months he steeped himself in the spirit and virtue of these men. This he needed to fortify himself for the trials ahead.

While at Marburg, Hamilton wrote in a balanced, antithetical style a treatise called *Patrick's Places,* which deals with the distinction between topics such as the law and the gospel, justification and holiness, faith and works. Hamilton wrote, "The law showeth us our sin, the gospel showeth us the remedy for it. The law showeth us our condemnation, the gospel showeth us our redemption. The law saith to the sinner, Pay thy debt; the gospel saith, Christ hath paid it. The law saith, Thou art a sinner; despair—thou shalt be damned; the gospel saith, Thy sins are forgiven thee; be of good comfort—thou shalt be saved."—Quoted by Robert F. Sample in *Beacon Lights of the Reformation,* pages 369, 370.

This brochure, written at Lambert's suggestion, has the distinction of being "the earliest doctrinal production of the Scottish Reformation," and it "became the cornerstone of Protestant theology in Scotland and England." Frith later translated it into English, and both John Knox and John Foxe include it in its entirety in their writings.

But Hamilton could not long remain away from Scotland, where he felt that God called him to deliver His message. Now he felt that he was prepared to face death, if necessary. He returned in the autumn of 1527 and began preaching to the nobility; to his own relatives in Kincavel, some of whom, including his brother and sister, joined him in the faith; as well as to a young lady of noble birth to whom he united himself in marriage. A daughter was born after his death.

Beginning with his family mansion, probably his brother's house, where he gathered his first congregation, he soon preached in all the surrounding country, as "he spared not to lay open the corruptions of the Roman Church, and to show the errors crept into the Christian religion; whereunto many gave ear, and a great following he had both for his learning and courteous behavior to all sorts of people."—Quoted by Lorimer, *op. cit.*, p. 105.

In January, 1528, he was invited by Archbishop Beaton to attend a conference of the heads of the church to consider "such points as might seem to stand in need of reform." Some of his relatives attempted to dissuade him from going, because they feared for their kinsman's life; but even though he knew he had not long to live, he resolutely turned his face to St. Andrews, "the Vatican of Scotland," to accept the archbishop's invitation. Here he lived in the lodgings provided for him by the archbishop.

The conference was held, and Hamilton defended his views. His opponents demonstrated such a conciliatory spirit that the young Reformer was permitted to teach in the university. This was all a part of the plan to get more evidence against him, for it was no easy matter to execute a member of such a noble family.

With utmost freedom he was permitted to go about the university for one whole month, instructing and disputing openly on all points he thought essential to bring about a reform in church doctrine and polity. Here at the ecclesiastical center and capital of Scotland he preached to students and faculty members, to various orders of monkhood—the Dominicans, Augustinians, the Franciscans—to noblemen, laymen, and priests, to all in the classrooms and the cathedral, and to all who sought him out in his apartment. In this one month he was able to strike at the very heart of the nation with his message of reform.

At the end of February he was seized and brought to trial in the cathedral. The charges made against him included his teaching that man is justified by faith and not by works, that faith, hope, and charity are so linked together that if an individual possesses one he has all, and if he lacks one he lacks all. Furthermore, he had stated that every true Christian must know whether he is in a state of grace, that no man is able by mere force of free will to do any good thing, that no one continues without sins in this life, and that corruption of sin remains in a child after baptism. He had exhorted the people to read the word of God, and he stated that the people were able to understand it. Worshiping of images and saints he had declared unlawful, as well as auricular confession, purgatory, and penance; all were contrary to the Scriptures, and he had called the pope antichrist.

After the mock trial he was deprived of all dignities and benefices of the church, and the secular government carried out the execution. Lest an attempt to rescue him prove successful, a guard of 3,000 men conducted him from the cathedral to the castle. It is said that when his brother James heard what was about to happen, he gathered a strong force to interfere with the plans of execution; but a storm on the Firth prevented him from reaching St. Andrews in time.

On the same day he was tried Hamilton was hastened to the execution in front of the gate of St. Salvador's College. At noon he was bound at the stake. As the iron chain fastened him to the pole, he prayed that the acute pain he might suffer would not cause him to say or do anything that would grieve his heavenly Father.

Hamilton died one of the most excruciatingly painful and prolonged deaths of any of the martyrs. He was tortured, not by intent but through carelessness, with a slow fire in which the pile had to be kindled three times because of green wood. When some powder which had been placed among the pieces exploded and a chunk grazed his flesh, Hamilton calmly said, "Have you no dry wood? Have you no more gunpowder?"

When the iron chain had nearly burned through the center of his body, one of the observers asked him to show whether he still believed, by giving them some sign of his faith. With that Hamilton held up three fingers of a partly burned hand, and held them high until he died at six o'clock in the evening, just six hours from the time he had been tied to the stake.

"On the day that he died the papacy unwittingly kindled a fire which shone over all Scotland, in the flames of which it was itself consumed," as "the reek of Patrick Hamilton infected all on whom it did blow."—Sample, *op. cit.*, p. 370.

JOHN HOOPER

Fighter Against Papal Errors

He WAS a tall man with a singularly repulsive appearance which kept his personal popularity at a minimum; and he was of an undeviating temperament, which allowed for little abandonment of opinions once espoused. Yet in spite of his rigorous doctrines and unprepossessing personality he easily filled churches to capacity.

Because he favored the English extremists in the Reformation and believed the views of Zwingli, he had less opportunity for escaping the stake than the Latimer-Ridley-Cranmer trio; and thus he became the first of the important bishops in England to die for his faith. His pronounced objection to the wearing of vestments, and his general nonconformist tendencies, developed a large circle of opponents.

Yet none of the English Reformers made a more profound impression on his hearers, nor aided the Protestant cause more by death, than did the former bishop of Gloucester and Worcester, John Hooper, sometimes referred to as "the father of the Puritans."

His ancestral home was Somerset, where he was born of wealthy parents near the close of the fifteenth century. As a student he has been described as diligent and prayerful, with a bent for reading the Scriptures.

In 1519 he was graduated with the bachelor of arts degree by the university of Oxford. That he was connected with the Cistercians, an order known for their austerity, seems to be quite certain; he probably received ordination to the priesthood under its sponsorship.

About the time the wealth of the monasteries lured Henry VIII to plan for their dissolution in 1536, Hooper went to live in London, where his leisure offered the opportunity for much reading. The writings of Zwingli, with his views on salvation, and Bullinger's efforts to promote the reforming spirit by a correspondence assuming international proportions, impressed him with their sincerity.

He returned to Oxford ostensibly with the intention of promulgating his newly acquired religious views. It was his opinion that a separation of church and state was desirable, but general acceptance of that idea did not come for more than a century. In one of his earliest writings he remarked, "As touching the superior powers of the earth, it is well known to all that have read and marked the Scripture that it appertaineth nothing unto their office to make any law to govern the conscience of their subjects in religion."—Quoted by Philip Schaff in *A History of the Christian Church,* vol. 6, p. 76.

Hooper came into national prominence about the time of the adoption of the Six Articles. His opposition to that set of regulations, accompanied by his growing Zwinglian bias, soon made him an object of suspicion among the leaders at Oxford, and led to his departure. It is also possible that about this time Sir Thomas Arundel, in whose house Hooper resided, suspected the Reformer's views and sent him to Dr. Gardiner, bishop of Winchester, to verify his suspicions. This forced Hooper to leave England.

At this juncture Hooper seems to have gone to Paris. He returned to England, however, before the danger was past, only to go back to the Continent again.

In Zurich, Heinrich Bullinger received him warmly. Other Reformers also welcomed him gladly, for the refugee brotherhood grew rapidly and carried with it an aura of mutual helpfulness. At Strasbourg he met Anne de Tserelas of Antwerp, whom he married in 1546 in Basel. There he made his home and devoted himself to an intensive study of Hebrew and to further indoctrination of Zwinglian beliefs.

The accession of Edward VI in January of 1547 paved the way for Hooper's return to England, but he did not remain long. He returned to Switzerland to stay two years, all the while associating with the Reformers Bullinger, Bucer, and Laski.

Once again in London, in 1549, his sermons renounced sin, castigated the evils and abuses of the church, and described the reprehensible iniquities prevalent in the world. Frequently he lectured twice a day and filled churches with eager listeners. By this time the Reformation stood on firm footing, though the country had not fully shaken off papal doctrines and abuses.

It was at this time that he occupied the place of a leader to the Reformers, constantly urging acceptance of the middle ground of Zwingli and Calvin, as opposed to Lutheranism and Catholicism. Apparently he felt that his preaching was effective, for he wrote to Bullinger: "The Archbishop of Canterbury, the bishops of Rochester, Ely, St. David's, Lincoln, and Bath, were sincerely bent on advancing the purity of doctrine, agreeing *in all things* with the Helvetic church."—Quoted by Thomas McCrie in *Life of John Knox,* page 336.

He now became Protector Somerset's chaplain and held the same position under Warwick. His views on the eucharist gained him the opportunity of presenting a series of sermons before the king during Lent, and as a result he was offered the bishopric of Gloucester. This he refused because it entailed the wearing of vestments, which he believed synonymous with popery and idolatry, and because the wording of the oath of supremacy did not meet with his approval.

After he spent a few weeks in Fleet prison, followed by some bitter wrangling, a compromise dispensed with Hooper's wearing the vestments after his consecration. The king had issued a statement permitting Archbishop Cranmer to ignore the use of vestments altogether in this particular service, but one side was as stubborn as the other: Cranmer refused to consecrate Hooper without the garb, and Hooper was ready to forgo the bishopric rather than accede to wearing the vestments.

Even the opinion of Bucer and Peter Martyr that vestments might be worn without sinning, did not convince Hooper that such apparel had any virtue except to enhance dependence upon popery. Hooper had for his support the opinions of many of the leading ecclesiastics of the time, who favored the dropping out of the church service all ceremonies savoring of the Church of Rome. And with these views the Puritans concurred.

Promptly after his consecration as bishop of Gloucester in 1551, Hooper left for his new post. His reforming zeal covered the entire diocese with its 311 clergymen. Often he preached four sermons a day, and he also outlined a series of lessons for the improvement of his clergy.

When the results proved unsatisfactory, he began a personal inquiry into the educational and theological preparation of these men. He asked questions relating to the Decalogue, to the Lord's Prayer, and the apostle's creed. The following list contains examples of this inquiry: "How many commandments? Where written? Can you say them by heart? What are the Articles of the Christian faith? Can you repeat them? Can you recite the Lord's Prayer? How do you know it to be the Lord's Prayer?"—J. J. Blunt, *A Sketch of the Reformation in England*, page 161.

The low educational state of the clergy is also indicated by Preserved Smith: "A reform of the clergy was also undertaken, and was much needed. In 1551 Bishop Hooper found in his diocese of 311 clergymen, 171 could not repeat the Ten Commandments, ten could not say the Lord's Prayer in English, seven could not tell who was its author, and sixty-two were absentees, chiefly because of pluralities."—*The Age of the Reformation*, page 314.

From this year to the time of his death Hooper was a member of the commission whose duty it was to report on canon law.

His elevation to the bishopric of Worcester in 1522 apparently did not raise such a furor as his consecration at Gloucester had done. He continued his strict discipline at Gloucester, and instituted a program of reform at Worcester as well. Constantly he fought against lapses from his ideals and strove to break down opposition, which occasionally led to mild violence.

With Mary's rise to power in July, 1553, Hooper's plans were undone. Less than two months after her reign began he was an inmate of Fleet prison on a vague charge of nonpayment of a debt to the queen. Possibly this charge was intended to bridge the gap until necessary laws against heresy could be passed by Mary's first Parliament, which was to meet from October 5 to December 6, 1553.

His imprisonment appears harsh and unjust, even for sixteenth-century standards. Hooper described it as follows: "... having nothing appointed to me for my bed but a little pad of straw and a rotten covering, with a tick and a few feathers therein, the chamber being vile and stinking; until by God's means, good people sent me bedding to lie in. On the one side of which prison is the sink and filth

JOHN HOOPER 81

of the house, and on the other side the town ditch, so that the stench of the house has infected me with sundry diseases."—John Foxe, *Book of Martyrs,* page 168.

He was degraded by the bishop of London early in 1554. On March 19 of that year he received a visit from the bishops of Winchester, London, Durham, Chichester, Llandaff, and other men listed collectively as the queen's commissioners, apparently to tell him that he had been deprived of his bishoprics.

On January 22, 1555, a group of bishops pleaded with him to return to the church and admit the pope's jurisdiction. He replied that he could not accept papal doctrine so contrary to Scriptures.

A few days later he was subjected to another examination by which his persecutors purposed to gain his recantation. With him at this hearing was John Rogers, who preceded him to the stake.

As the ineffectiveness of this interview became apparent, they were both taken to the Clink, a prison in Southwark, preparatory to their transfer to Newgate, a prison more detestable than the Fleet.

The following day, after still another examination, he was delivered to the secular power to be taken to Gloucester to die among his parishioners, where his assistance to the poor had won him a place of high esteem, in spite of his harsh demeanor.

The night before the execution he said to the officials, "My request, therefore, to you shall be only that there may be a quick fire, shortly to make an end; and in the meantime, I will be as obedient unto you, as yourselves would wish."—Quoted by Ruth G. Short in *Stories of the Reformation in England and Scotland,* page 144. On February 9, 1555, he was fastened to the stake with an iron hoop. Though the fire was kindled three times, and though he had three bags of powder on his body to hasten the end, it took three quarters of an hour of agony, in the presence of thousands of people, before he perished.

And what had been his crimes? He had married and refused to relinquish his wife; he did not believe in the bodily presence of Christ in the bread of the Lord's Supper; he denied the pope's authority as the head of the church; and he opposed the wearing of the priestly costume.

JOHN KNOX

Fearless Scottish Reformer

JOHN KNOX, the man who out-Calvined Calvin, brought all Scotland to her knees, and even made kings and queens bow to his will, began his work as a reformer after his forty-fourth birthday. None other among his colleagues is so sharply and dramatically outlined in the Reformation, unless it be Martin Luther.

It is supposed that he was born at Haddington, a few miles east of Edinburgh, in 1505. He came from below middle-class parentage and entered the University of Glasgow in 1522, the year Luther published his first translation of the New Testament. Here, it is said, he manifested no particular evidence of scholarship, but undoubtedly what he learned sufficed for his purpose. He knew Latin, for this was the language used in the universities. He also knew French and English, and acquired Hebrew after he was forty.

Little is known of him between 1522 and 1544. Sometime during those years he was probably ordained to the priesthood, and it is also thought he studied and practiced law between 1540 and 1543. During his tutoring days he came in touch with George Wishart, the Reformer, who was cloaking "the kirk" in Calvinistic garb.

After George Beaton, cardinal archbishop of St. Andrews, had been murdered for burning Wishart at the stake, Knox joined the murderers' sympathizers in St. Andrews. These men selected Knox as their preacher, and in his first sermon he denounced the pope as antichrist and the mass as a form of idolatry. Of this sermon one of his listeners remarked, "Others lop off the branches of the papacy, but he strikes at the root, to destroy the whole."—Quoted by James Stalker in *John Knox*, page 23.

In July, 1547, St. Andrews fell before the French fleet, and Knox was taken to France to be confined as a galley slave for almost two years. But throughout this trying ordeal he never lost courage, but believed confidently that he would yet preach in Scotland.

When he was released from the galley in 1549, he went to England rather than Scotland, and remained there five years. He preached under English protection at Berwick for two years, and as royal chaplain he addressed the most distinguished and influential audiences in England. In 1552 he had a hand in the compilation of the *Book of Common Prayer,* thereby putting in his bit to make it more Protestant. Finally, as a crowning glory, he was offered the bishopric of Rochester. This, however, he declined, and for his refusal was called to make an explanation before the Privy Council. When the council expressed its regret that he was of a contrary mind to the common order, Knox replied that he was more sorry that a common order should be contrary to Christ's institution.

With the death of Edward VI, under whose reign Protestantism had "sprung up like the gourd of Jonah in the sunshine of the court," and the ascension of Mary Tudor, "Bloody Mary," to the throne, with the resultant reversal of religious affiliations, Knox had to flee to Geneva, which had become a city of refuge for Protestant divines from all over Europe.

For a time he shepherded a congregation at Frankfort on the Main and also one at Geneva. These churches were composed of refugees from England. But not for long did he remain here, for Scotland was calling him. When he returned to his homeland he was welcomed with open arms wherever he went. Scotland seemed to be crying to be released from the Catholic yoke, and the nobles who had laid the groundwork gathered around John Knox to lend their support. It was a heartening experience for the Reformer.

Everywhere he went he celebrated the Lord's Supper in its simple form and forbade the people to attend mass. From this time on the mass became the distinguishing feature between Protestant and Catholic adherents.

Geneva was calling him to return; but, before answering this summons, he established the Protestant cause as far as he was able. He also gave instructions that the Scriptures should be read to the edification of all in devotional meetings. When he returned to the Continent he took with him a bride.

Apparently little record remains concerning the actual relationship between Knox and the great Reformer John Calvin, but their association must have been intimate. Of Knox's opinion of Calvin and of Geneva we are not left in doubt, for he spoke of Calvin as "that singular instrument of Christ Jesus in the glory of His gospel," and of the city as "the most perfect school of Christ that ever was since the days of the apostles." This was the model, with some political adaptations of his own, that he used in his own country.

Here at Geneva he had time to read, think, and study, and to associate with some of the most learned men of the age. As a result, most of his works were written during these three years. He helped in the translation of the *Geneva Bible*. The preachers of Geneva assigned him the task of writing a treatise on predestination, and when it was completed, it received the sanction of Genevan authorities.

One pamphlet, however, which he published in Geneva gave him untold trouble. It was the *First Blast of the Trumpet Against the Monstrous Regiment of Women*. Aiming it at Mary of Lorraine, regent of Scotland, Mary Tudor of England, and Catherine de' Medici of France, he argued that women had no right to rule. But the tract acted as a boomerang to the Protestant cause when Elizabeth, the Protestant queen, under whom England experienced her most glorious period, came to the throne. Knox was called upon to explain his tract both to Elizabeth and also to Mary, Queen of Scots.

It is said Elizabeth never forgave him and hated the place it was published. Calvin, when he sensed the harm that the tract was doing to the Protestant cause, took exception to Knox's writing it; but Knox, it is said, never retracted his opinion on women rulers.

From Geneva, Knox guided the Protestant party in Scotland, and when Mary Tudor of England died in 1558 and Knox was left without a congregation as the exiles returned to England, he made his way to Edinburgh, arriving there in May, 1559.

Here he found himself in the midst of the contest, one that he himself had helped produce. Mary of Lorraine, regent of Scotland, adopting a policy of expediency, had encouraged the Protestant nobles, who had formed the "Lords of the Congregation." Under their jurisdiction many churches were established openly. But Mary of Lorraine, a Frenchwoman of the house of Guise, and a papist at heart, determined to see that Scotland should bow to France politically and to Rome religiously.

With that intent she filled Scotland with French soldiers, who ravaged the country. She thought that now was the time to strike. She summoned the Protestant preachers to appear before her May 10, 1559. These, however, with John Knox among them, were accompanied by a contingent of troops. So was introduced a state of civil war which did not end until Mary's death, June 10, 1560.

Knox kept on preaching, continually thundering against the mass and everything connected with the papacy. He openly denounced the archbishop, and things got out of hand when mobs tore down images, sacked the monasteries and the churches, and brought about a general state of disorder and confusion. Knox condemned the rioters; but when Mary of Lorraine wanted to punish them, he told her she was fighting against God and not man.

The Reformation in Scotland seems to have been accompanied by greater violence than elsewhere in Europe. It has also been stated that the corruption of the Catholic Church had reached a greater height in Scotland than in any other country, unless it was in Italy.

Catholics and Protestants were now under arms, and Knox played a strange part in the movement. He appealed to Elizabeth of England for a fleet to help the Protestants in Scotland, and she sent both a fleet and an army. He was at once the army chaplain speaking courage to his forces. He was the secretary of the Congregation, giving instructions and writing commands. He was also the liaison officer, negotiating with the English government. Thus he worked unceasingly in order that the sacred cause of Protestantism might triumph.

With the death of Mary of Lorraine all this ended. The Treaty of Edinburgh, which followed immediately, stipulated that all foreign arms and troops should be removed and that no Frenchman should hold any office of importance. It was a distinct Protestant victory.

On July 1, 1560, began what has been pronounced the most important parliament that ever met in Scotland. This parliament, attended by a large number of lords, barons, and nobles, Knox among them, abolished the jurisdiction of the pope and the celebration of the mass. So stringent did they make the law against the

mass that offenders were threatened with death upon the third conviction.

Knox and his five assistants drew up a *Confession*, the doctrinal
standard for Scotland, in four days, and this was adopted by Parliament. This *Confession* was written on extreme Calvinistic lines, as
was Knox's *First Book of Discipline*, declared a masterpiece in organization, completed immediately upon the adjournment of parliament.

In order to establish church schools, to provide for the poor, and
to pay the clergy, Knox hoped to divert the property of the Catholic
Church, but here he was blocked. The avarice of the nobility
thwarted his purpose. They had grabbed the lands of the church
and refused to relinquish them, except such a portion as they themselves thought necessary to support the ministers.

As a consequence, Knox's remaining years were embittered as
he saw a starved ministry attempting to carry on, and Protestantism
in Scotland remained stunted for years. Yet to Knox's ideal as propounded in his *Discipline* may be ascribed the present-day reputation Scotland has attained in the field of education.

Knox had still another battle to fight. Mary, queen of Scots, the
unfortunate Mary who by her own unwise acts lost her crown and
later her life, returned from France as a widow of eighteen to Scotland in August, 1561. She was determined to restore Scotland to
the Catholic Church.

The most dramatic period of Knox's life doubtless falls during
her reign as he tilted and sparred verbally with Mary when she
repeatedly summoned him into her presence. The first such skirmish
resulted when Knox condemned the mass which she had celebrated
her first Sunday after arriving in Scotland. He had said that one
mass was more terrible to him than 10,000 armed invaders. Five
times, some say six, she called him before her.

The second occasion was Knox's sermon against the persecution
of the Huguenots in France, an event Mary celebrated with a ball
at Holyrood. The next also concerned the mass. The fourth, which
left an aftermath of peril, resulted when Knox had vehemently
spoken against her proposed marriage to a Catholic, the son of the
king of Spain. This time she dissolved in tears and sobs as she railed
against him; but Knox maintained he was preaching not his own
words, but the words that were given him out of the Scriptures.

Knox and his friends knew full well that his life now was in great danger. When the privy council called him in December, 1563, to answer for the crime of gathering a number of friends to support those who had been arrested for spying upon a mass at Holyrood, his friends urged him to make his peace with the queen beforehand, but Knox in typical fashion, refused, saying, "I praise my God, through Jesus Christ, I have learned not to cry conjuration and treason at everything that the godless multitude does condemn, neither yet to fear the things that they fear."—Quoted by James Stalker in *John Knox*, page 75.

After the queen, arrayed in all her worldly pomp, had assumed her seat, she saw Knox and burst out laughing. "Know ye whereat I laugh?" she asked the council. "Yon man made me weep, and wept never a tear himself; I will see if I can make him cry."—*Ibid.*, pp. 75, 76.

The crime they attempted to fasten upon him was that he had called the queen's lieges without her permission. Knox defended himself by saying that he had a perfect right to do so, that he did so every week when he invited people to church, and that there were some before him who had answered the summons. In spite of the efforts to pronounce the death sentence upon him, Knox remained cool and collected. In the end the council acquitted him, but this was doubtless the closest Knox ever came to wearing the martyr's crown.

Mary had, however, won for herself many friends, among them a group of nobles who were still Catholic, and by her practice of Catholicism many Catholics who had been driven under cover, now came out openly again to practice their religion. Many argued that the mass was not such a terrible thing after all, and even the Earl of Murray, Mary's half brother, future regent, and Knox's close associate, asserted that the queen had a right to follow her own religion unmolested.

It seemed for a time that the Protestant movement was destined to fail, had it not been Mary's own conduct, as it had been Mary of Lorraine's death, that proved to be Knox's greatest ally. Her marriage to her cousin Henry Darnley, her favoritism toward the Italian, Rizzio, and her later marriage to the Earl of Bothwell who helped instigate the murder of Darnley, lost her the sympathy of her best counselors and later the friendship of Elizabeth of England. The country revolted in disgust and loathing at her indiscretions, for which she was imprisoned and dismissed from the crown. And to Knox was given the privilege and high honor of preaching at the coronation of her infant son, the future James I of England.

The Earl of Murray, Scotland's most eminent Protestant lay leader, was made regent, and the Protestant church of Scotland attained full legal status by order of the Scottish parliament in 1567.

An evaluation of Knox, in order to be just, must accord to him the position of a great national hero, both politically and religiously. He led Scotland as none other in her entire history has done. It was his dynamic, fearless personality that brought Scotland out of its political chaos and established a degree of unity, compactness, and order in its national life.

The weapon Knox used to accomplish his purpose was the word of God. His sermons, of which few have come down to us, were full of vigorous, plain speech, wit, and sarcasm. He did not hesitate to flay rulers, nobles, and princes from the pulpit if what they did failed to measure up to his standard. His sermons have been described like "a match set to kindling wood," and his words have been compared to hail and bullets because of the forcefulness with which they were spoken. Even during the last year of his life when he was so helpless that he needed to be lifted into the pulpit, James Melville, his successor, wrote, "He was so active and vigorous that he was like to ding the pulpit in blads (break in pieces) and fly out of it."—*Ibid.*, p. 87.

The assassination of Regent Murray in 1570 was a most heartrending experience for Knox, and as he moved more than three thousand persons to tears by his funeral oration, he felt that his own days were numbered. He suffered an apoplectic stroke shortly after.

His last sermon, preached in Edinburgh, in August, 1572, a few months before he died, execrated the perpetrators of the Massacre of St. Bartholomew. His last days and hours were spent in meditation, reading the Scriptures, and visiting with friends who came to see him. The end came peacefully and without pain. Regent Morton, who spoke at his grave, asserted, "Here lies one who never feared the face of man."—Quoted by Williston Walker in *The Reformation*, page 334.

HUGH LATIMER

Preacher of the Gospel

A CANDIDATE for the degree of bachelor of divinity was delivering a Latin discourse at the University of Cambridge in 1524 as part of his requirements. In the audience was seated a young man so small in stature as to be almost hidden from view, who listened interestedly as the young graduate-to-be eloquently assailed the doctrinal views of Philipp Melanchthon.

The lecturer was Hugh Latimer, a zealous Catholic. The little man was Thomas Bilney, leader of the Society of Christians, the hotbed of heresy at the university.

Counseling with himself, the prudent and discerning Bilney determined by subtlety and tact to win this ardent Catholic to his beliefs. Knowing that the haughty, opinionated Latimer disdained evangelical preaching, Bilney decided, after much prayer and reflection, to call on Latimer in his room.

"For the love of God, be pleased to hear my confession," pleaded Bilney, as he entered through the door.

Latimer, startled but pleased to think that this heretic had been converted by his sermon, consented, and Bilney knelt before him.

Bilney related the torture of spirit he had once felt, and the unsuccessful search he had made for relief through the methods prescribed by the church. However, when once he believed that Jesus Christ, the Lamb of God, forgave his sins, great peace had come into his soul.

Latimer, not doubting the genuineness of the confession, listened with an open mind. As Bilney continued talking about divine love, the grace of God, and the healing power of Christ, the Holy Spirit gave Latimer a new heart.

When Bilney ceased, Latimer broke down and wept bitterly.

Bilney assured him that scarlet sins become white as snow when washed in the blood of the Lamb.

This was one of the strangest conversions in history.

Later, in one of his sermons, Latimer said, "I learnt more by this confession than by much reading and in many years before. . . . I now tasted the word of God, and forsook the doctors of the school and all their fooleries."

Both of these young men were destined ultimately to die at the stake for their faith. Latimer was to become one of the greatest preachers in England, and was to sit among the mighty in ecclesiastical circles of his country. By some he is called "the second John Knox."

Hugh Latimer was born about 1485 at Thurcaston in Leicestershire. He was sent to the country schools and then to Cambridge, where he became a fellow at Clare Hall and attained the master of arts degree. Following the completion of his classical studies he completed the bachelor of divinity degree, but because he failed to pay his fees, the degree was never conferred.

Of himself at this period he later said, "I was as obstinate a papist as any was in England, insomuch that when I should be made bachelor of divinity, my whole oration went against Philipp Melanchthon and against his opinions."—Hugh Latimer, *Works*, vol. 1, p. 334. He attacked the Bible readers among both professors and students. He railed against Dr. George Stafford, an illustrious teacher who explained the Greek New Testament to his classes. Latimer asked the students to remain away from Stafford's lectures.

All this was changed after "little Bilney" visited him. He became Bilney's disciple, and daily they were seen together, conversing and taking long walks. Practical in their Christianity, they visited the lazar house, the insane asylum, the jail, the poorer students in their narrow rooms, and the underprivileged working classes. They preached the gospel among these unfortunate people, and made many converts.

Latimer's character underwent a marvelous transformation. One of the first things he did was to apologize to Dr. Stafford. Meekly and humbly he spent much time in solitude studying the Bible, often arising at two o'clock in the morning for this purpose. He was energetic, humorous, plain of speech, and at times ironical, but honest, devoted, and courageous, frequently disregarding consequences as he spoke what he deemed to be right.

In 1522 he was one of the twelve licensed by the university to preach in all parts of England. After his conversion in 1524 the people regarded his preaching as something new and different. He preached boldly that Jesus Christ provided salvation for sinners, and that human traditions were unreliable guides. Large crowds gathered as he told them that the word of God was to be obeyed by prince and peasant alike. Even those who came to scoff and criticize went away saying that they had never heard any man speak as he did.

"Thus Latimer joined his contemporaries in championing the movement for a rebirth of feeling and in crying to the world the promise of justification by faith."—C. M. Gray, *Hugh Latimer and the Sixteenth Century,* page 20.

Priests became alarmed as they saw their parishioners begin to study the Bible, and university professors threatened to withhold advancement from students who turned evangelical. Nonetheless, the Reformers kept on; to Stafford's teaching, Latimer's preaching, and Bilney's praying were added Robert Barnes's scholarly exhortations and John Frith's stirring discourses on Jesus' saving love.

As the priests and professors at Cambridge saw Latimer's increasing popularity, they said that he must be stopped. For this purpose they appealed to Dr. West, bishop of Ely. After listening to one of Latimer's sermons on the evil ways of the clergy, West asked him to preach a sermon against Martin Luther, as an effective means of checking heresy. He could hardly have been pleased with Latimer's reply, "If Luther preaches the word of God, I cannot oppose him. But if he teaches the contrary, I am ready to attack him."

Since he had been forbidden to preach in either the university or the diocese, Latimer now went from house to house. Unhappy without a pulpit, he welcomed the invitation to preach in a monastery chapel. Barnes was another convert of "little Bilney" and was the newly appointed prior of St. Augustine's Monastery, which was outside the church control.

Called before Cardinal Wolsey, Latimer told what he had been preaching, but disavowed having Lutheran tendencies. Since Wolsey was no friend of West because of a private feud between them, and since he saw in Latimer the learning he so greatly admired, he granted the Reformer a special license to preach, much to the chagrin of Latimer's papist enemies.

When he was called to be the chaplain of Henry VIII, it can be said to Latimer's credit that he did not mute his message to tickle the ear of either king or prelate. At one time he stated, "Do you know who is the most diligentest bishop and prelate in all England? . . . It is the devil. . . . Ye shall never find him idle, I warrant you. Where the devil is resident—there away with books and up with candles; away with Bibles and up with beads; away with the light of the gospel and up with the light of candles; yea at noondays; down with Christ's cross, up with purgatory pickpurse; away with clothing the naked, the poor, and impotent, up with decking of images and gay garnishing of stocks and stones; down with God's traditions and His most holy word. . . . Oh! that our prelates would be as diligent to sow the corn of good doctrine as Satan is to sow cockle and darnel!"

Latimer also deplored the evils which accompanied the Reformation. As he deplored the low state to which the clergy had fallen because of a lack of funds to give them a decent living, he wanted to introduce a method whereby the ablest and most consecrated men would find election to the pulpit.

Latimer's way was beset by pitfalls into which at times he stumbled. Cited for heresy in 1532, he made what was considered a complete submission; but, later, when he stated that he had merely confessed errors in discretion and not in doctrine, he was again cited, and this time he recanted fully.

With Cranmer's ascension to the archbishopric of Canterbury, Latimer's way became easier. When Henry formally repudiated the authority of the pope in 1534, Latimer became a principal consultant with Cranmer and Thomas Cromwell as they advised the king concerning governmental and ecclesiastical procedures arising out of the abrogation.

At first favorable to Protestant views, the king subscribed to the Ten Articles, which the Protestants considered a long step forward. The opposition of the Catholic party led, however, in 1539, to the adoption of the Six Articles, which established transubstantiation, excluded Communion in both kinds, forbade marriage of priests, made obligatory vows of celibacy, upheld private mass for souls in purgatory, and necessitated auricular confession.

Feeling that his conscience would not allow him to uphold these rules, Latimer resigned his bishopric, and it may be that Cromwell saved him from the stake. It is said that Cromwell told the king, "Consider what a singular man he is, and cast not that away in one hour which nature and art hath been so many years in breeding and perfecting."

For a while he lived as a private citizen with Cranmer, and for a time he was imprisoned in the Tower of London. Upon his liberation in 1540 he was charged to leave London and desist from all preaching and from visiting the universities or his old diocese.

Six years later he was heard from again, this time also in the Tower because of his association with another Reformer, Edward Crome. When Edward VI came to the throne, Latimer was released, and immediately he began to preach again with even more vigor and power than before, although he refused to return to the bishopric of Worcester. Larger crowds gathered at Paul's Cross and other places to listen to him, and he made many converts.

When Mary Tudor followed the boy Edward to the throne in 1553, all this was over. A reactionary movement set in, and the restoration of the Catholic regime began.

Sent once more to the Tower, which was at this time overcrowded with many opponents of Catholicism, Latimer was confined in the same room with his friends Ridley and Cranmer, and with another man. Here they comforted each other by reading and discussing the New Testament. Latimer, old and sick, found prison life extremely difficult.

After six months, on March 8, 1554, Latimer was removed to Bocardo Prison at Oxford. With Ridley and Cranmer, he was examined at St. Mary's Church, April 14, on the charge that he had denied the doctrine of transubstantiation. Eighteen months later, on October 16, 1555, Latimer and Ridley were led to the stake. Cranmer's fate was postponed five months.

After both had been tied to the same stake in a ditch near Baliol College and a fagot lighted under Ridley, Latimer spoke the words which have since strengthened the faith of countless Christians the world over: "Be of good comfort, Master Ridley, and play the man. *We shall this day light such a candle, by God's grace, in England, as I trust shall never be put out.*"

ANDREW MELVILLE

A Living Epistle for God

"A S A PREACHER of God's word, he was talented in a very high degree—zealous, untiring, instant in season and out of season, and eminently successful—and as a saint of God, he was a living epistle of the power of religion on the heart. Sound of faith, pure in morals, he recommended the gospel in his life and conversation—he fought the good fight. . . . If John Knox rid Scotland of the errors and superstitions of popery, Andrew Melville contributed materially, by his fortitude, example, and counsel, to resist, even to the death, the propagation of a form of worship uncongenial to the Scottish character."—Quoted by McClintock and Strong in *Cyclopedia of Biblical, Theological, and Ecclesiastical Literature,* article, "Melville."

This testimony was spoken about Scotland's greatest educator and "the father of Scottish presbytery." The youngest of Richard Melville's nine sons, he was born in 1545 at Baldovie, a small estate near Montrose, Forfarshire, Scotland, of a family deeply attached to the reformed religion. When about two years of age he lost his parents, and his oldest brother, a minister, accepted the responsibility of the lad's rearing and education.

He attended grammar school at Montrose, where he was introduced to the study of Latin, Greek, and French. With this background, at fourteen he entered St. Mary's College at St. Andrews University with a knowledge of Greek that astounded his teachers. At the termination of his four-year course at St. Andrews, at nineteen, he had earned the distinction of being "the best philosopher, poet, and Grecian of any young master in the land." His intellectual insight and scholarly precision caused Douglas, the rector of St. Andrews, to remark with pleasure and unconscious prophetic foresight, "My silly fatherless and motherless boy, it's ill to wit what God may make of thee yet."

Melville enrolled in the University of Paris in 1564, where he studied philosophy, mathematics, Latin, Greek, Hebrew, and the Oriental languages until 1566, when he journeyed to Poitiers to gain an understanding of civil law. He was possessed with extraordinary learning, and at the age of twenty-one he was offered the regency of the College of St. Marceon. There his understanding of the classics, his ability as a Latin poet, and his oratorical prowess soon made his college superior to the College of St. Pivareau as the two vied for literary honors.

He remained at Marceon until his attitude during the Huguenot wars led the officials to suspect him of Huguenot sympathies. Lest he be apprehended, he went to Geneva. On the way he encountered grave difficulties, but these were soon forgotten under the spell of the warm welcome accorded him by Beza, who influenced the Genevan officials to grant him the vacant chair of humanities in the academy. Besides teaching, he attended many of his colleagues' lectures and began to be known for his scholarship in Oriental learning, as well as for his zeal for religious and civil liberty. Of the last he learned still more when the refugees of the St. Bartholomew Massacre began pouring into the city.

From the time of his arrival in Paris in 1564, until 1572, he had virtually cut himself off from his homeland and friends, but at this time, apparently because of his renown as an instructor in both France and Switzerland, he began to be besieged with appeals to return to Scotland and there to give his energies and organizing ability to the development of the educational standards, then at a rather low ebb.

When Melville decided to return home, Beza wrote to the general assembly in Scotland that the young man was "equally distinguished for his piety and his erudition, and that the Church of Geneva could not give a stronger proof of affection to her sister Church of Scotland than by suffering herself to be bereaved of him that his native country might be enriched with his gifts."

Upon his arrival in Edinburgh in 1574, Regent Morton asked him to be tutor in his family, but Melville preferred college to court life, and shortly thereafter the general assembly appointed him principal of Glasgow College. It was about this time that he met the young king, James VI, with whose opinions on church government he was later to come into conflict.

Melville soon distinguished himself as an educator as he introduced his six-year plan of an enlarged curriculum, including departments of philosophy, language, science, and divinity. The last he reserved for himself. His program also called for the training of regents, or deans, to supervise these departments. By his work he assured this university of an eminent literary history and a high reputation for scholarship throughout all Europe.

His enthusiasm paralleled his ability and energy. Soon the empty classrooms were filled to capacity; students enrolled from all areas in Scotland, as well as from abroad, as with singular success he developed an unusual ardor among them by his teaching and discipline. Within one year after his return to Scotland his renown as a reformer for Scottish education had reached Aberdeen, to which place he was called as consultant to Principal Alexander Arbuthnot of King's College, to assist with the formation of a new university constitution.

In 1577 the charge of Govan, near Glasgow, was placed under his supervision, and in the same year his stature as an educator again increased when a royal charter ratified his revised course of study for the University of Glasgow.

Scotland's low educational standards became more and more apparent as this university under Melville's guidance attained an excellent status of discipline and scholarship. Recognizing the need of immediate action, the general assembly, with the approval of the Scottish parliament, appointed Melville the director of improvements for all colleges and universities in Scotland. He was also made commissioner for the examination of St. Andrews University, the school of greatest wealth and enrollment; and in 1579 the parliament sanctioned his recommendations for its scholastic improvement. For the first time, St. Andrews as a seat of liberal learning became attractive to foreign students.

One distinction called for another, and in 1580 the assembly, by royal letter, was requested to permit Melville's transfer from his position in the Glasgow university to a similar post in St. Mary's College, at the University of St. Andrews. This college had by an act of parliament been created a school of divinity the same year. In less than two years after beginning his duties, his acknowledged ability and zealous enthusiasm brought noted improvements, in spite of internal opposition. The enrollment increased, and the cause of religion made exceptional progress, as his instruction in Syrian, Chaldee, and Hebrew, and his theological lectures drew students and teachers from other colleges. As a Scottish educator he stood without a peer.

Paralleling and often inextricably intertwined with his work as an educator were the religious and political issues of the period, in which he became completely involved. This man, described as "low in stature and slender in his person, but possessed of great physical energy," automatically donned the toga of John Knox. His vibrant voice, his fluency and power of words, his expressive gestures, his possession of a mind and determination of superior rank, and his reputation as a divine and a scholar, all aided in his introducing an austere presbyterianism into the tentative framework of church organization begun by Knox. His organizing genius in church affairs reflected his earlier educational successes.

Barely had Melville arrived in Scotland before he began to prove the unscriptural status of prelacy, with its three gradations of ministers; and he advocated its abolition. In its stead he recommended that all ministers have equality in authority and rank. His chief purpose was to make the populace conscious of Christianity as a criterion of behavior for nations and people, rather than as the victory of any form of church government over another. He was not sentimentally religious, self-seeking, nor fearful of consequences to himself; consequently a struggle with James VI and his ideas of divine rights was inevitable.

By 1575 he had become a member of the general assembly, where he served on the committee formed to study the polity of the church and to formulate an outline of ecclesiastical administration for the information of the general assembly. The result was what came to be known as the *Second Book of Discipline,* in the preparation and defense of which Melville took an active part; and in 1578, as moderator of the assembly, he received a unanimous vote which made the *Second Book* the guide for the government of the Presbyterian Church.

In brief, this book "discarded every vestige of prelacy, ended patronage, placed ordination in the hands of the eldership, and established a gradation of church courts. The church courts had a jurisdiction independent of the civil magistrates. . . . It did not, however, complete the development of the Scottish 'presbytery,' for it recognized no intermediate court between the eldership of the particular congregation and the assembly of the province; though it pointed the way to 'presbyteries' by allowing three or four contiguous congregations to have an eldership in common."—*The Dictionary of National Biography*.

His advocacy of the presbyterian system, as opposed to prelacy, was doubtless predicated on his Genevan experience; and what he had learned there he purposed to transplant to his homeland.

Cleverly and fearlessly he circumvented the plan of the astute Regent Morton to make the church subservient to the crown; and for this work he had ample opportunity, for as professor of divinity he took a leading part in the disputes on theology and polity, which often gave him access to the members of both the parliament and the privy council; but not without encountering the regent's temper. Melville's courage, however, was remarkable. One day when Morton had threatened him, Melville remarked, "Tush, man! threaten your courtiers so. It is the same to me whether I rot in the air or in the ground; and I have lived out of your country as well as in it. Let God be praised; you can neither hang nor exile His truth!"

As moderator of the general assembly he lost no opportunity to promote his specific plans for church government and to oppose the royal supremacy in ecclesiastical affairs. Because of his vehemence and reference to "a new popedom in the person of the prince," he was cited for high treason before the privy council, which, in spite of lack of evidence to support the charge, gave him a prison sentence for contumacy. He argued that a minister's utterances from the pulpit were not subject to a civil court until a church court had ruled on the case. Then, before he could be imprisoned, he fled to London.

While at the court of Queen Elizabeth he enlisted the sympathies of its adherents in behalf of the Scottish Presbyterian cause. Subsequently the group which supported his views in Scotland on church polity came into power, and after about two years Melville returned to his country and was reinstated in his office.

From 1585 to 1590 his status with the government fluctuated. At the beginning of this period he was ordained to the Presbyterian ministry, and James VI made him vicar of Abercrombie. In 1587, and again in 1589, he was chosen moderator of the general assembly. He attended conference after conference and assembly after assembly, boldly speaking in behalf of what he termed the New Testament form of church government, and denouncing the bishops and their system. Time after time the king sought to circumvent him, even keeping him from speaking at the assembly at Dundee in 1588 and forcing his withdrawal from the convention.

Yet some progress toward ending episcopacy was made. By May, 1590, at the coronation of the queen, Melville had risen to such power that only Presbyterian ministers were permitted to officiate; and Melville, himself, recited a Latin poem of his own composition, which was later printed by the king's orders.

All his difficulties, including vile calumnies, trials for treason, and sentence to imprisonment were forgotten in his satisfaction at seeing the parliament of 1592 pass an ecclesiastical act which placed church government under the control of general assemblies, kirk sessions, presbyteries, and provincial synods. This action constituted the legal basis of Presbyterian church government.

But even this decision of parliament did not stop the machinations of James VI in behalf of episcopacy. He insisted, among other stipulations, that state affairs be excluded from sermons, that assemblies must obtain his sanction for convening, and that church courts should disregard cases punishable under the criminal code. Furthermore, he declared the power of Melville and other officials of the assembly illegal and ordered them to leave Edinburgh.

At a later meeting a group of ministers was selected to confer with the king on affairs of the church, and this body was called "the needle which drew in the episcopal thread." But the king's enmity for Melville did not affect the clergy's estimate of him, for in 1594 he was again the moderator of the Edinburgh general assembly.

The king, ever anxious to find a cause against Melville, took advantage of a disturbance in Edinburgh, in 1596, to effect a change in the constitution of church government, an alteration violently opposed by leading clergymen and the Synod of Fife. Melville, who had not lost his fearlessness, headed a deputation to wait upon the king. The same spirit he had shown to the infuriated Morton he now showed to the king.

When James reminded him that he was his vassal, Melville replied, "Sirrah, ye are God's silly vassal; there are two kings and two kingdoms in Scotland: there is King James, the head of the commonwealth; and there is Christ Jesus, the King of the church, whose subject James the Sixth is, and of whose kingdom he is not a king, nor a lord, nor a head, but a member."

Such words were not the soft answer that turneth away wrath, and the king finally succeeded in getting Melville discharged as rector of St. Andrews University, in 1597, although Melville did return as dean of the faculty of theology in 1599. Determined to dismiss Melville entirely, to eliminate his constant opposition, the king succeeded in having it declared illegal for teachers of philosophy and theology, who were not at the same time pastors, to sit in any church courts "under pain of deprivation and rebellion."

By 1601 the king had become thoroughly exasperated at Melville's fearless insistence upon his rights by his appearance at assemblies in Falkland, Montrose, and other places, and went to St. Andrews University, where, without the privy council's sanction, he ordered Melville not to leave the college premises; "if he fail and do in the contrary, that he shall be incontinent thereafter, denounced rebel, and put to the law, and all his movable goods escheat to his highness's use for his contemption."

With the accession of James VI to the English throne, there to become James I, the quarrel between the two antagonists seemed to subside. Melville wrote a number of odes showing his agreement to the union of the two nations, but during the next two years Melville again opposed the restoration of episcopacy into Scotland. And when in 1606, during his attendance at the Hampton Court conference, he wrote a Latin epigram contemptuously ridiculing some rites of the high church, the privy council found him guilty of *scandalum magnatum.*

For the larger part of the next year he was a prisoner in the homes of the dean of St. Paul's and of the bishop of Winchester. Following that, "in violation of every principle of justice," he was kept in the Tower for more than four years, during the first of which he was in virtual solitary confinement. Pen, ink, and paper were denied him, and he saw no one but the person who brought him his food. "But his spirit was free and unbroken, and he covered the walls of his cells with verses beautifully engraved with the tongue of his shoe buckle." For the remainder of his prison term his treatment was less rigorous.

Upon his release he left for France, in 1611, to join the staff of the University of Sedan as professor of theology. Melville, now in his sixty-sixth year, wanted to return to Scotland, but the king refused, and he remained in Sedan until his death in 1622. The bitterness of his enforced exile was somewhat eased, however, by the kindness of some of his fellow countrymen who were living in France; but the hardness of the king was "one of the greatest blots on that reign."

NICHOLAS RIDLEY

Martyr for His Faith

"I MARVEL that you will trouble me with any such vain and foolish talk. You know my mind concerning the usurped authority of that Roman antichrist. As I confessed openly in the schools, so do I now, that both by my behaviour and talk I do no obedience at all to the bishop of Rome, nor to his usurped authority, and that for divers good and godly considerations."

Those were the words of Nicholas Ridley on October 1, 1555, a few days preceding his execution, in answer to the suggestion that he confess the pope to be the chief head of the church, and that he recant his view that salvation was possible outside the Catholic Church.

Nicholas, the second son of Christopher Ridley, was born about 1500. His comfortably situated parents lived in Northumberland near Willimoteswick, England. He attended grammar school at Newcastle upon Tyne and began his university studies in Pembroke Hall, Cambridge, about 1518. Here his ability as a student, and particularly his grasp of Greek, won him scholarly distinction. Following his honors graduation from Cambridge, he continued his studies and received the master of arts degree in 1526. He also attended Continental schools, such as the Sorbonne at the University of Paris, and the University of Louvain. Eventually he became proctor and chaplain of Cambridge University.

Up to 1534 he had not severed his affiliation with the Catholic Church, but his success in obtaining a university opinion opposing the spiritual power of the papacy and his part in signing a decree removing England from the sphere of papal jurisdiction, were indications of his trend of thought.

His reading of Bertram's *Book of the Sacraments,* and subsequent interviews with Thomas Cranmer and Peter Martyr regarding the gospel of Christ, "not a little confirmed him." Before the close of the year he openly supported the claim of Henry VIII to having supreme ecclesiastical jurisdiction of the English kingdom. Ridley had an uncle, an enemy of the Reformation, who paid all of the young man's university expenses. After this uncle died in 1536, the way opened for Ridley to demonstrate Protestant tendencies.

As he came into prominence, honor after honor followed in quick succession. When Ridley received his bachelor of divinity degree in 1537, Cranmer made him his chaplain. Cranmer had a high opinion of Ridley's erudition and discretion, and the following year he installed him as vicar of Herne, Kent.

Gradually Ridley began to reject the faith of the Catholic Church. He opposed the Act of the Six Articles in 1539, which enumerated important doctrines and policies of the church. The following year came the conferring of the degree of doctor of divinity and his election as master of Pembroke Hall, where he had begun his educational career. The canonry of Canterbury was given to him in 1541.

In 1543 the first open acts of ecclesiastical hostility against him began. Dr. Stephen Gardiner, bishop of Winchester, preferred charges against him for nonconformist practices, and for teaching heresy. Ridley was acquitted, however, perhaps by the king's favor. Before the death of Henry VIII, Ridley renounced the doctrine of transubstantiation, which teaches that the bread and wine are changed into the very body and blood of Christ.

His status with higher authorities continued to improve, and in 1545 circumstances enabled him to add the canonry of Westminster to the one of Canterbury, which he had received four years before.

His gradual deviation from the Catholic fold did not, however, lead to carelessness in the performance of his duties, nor to neglect of proper recognition of the established order. Ridley "stickled more for the ceremonies of the church than any of his brethren in the reign of Edward VI." This was particularly true as he followed the liturgy of the developing Anglican Church. During Henry VIII's last year he received a preferment with some liberality and became the bishop of Rochester.

The reign of Edward VI (1547-1553) gave Ridley an opportunity to step into even greater public prominence than he had before. His scholarly attainments fitted him eminently as a collaborator in compiling the *First Prayer Book*. Protestantism moved aggressively during Edward's time. Near the close of 1548, Ridley received the appointment of visitor to Cambridge, a position which privileged him to reorganize the university so as to ensure the firm entrenchment of Protestantism. This task began in May, 1549.

About this time occurred an episode of a type which was altogether too frequent in the history of the Reformation, and which the twentieth-century mind has difficulty in understanding. Ridley, in accord with Cranmer and others, pronounced death sentence on Joan of Bocher for an act considered detrimental to the religious beliefs of the period. Ridley knew definitely that she would be delivered to the secular power to meet death at the stake. It is true that "it was the dogma of the church in which Cranmer had been born and bred; from which even yet [he] had not wholly emancipated himself," but such an argument is neither a justification of, nor an acquiescence in, such acts.

Ridley was hostile to Princess Mary because of her lack of zeal in religious reform. He preached against Mary's succession at Paul's Cross on Sunday, July 9, after Edward's death. Here he railed on her as a usurper, not on the grounds of the supposed illegality of her birth, but on her lack of dependability in matters of "truth, faith, and obedience."

To this insult he added his support of Lady Jane Grey, who actually became the queen for nine days, to succeed Edward VI. Possibly in his support of Lady Jane Grey he was motivated by the duke of Northumberland, who headed the movement to put her on the throne.

As soon as circumstances showed that Northumberland sponsored a lost cause, Ridley went to Queen Mary at Framlingham, fell at her feet, and asked for mercy. This he did not receive.

On July 20, 1553, he became a prisoner in the Tower, along with Latimer and Cranmer. This incarceration did not keep him or the others from working constantly in the defense of, and for the promulgation of, the reformed doctrines. They wrote many letters of counsel on doctrines and Christian living to the brethren outside, and these letters were effective in forwarding the Reformation.

From this date to his death, more than two years later, he remained under guard at the Tower, at Bocardo in Oxford, or in the home of a Mr. Irish. The three prisoners were brought to trial in St. Mary's at Oxford, April 14, 1554. Here, it is said, Ridley carried off the honors in presenting the Protestant view.

"He adheres to one line of argument—that of explaining all the authorities advanced against him of the *spiritual* presence only; and this he does with a knowledge of his subject, as well as a readiness in applying it, such as argue an extent of reading, a tenacity of memory, and a presence of mind, quite wonderful. Be they passages from Scriptures, from fathers, or from the canons of councils, with which he is plied, they appear to be the last things which he had examined, so that a false reading, or a false gloss, or a packed quotation, never escapes him: and either a minute knowledge of an author's text, or (what is often quite as certain a proof of scholarship) an accurate perception of the general spirit which influences him, enables him to wrest the weapon from the hands of his adversaries, and to turn it against themselves."—J. J. Blunt, *A Sketch of the Reformation in England,* pages 284, 285.

Under the heresy laws passed by Parliament in 1555, Ridley, on September 30 of that year, received confirmation of his sentence on the capital charge of heresy. His formal degradation was scheduled for October 15.

His calm behavior at his execution also furthered, rather than hindered, the cause of the Reformation. His serene bearing and his encouragement to the aged Latimer, "Be of good cheer, brother, for God will either assuage the fury of the flame, or else strengthen us to abide it," created a lasting impression that here were men who stood willing to die for a great ideal. And Latimer's reply, as they were being fastened to the stake, "We shall this day light such a candle, by God's grace, in England, as I trust shall never be put out," was a prophecy which lingered long in the minds of those who witnessed the ordeal October 15, 1555, in the ditch opposite Baliol College. Cranmer, whose sentence had been deferred for five more months, saw their martyrdom from his prison window.

A memorial near the scene of execution was built in 1841.

JOHN ROGERS

Scholar and Translator of the Bible

SELDOM have church historians bestowed so many "firsts" upon anyone, regardless of era or nationality, as they have upon John Rogers, the first to write a Bible commentary, the first to write an English concordance, the first to compile and edit an authorized English Bible, and the first Protestant during Mary's reign to perish as a martyr.

He was born sometime between 1500 and 1505, probably at Deritend, in the parish of Aston, near Birmingham. He attained the A.B. degree at Cambridge in 1525. It is conjectured that in order to accomplish the monumental task to which he later set himself, which won him a place among the first scholars of his age, he must have been a rather "severe student" during his undergraduate days.

Upon completion of his college work he became a junior canon at Christ's College at Oxford and assumed holy orders shortly after. For nearly two years he officiated as rector at Holy Trinity in London, from 1532 to 1534, and for a part of his life he served as a priest in the Catholic Church close to the spot where he was later martyred.

Late in 1534 he resigned his rectorship in London and went to Antwerp, where he had been invited to become the chaplain to the Merchant Adventurers. Here he met William Tyndale, who was then translating the Old Testament. Some biographers affirm that Rogers met Coverdale at this time also, but Joseph L. Chester maintains that Coverdale was in England the whole period Tyndale was in Antwerp, and that therefore no connection existed between Coverdale and Rogers, or between Coverdale and Tyndale, at this time.

Having been deprived of the aid of Frith, who had but a short time preceding been martyred at Smithfield, Tyndale asked Rogers to join him in translating the Bible. Happy to employ his Greek and Hebrew, Rogers willingly assented, although he continued his ministrations as a Catholic chaplain.

While translating the Holy Scriptures, Rogers experienced his conversion to Protestantism. "I have found the true light in the gospel," he remarked one day to Tyndale; "I now see the filthiness of Rome, and I cast from my shoulders the heavy yoke it has imposed upon me." From that moment Tyndale received from Rogers the help which formerly had been given him by Frith.

But this association did not last long; Tyndale was soon arrested, and then was executed near Vilvorde Castle, in 1536.

Upon Tyndale's arrest Rogers saved the manuscript of the Old Testament, and immediately set to work to print the translation, possibly on a press owned by the Merchants of Antwerp. Because of his apparent submissiveness to Romish practices, suspicion did not attach itself to him at this time. Consequently he was able to bring Tyndale's work to fruition. And this, his biographer, Chester, remarked, "was no schoolboy's task. . . . Apart from the actual labor of placing the text in a complete state, and probably comparing every verse with the original there was a vast amount of mental effort to be bestowed upon the marginal illustrations which he added, as well as upon the various prefaces and other articles, prefixed to the whole work, and to individual portions of it. The marginal notes alone would fill a volume of considerable magnitude." Furthermore, Rogers "sat in judgment on every page," and "the mere labor of thus examining and revising . . . must have been nearly, if not quite, equivalent to a first translation."—Joseph L. Chester, *John Rogers*, pages 47, 33. Perhaps even more so, for it is usually easier to make a new garment than to remodel an old one.

Coverdale's part in this Bible is much less than some have supposed it to be. Rogers doubtless referred to his translation among others, but the Coverdale portions are said to be "not very numerous."

Since Coverdale's translation of the Bible in 1535 failed to gain official approval, Grafton and Whitchurch, English printers, came to Antwerp to see what terms they could make with Rogers. They were prompted primarily by business motives. Grafton especially was so pleased with what he found that he staked nearly his whole fortune in the printing of the new Bible. When they assumed the job it seems certain that the translation and printing of all the books preceding that of Isaiah had already been completed.

These sheets Grafton and Whitchurch purchased from whatever printer had done the work, and hired Rogers to translate and edit the remainder as fast as he could. Tyndale had supposedly translated all of the New Testament and all of the Old from Genesis through 2 Chronicles, and perhaps also the book of Jonah. It is even possible that he had translated all. But it may be taken for granted that some partially completed manuscripts and numerous notes, probably in a state of confusion because of Tyndale's sudden arrest, were left for Rogers's editing.

By July, 1537, the entire volume, under the pen name of Thomas Matthew, was printed and delivered in England, a little more than two years after Rogers began helping Tyndale work on it.

Cranmer liked the new translation, and the king granted a royal license for its publication and distribution. Soon the king proclaimed that every parish church in England should possess a copy of this Bible, that the people should have unrestricted access to reading it, provided they did not argue about its merits or doctrines but took their questions to their ministers and instructors. Within four years and four months 24,000 copies of the whole Bible were sold in London.

The question may be asked, Why did not Rogers sign his own name to the Bible, rather than that of Thomas Matthew? Chester explains that to have done so would not have been honest, for the work was not all his. Tyndale was dead and his name in disrepute among the papists; Frith, likewise, was dead and his name odious. Coverdale's name was out of the question, for his Bible had failed to win approval. This new Bible needed an author's name to throw the papists off their guard, and it may be that Rogers selected the names of his two favorite Scripture characters, Thomas and Matthew, to serve as the nom de plume for this whole Bible, "the greatest enemy . . . the papacy had yet encountered in England," and by which it ultimately received its deathblow.

About 1537 Rogers married Adriana de Weyden, a Protestant, in Antwerp. Soon afterward he departed for Wittenberg, where he learned the German language well enough to take charge of a German congregation. For ten years he preached in that city, and there most of his children were born. But at heart Rogers always remained an Englishman. When he was permitted to return to the land of his birth during the reign of Edward VI, his wife, and those of his children who were born in Germany were naturalized as British citizens by an act of Parliament.

Rogers probably returned to England in 1548, living at first in the house of his friend Whitchurch, where he translated Melanchthon's *A Weighing and Considering of the Interim* and thereby helped quell the rumor that the German Reformer had renounced Protestantism and returned to the Catholic Church. In 1550 Rogers became simultaneously the rector of St. Margaret Moyses and the vicar of St. Sepulchre, both in London.

In 1551 Nicholas Ridley, then bishop of London, made him a prebendary at St. Paul's. It is said that his duties were "severe and important." Two years later Ridley had him appointed as divinity lecturer or reader in the same cathedral, a position of prominence which was to catch the eye of the papist Mary as she ascended the throne soon after.

From the beginning of his Protestant ministry in England Rogers was a nonconformist, wearing only a little round cap rather than a priest's coat and square cap; and he would not wear the gown and the tippet, as was the custom of the regular clergy. He also lashed out against the Protestants in high places who enriched themselves from the spoils of the Catholic Church, criticism which did not tend to make him popular with the chief courtiers during the time of Edward VI.

Mary came to the throne August 3, 1553. On the Sunday after, on August 6, Rogers was asked to preach at Paul's Cross. It was not his turn to do so, and it is thought that his selection at that time was a contrivance of the papists to hasten his downfall.

It would have been expedient from an opportunist's point of view had Rogers preached a noncommittal, temporizing sermon, one filled with platitudes and overtures, but he never was one to conform his faith to the demands of his enemies. And he chose rather to give his message a "certain sound" at that crucial hour. He denounced the papacy and cautioned the people "to beware of all pestilent popery, idolatry, and superstition," and urged them to remain steadfast to the Protestant faith as taught during the reign of Edward VI.

Luther had the assurance of a safe conduct at Worms, but Rogers knew he was facing death when he preached as he did that Sunday at Paul's Cross. And what a pity it would have been had he preached other than he did, for at that particular moment the whole Protestant movement in England depended upon his words. "What a crushing blow would he have inflicted upon the cause of the Reformation, and how his example would have deterred others from maintaining their steadfastness when it should come their turns to be in peril, had he temporized with the ruling powers, or compromised himself. There never was any position in the whole history of the Reformation, all things considered, where the responsibilities thrown upon a single man were greater and the results more important, or where they were more nobly sustained. Surely, his conduct was more than noble—it was magnificent."—*Ibid.*, pp. 104, 105.

He was brought before Mary's council to answer for his doctrines of marriage of the clergy, the supremacy of Jesus Christ instead of that of the pope, and the abolition of the mass. He was imprisoned six months in his own home, from which he made no attempt to escape; and then Bonner, bishop of London, transferred him to Newgate prison, January 27, 1554, where he was confined among thieves and criminals and all kinds of low-class prisoners.

In January, 1555, he was examined before Gardiner, bishop of Winchester. Rogers stated his desire to be heard in writing, but this request was denied him. Nonetheless, there is preserved a minute account of his trial as he wrote it daily in prison.

On the doctrine of the eucharist he stated, "For I cannot understand 'really and substantially' to signify other than corporally, but corporally Christ is in heaven, and so cannot Christ be corporally also in your sacrament." He denied having preached against the Queen, even though he had stated that neither she nor Henry VIII was the head of the Church. He also denied ever having dissented from the Catholic Church; to him "catholic" signified, not the Roman Catholic Church, but "the consent of all true teaching churches of all times and all ages."—John Foxe, *Acts and Monuments*, vol. 6, p. 595.

On January 29, 1555, he was condemned to be burned at Smithfield. While awaiting execution he remained cheerful to the end, even drinking a toast to Hooper's health the day before he died. Hooper had been imprisoned in another apartment, and since his trial had been held the day before Rogers's, Rogers supposed they would be sentenced together.

Rogers also asked permission to talk to his wife that he might advise her what to do with the children, but this Bonner refused him on the basis that he had no wife, that his marriage to her was contrary to the teachings of the Romish Church. Rogers replied to the bishop, "Ye make yourself highly displeased with the matrimony of priests, but ye maintain their open whoredoms; as in Wales, where every priest hath his whore openly dwelling with him, and lying with him: even as your holy father suffereth all the priests in Dutchland and in France to do the like."—*Ibid.*, p. 603.

As the sheriffs led him to Smithfield, he encouraged the large crowd lining the path to remain steadfast in the faith of Jesus Christ. His wife and eleven children, including one infant, met him on the way. The temptation to renounce heresy, to remain among the living to provide for and enjoy his family, must have been even greater than all previous temptations; but Rogers withstood this test also. And he likewise resisted all attempts of the papists to get him to recant just before the execution. One cannot help standing in awe at such steadfastness.

As the flames kindled about him, "he, as one feeling no smart, washed his hands in the flame, as though it had been cold water," and then held them up to heaven until the fire consumed them.

The French ambassador at London, a loyal Roman Catholic and an eyewitness of the execution, wrote to Montmorency, chief minister to Francis I, immediately following the execution: "This day was performed the confirmation of the alliance between the pope and this kingdom, by a public and solemn sacrifice of a preaching doctor named Roger, who has been burned alive for being a Lutheran; but he died persisting in his opinion. At this conduct, the greatest part of the people took such pleasure, that they were not afraid to make him many exclamations to strengthen his courage. Even his children assisted in such a manner that it seemed as if he had been led to a wedding."—Chester, *op. cit.*, p. 202.

But those who rejoiced most that Rogers had remained true to his faith were the other doomed prisoners, among them Bradford, Cranmer, Ridley, and Latimer. To them Rogers was the bellwether who had trodden the path ahead and marked it well. He had not failed them, and they were glad. "I thank our Lord God and heavenly father by Christ," Ridley wrote to Bradford, "that, since I heard of our dear brother Rogers' departing and stout confession of Christ and His truth even unto the death, my heart, blessed be God! so rejoiced of it, that, since that time, I say I never felt any lumpish heaviness in my heart, as I grant I have felt sometimes before." And four days after Rogers's execution Bradford wrote to Cranmer, Ridley, and Latimer, expressing his happiness that their "dear brother" had "broken the ice valiantly."—*Ibid.*, pp. 213, 214.

Something more needs to be said about Rogers's writings. While in prison he wrote not only the account of his trial, but also a treatise entitled *Admonitions, Sayings, and Prophesyings*, which contained much instruction for the Protestant church. Among other things, he had a burden that well-qualified ministers be placed in the churches to shepherd the flocks. The manuscript of his writings Rogers had left behind him in prison as "a black thing" lying under the stairs in a dark corner. There his wife and son Daniel found it when they returned from witnessing his death. Others had searched the room but had found nothing.

Rogers wrote two more treatises, either one of which considered alone would place him in the front ranks of the heroes of the Reformation. One is a general English commentary upon the Bible, the first of its kind, which in turn led the way for many others to imitate. His other claim to fame is his preparation of the first concordance, *A Table of the Principal Matters Contained in the Bible, in Which the Reader May Find and Practice Many Common Places*. This was written for the purpose of directing attention to those parts of the Scriptures which opposed the Romish doctrines, with stress upon marriage, mass, and the eucharist, which were doubtless the most disputed subjects of the time between the Reformers and the Catholic Church.

WILLIAM TYNDALE

Kingpin of the English Reformation

WILLIAM TYNDALE occupies the paradoxical position of a man who made two great strategic contributions to English thought, one in the field of religion and the other in the field of literature—yet for some four hundred years he held one of the lesser acclaimed places both as a reformer and as a man of letters.

It may be said at the risk of using superlatives that he gave more to the English Reformation than any other Reformer, for without his translation of the New Testament into the clear English of his day, so that the common man could read and understand, such great preachers as John Colet, Hugh Latimer, Nicholas Ridley, and others could have preached until doomsday, yet there would have remained little understanding of the Scriptures.

Tyndale's translation of the Bible was the fulcrum on which balanced the entire English Reformation. He was the kingpin, as it were, that held together the framework of spiritual advancement in England during the sixteenth century. And with his translation, furnishing the chief source material for the Authorized Version of 1611, Tyndale's influence upon English literature likewise became greater than that of any other man.

Little is known of Tyndale's family. Born sometime between 1483 and 1495 in the western part of Gloucestershire, near the border of Wales, he early applied his mind to acquiring an education. As a boy he entered Oxford, where it is thought he gained a love for Bible study from Colet; at least he demonstrated a peculiar bent toward spiritual things. He likewise studied other liberal arts, and he acquired the mastery of seven languages—Greek, Hebrew, Latin, Italian, Spanish, English, and French—so that he spoke in each with a degree of native fluency.

He took his M.A. degree in 1515, and then he went to Cambridge, where he fell under the influence of Erasmus. One of his first appointments was that of tutor-chaplain at Little Sodsbury in the family of Sir Thomas Walsh. He was apparently already ordained at this time. Here he entered into ecclesiastical disputation with the church dignitaries. Later, when he preached at Bristol, he set the tongues of the clergy wagging because of what they considered his heresy. For his divergent views he was summoned to appear before the chancellor.

Disturbed in heart and mind by the gross ignorance and sordid living of the priests and monks, Tyndale sought advice from an old chancellor, and in return this man told him that the pope was the antichrist of the Scriptures. This startled the young priest so much that he prayed and studied anew, taking Erasmus's Greek New Testament still closer to heart.

He soon began to be convinced as to what his lifework was to be. Realizing that the church would rather have thousands of books written against its teachings than to have the common people have access to the Bible, he determined to translate the New Testament. As his mission in life became clearer to him, he remarked, "I perceived by experience how that it is impossible to establish the lay people in any truth, except that the Scriptures were plainly laid before their eyes, that they might see the process, order, and meaning of the text."—Quoted by Luke S. Walmsley in *Fighters and Martyrs for the Freedom of the Faith*, page 73.

To one of his opponents who had expressed the thought that the pope's laws were better than God's, Tyndale replied, "I defy the pope and all his laws; and if God spare my life, ere many years, I will cause a boy that driveth the plow shall know more of the Scripture than thou dost."—Quoted by J. F. Mozley in *William Tyndale*, page 35.

So Tyndale began looking around as to who might help him with his task. He felt that surely the bishop of London would do so; but when he appealed to him in 1523, the bishop would have nothing to do with it. Another on whom he thought he could count opposed it, namely, Sir Thomas More, who advocated that only a group of responsible scholars, and not an individual, should undertake such a task, furthermore, that the ignorant man of the street should not have access to the Bible, lest some fanciful interpretations result.

However, one day as Tyndale was preaching at St. Dunstan's, a wealthy cloth merchant and London alderman, Sir Humphrey Monmouth, heard him, became his friend, and offered him his London home to write in. Here for a year Tyndale found shelter where he could work to his heart's content.

Then the priests were after him. As a consequence he came to the conclusion that there was not a place in all England where he could translate the Scriptures; and he sailed in May, 1524, for the Continent, and he never saw his beloved country again.

For the next twelve and a half years Tyndale lived the life of a persecuted, hunted, and disappointed man, as he fled from one city to another to evade his oppressors. He moved frequently among the cities of Wittenberg, Cologne, Hamburg, Worms, Strasbourg, Marburg, and Antwerp.

He is supposed to have visited Luther in Wittenberg in 1524, where he stayed nearly a year, working at his translating. In Cologne in 1525 the printing started, but a careless word to the effect that England would soon rub her eyes caused the news to travel to the bishops of England. Tyndale fled to Worms, taking what precious sheets he could with him.

Here his New Testament was printed in 1526, and six thousand copies were said to have been sent to England in the winter of 1526-27, in spite of the fact that the bishops were zealously watching the ports. It was the small size of the edition which made it possible to pack the copies in cases, sacks of flour, bales of merchandise, and barrels. It is recorded that in the four years following, some fifteen thousand copies passed into England.

The Roman Catholic Church immediately seized one thousand copies and had them burned in 1527, and later the bishop of London bought up all he could find. He also called on Sir Thomas More publicly to expose the errors in the translation.

To have the old edition disposed of by purchase was all to Tyndale's favor, for it enabled him to publish a revised edition, much better than the first. And the second soon came out "thick and threefold," as well as did seven more editions during the next ten years.

The bishops were incensed. One reason was that Tyndale's

translation had lost for them some of their choice Christian words. He had used *repentance* for *penance, acknowledge* for *confess, favor* for *grace, image* for *idol, elder* for *priest, love* for *charity, congregation* for *church,* to give a few examples. For his text he had taken Erasmus's Greek New Testament, and he had doubtless followed Luther's German translation, which had been completed at the Wartburg a short while before.

At the time Tyndale made his translation, there was no English Bible for the common people. Wycliffe's Bible, which that Reformer had translated into the early Middle English, was largely obsolete, and it had been taken from the Latin Vulgate, itself a translation. Then, too, there was much opposition to Wycliffe's doctrines.

Tyndale said of his own translation, "I had no man to counterfeit (imitate), neither was helped with English of any that had interpreted the same, or such like thing in the Scripture beforehand." His objective was to produce an absolutely honest, simple, straightforward translation of the Scriptures into English so all England could read it. To the translator's credit it can be said that he shunned the use of the overornate, euphuistic, or Arcadian stylistic devices so prevalent in the sixteenth century. Had he succumbed to the temptation, his translation would doubtless not have served as the basis for the Authorized Version of 1611.

Concerning Tyndale's part in this Authorized Version, authorities state that when the English Bible of 1611 left the hands of the revisers, the work of Tyndale remained largely undisturbed, and where the King James committee had departed from Tyndale's translation the revisers of 1881 restored the original words. "These revisers of the Authorized Version had indeed many virtues, but above all they had that great and rare virtue of not meddling with what was too good to be improved. They were the last of a long series of revisers who had based their work on Tyndale with comparatively little modification: for indeed, where one reviser had altered Tyndale's wording, his successor had often returned to the original. And Tyndale had fixed the pattern upon which they had all alike worked."—R. W. Chambers, *Man's Unconquerable Mind,* page 191.

It has been said that at least 90 per cent of the King James Version may be attributed to Tyndale, thus establishing Tyndale's position among the literary immortals of England. He is "the man whose choice of words has for four hundred years exercised supreme influence upon English prose." Froude is given credit for the following tribute to the translator's literary faculty: "The peculiar genius which breathes through the English Bible, the mingled tenderness and majesty, the Saxon simplicity, the grandeur, unequaled, unapproached in the attempted improvements of modern scholars, all are here, and bear the impress of the mind of one man and that man William Tyndale."— Luke S. Walmsley, *Fighters and Martyrs for the Freedom of the Faith*, pages 77, 78.

The question that will doubtless arise in the minds of many is, Why have not scholars discovered before now the great debt English Protestantism owed to Tyndale? The answer is that Tyndale published his translation when such translations were still forbidden by the English government. Tyndale's enemies said that Tyndale had deliberately put heresies into his work in order to get his false doctrines before the people. Consequently, shortly after Tyndale's martyrdom, when translations were authorized, Tyndale's name was deliberately withheld by his publishers in order that his cause might triumph.

Before his death Tyndale translated not only the New Testament, but the five books of Moses, the book of Jonah, and probably everything from Joshua to Second Chronicles. It is even possible that he translated all of the Old Testament, although some contend that the books from Ezra to Malachi were taken from the Coverdale Bible of 1535. Still others maintain that whatever untranslated portions remained when Tyndale died were supplied by John Rogers, who doubtless used the Coverdale version as a guide. A year after Tyndale's martyrdom Rogers took the manuscript, edited and published it as the Matthew Bible. This Bible was used as a basis for all later revisions, but Tyndale's name was separated from his work.

For the four-hundredth anniversary of Tyndale's death, in 1936, Great Britain honored her Reformation hero by publishing his New Testament for the occasion and asking the British people in thousands of churches and schools to read from his translation. Many of them, it is said, for the first time recognized the close resemblance between Tyndale's version and that of the Authorized. Isaac Foot, in his introduction to this New Testament of Tyndale's, wrote, July, 1938, "The persistence of Tyndale's work is in fact the outstanding miracle of English letters."

That Tyndale is among the most heroic of English figures cannot be gainsaid. As a good humanist and a stanch defender of the principles of the Reformation during the days when kings championed the papacy, he brought his great learning to the service of a great cause. Besides the translation of the Bible he also wrote a number of treatises in which he scathingly and contemptuously held the clergy up to ridicule for their departure from the early simplicity of the church. In them he indicted the whole church, and in one of his pamphlets he expounded on the doctrine of justification by faith.

Tyndale's life conformed to his preaching. From his first declaration of intention to make the plowboy know more than the priest, until his last words, "Lord, open the king of England's eyes," his life shone like a pure white light leading to his set goal. He was at the same time humble and heroic. He remained a celibate priest all his life.

It has already been mentioned that the bishops in England attempted to keep Tyndale's translation out of the country; but when he succeeded to the extent he did, they smarted greatly under his victory. In spite of their efforts at repression, many thousands of copies eluded their vigilance and reached the common masses. The bishops had burned some of his books; now they resolved that he must be burned at the stake.

Tyndale was not unaware of the fate awaiting him. Eight years before the end he wrote, "If they shall burn me, they shall do none other than I look for."

Around the 1530's Henry VIII lent his aid that Tyndale might be brought to trial, but when he attempted to gain possession of Tyndale's person by asking Charles V to deliver him, the emperor refused. Sir Thomas Elyot, author of the *Governor,* was sent to trap him, but he was unsuccessful.

The papal party did not give up. They were in league with the papal party in the Low Countries. They were likewise astute enough to realize that Charles V, whom Luther defied at Worms, would not stand in their way to take the life of an English Reformer, particularly with Henry VIII having treated Charles V's aunt, Catherine of Aragon, the way he had.

So it was a man by the name of Phillips who undertook the job of luring Tyndale from the house, where he was staying, on the pretext of taking him out to dine. On the way Tyndale was captured and taken to the castle of Vilvorde, a state prison of the Low Countries, in which dungeon he remained sixteen months.

Among the charges preferred against him were that he maintained that faith alone sufficed for justification, that conscience should not be established on human traditions, that there was no purgatory, and that neither the Virgin nor the saints interceded for human beings.

He was taken out of prison Friday, October 6, 1536. First he was strangled, and then he was burned at the stake.

Some five years later a Bible purportedly translated by "divers excellent learned men" reached the desk of Henry VIII. He ordered that every church within his kingdom receive a copy. Thus Tyndale triumphed over the noose and the flames!

GEORGE WISHART

He Kindled the Flame of Truth

G̲EORGE WISHART, the forerunner
and teacher of John Knox, popularized the Calvinistic form of Protestantism in Scotland. He laid the kindling to which Knox later
applied the match and made all Scotland glow in the warmth of
the knowledge that salvation comes by grace and not by works, that
veneration of saints is useless, and that purgatory is nonexistent.

Born about 1513 of an aristocratic family at Pittarrow, near
Montrose, he was among the first to teach Greek in the country.
This he did at the seminary at Montrose, where he was either the
assistant or the successor to his master. His teaching the New Testament Greek brought against him the charge of heresy in 1538 and
caused him to flee to England.

It is probable that while in England he was convicted of heresy,
of which he supposedly recanted, sometime in 1539 in St. Nicholas
church in Bristol. During the same year he visited both Germany
and Switzerland, and then returned to England.

He taught at Cambridge and associated with such eminent Reformers as Bilney and Latimer. One of the finest tributes ever paid
a teacher was given Wishart by one of his students, Emery Tylney.
Tylney delivered it to John Foxe, who preserved it in his *Book of
Martyrs*.

"About the year 1543, there was in the University of Cambridge
one Master George Wishart, commonly called Master George of
Benet's College, a man of tall stature, judged by his physiognomy
to be a melancholy disposition, black-haired, long-bearded, comely
of person, well spoken after his country of Scotland, courteous,
lowly, lovely, glad to teach, desirous to learn, and well traveled;
never having on him for his habit and clothing but a mantle or frieze

gown to the shoes, a black millian fustian doublet, and plain black hose, coarse new canvas for his shirts, and white falling bands, and cuffs at his hands. All which apparel he gave to the poor, some weekly, some monthly, some quarterly, as he liked, saving his French cap, which he kept the whole year of my being with him.

"He was a man modest, temperate, fearing God, hating covetousness—for his charity had never end, night, noon, nor day; he forbore one meal in three, one day in four for the most part, except something to comfort nature. He lay hard upon a puff of straw, and coarse new canvas sheets, which, when he changed, he gave away. . . . He taught with great modesty and gravity, so that some of his people thought him severe, and would have slain him, but the Lord was his defense. And he, after due correction for their malice, by good exhortation, amended them and went his way. O that the Lord had left him to me, his poor boy, that he might have finished what he had begun."—Page 138.

About 1544 Wishart returned to Scotland and began preaching with fervor at Montrose, Dundee, Ayrshire, and East Lothian. At Montrose he expounded chapter by chapter the book of Romans. Frequently when he found himself deprived of a pulpit he betook himself to the market place, the wayside, and the moor. He said, "Christ is as potent in the field as in the kirk."

It was about this time that John Knox began to identify himself with the Reformer and accompany him on many of his trips. From him Knox doubtless learned Greek, and Wishart influenced him in his religious convictions.

Wishart's religious views included that only sacraments which had been introduced by Christ as shown in the Gospels should be celebrated, that auricular confession, infant baptism, and prayer to the saints were invalid, purgatory did not exist, and prominent church councils meant nothing unless their pronouncements were in harmony with the Bible. He also maintained that salvation sprang from the word of God, the bread of the eucharist did not contain Christ's body, prayer to images was idol worship, self-affliction was not of God, every man was a priest, the pope had no more power than any other man, eating flesh on Fridays was lawful, and marriage of priests was Biblical.

As Wishart continued his ministry, he enjoyed great popularity among both the common people and the upper classes. Thomas McCrie wrote of him, "Seldom do we meet in ecclesiastical history, with a character so amiable and interesting as that of George Wishart. Excelling all his countrymen at that period in learning, of the most persuasive eloquence, irreproachable in life, courteous and affable in manners, his fervent piety, zeal, and courage in the cause of truth were tempered with uncommon meekness, modesty, patience, prudence, and charity. In his tour of preaching through Scotland, he was usually accompanied by some of the principal gentry; and the people, who flocked to hear him, were ravished with his discourses."—*Life of John Knox,* page 21.

So fervent and influential were his sermons that at Dundee the people destroyed the convents and churches of the Black and Gray Friars. Naturally this aroused opposition among the papal adherents, and particularly of Cardinal David Beaton, whom Knox called the devil's own son. One day while Wishart was in the pulpit, one of the most prominent citizens, at the cardinal's behest, interrupted him and bade him in the name of Mary of Guise to leave town. This Wishart did, but not before he predicted that, if he was Christ's true representative, trouble would come upon them for rejecting him and God's message for them.

He then went to Ayrshire, where there still remained some of the followers of the Lollards. Here the bishop of Glasgow raised his voice against him from the pulpit, and the Reformer then went to the market cross and preached so powerfully that even his enemies were confounded.

A few days later the plague broke out in Dundee. Wishart, against the advice of his friends, returned to the town to help the sick. He felt that perhaps now that they were ill and afflicted they would give more heed to the word of God.

One of the first things he did was to preach to them. Selecting the head of the East Port at the Cowgate as his pulpit, with the healthy on the inside and the plague-stricken outside, he spoke on Psalm 107:20: "He sent His word, and healed them." Declaring that punishment comes from disobedience to God's commandments, he gave them the promise of God's mercy to the repentant.

Then he went among the sick and organized relief measures within the town so that it was said, "The poor were no more neglected than the rich." He remained until the plague ceased.

But hostility against him became more pronounced; at least two attempts were made to kill him. One day as he was leaving the church after preaching to the afflicted, a priest stood waiting at the lower step to kill him. Either forewarned by the Spirit or suspecting the priest's intent, Wishart approached him, took the dagger from underneath his loose gown, and remarked, "My friend, what would ye do?"—Ruth G. Short, *Stories of the Reformation in England and Scotland*, page 180.

The priest, frightened and cowering, knelt and acknowledged his purpose; but when the crowd wanted to mob him, Wishart put his arms around the would-be murderer and forbade the multitude to touch him, saying that a service had been performed in letting both the people and the Reformer know what there was to fear, and that henceforth he, Wishart, would be more alert.

The next attempt the cardinal made to have Wishart slain was in the form of a forged letter, purportedly from a sick friend, John Kinnear in Fife, which said that Wishart should come with full speed.

After Wishart, who was now back at Montrose, had gone only a short distance, he refused to go farther, stating that the Lord had forbidden him to do so. He sent some of his friends who accompanied him to determine what lay ahead, and they returned with the information that some sixty armed men had been lying in ambush ready to take his life. Wishart observed, "I know I shall end my life by that bloodthirsty man's hands [meaning Cardinal Beaton], but it will not be in this manner."—*Ibid.*, p. 181.

Nonetheless, Wishart knew that his hour was fast approaching; but he continued preaching in various churches. From Montrose he went to Edinburgh, where he stayed at the home of one of his disciples, James Watson. Here, after having spent the greater part of a night praying in the garden, friends who had watched asked where he had been. He replied, "I am assured that my warfare is near at an end, and therefore pray to God with me, that I shrink not when the battle waxeth most hot."

After Christmas he went to Haddington, where his audience, usually large, had greatly dwindled in size because of Catholic opposition. He roundly denounced the absentees and predicted retribution that would come upon the town—and this prediction was later fulfilled.

From Haddington he went to a friend's house near Ormiston in East Lothian. Here one night about midnight he was arrested by the Earl of Bothwell, again at the instigation of Cardinal Beaton. At this time Wishart asked that the sword which Knox had been carrying ever since the attempt upon Wishart's life at Dundee be taken from him. And he also told Knox, who pleaded to go with him to Ormiston, to go back to his pupils, and declared that one was sufficient for the sacrifice.

When arresting Wishart, Bothwell promised to protect the Reformer from violence and from deliverance into the cardinal's hands, a promise he did not bother to keep. Near the close of January, 1546, he released him to the cardinal, who incarcerated him in the dungeon of his castle at St. Andrews.

Here Wishart was tried February 28 in the cathedral before the bishops and other clergy. They accused him of being a heretic, renegade, traitor, thief, deceiver of the people, and despiser of the holy church. Wishart, with meekness and sweetness, it is said, reiterated his position on the doctrines of the Bible.

Condemned to be burned, Wishart said to his friends, "Consider and behold my visage. Ye shall not see me change my color. This grim fire I fear not."—*Ibid.*, p. 183.

With hands tied behind his back, a rope around his neck, an iron band around his waist, with bags of gunpowder tied to various parts of his clothing, and with gunners pointing at him to make certain the people, with whom he was still greatly popular, would not help him escape, he stood at the stake prepared at the foot of the castle gate. Beaton, with the other bishops, watched the execution from the castle tower.

It was at this moment, according to a number of historians, that Wishart predicted the death of Cardinal Beaton. "God forgive yon man that lies so glorious on yon wall; but within a few days he shall lie as shameful as he lies glorious now."—*The Dictionary of National Biography*. Beaton met his death three months later when a group of fanatics avenged the death of Wishart and other martyrs.

Wishart has at times been identified with the Wishart who was connected with a plot to assassinate Cardinal Beaton. This may or may not be true, but in fairness it must be said that there was violence on both sides.

Before the Reformer was tied to the stake, he exhorted his hearers to love God's word, to obey it, to stand nobly in face of persecution, and to urge their prelates to learn the Bible so that they might be ashamed to do evil, but willing to do good. He forgave his enemies, including those who brought about his death. His last words were directed to the hangman, who had asked forgiveness. This Wishart gave with a kiss. Wishart was first hanged and then burned.

Among the witnesses stood one on whom the spectacle made a profound impression; and from then on the fate of the Protestant Reformation in Scotland was determined to a large degree by that observer, John Knox.

JOHN WYCLIFFE

Morning Star of the Reformation

JOHN WYCLIFFE, first of the noted Reformers, lived from about 1320 to 1384, during a period covering the reign of three kings: Edward II, Edward III, and Richard II. This age bristled with numerous political ferments and national difficulties, such as the Hundred Years' War, three attacks of the dreaded Black Death, the Peasants' Revolt, and the political and ecclesiastical repercussions attending the "captivity" of the church at Avignon, France.

Because of the prominent place achieved by Wycliffe in England's political and religious growth it may be supposed that his background and activities can be traced with ease and clarity, but such is not the case. To write a biography of any man of this period presents a difficult task, and to gather materials concerning John Wycliffe is no exception. The fact that in all his writings not a single personal letter remains gives evidence of the difficulty of finding intimate glimpses of his character. To add confusion, it has been asserted that at least twenty different spellings of his name appear in scattered records. The extreme paucity of authentic material covering details of his life has effectively thwarted the efforts of capable scholars; but in spite of such obstacles, some facts are known.

John Wycliffe was born to a devout Catholic family of northern England who remained loyal to the church despite the teachings of its illustrious son. It has been presumed by some writers that John's parents may have been Roger Wyclif, lord of Wy, and his wife Cathrine.

Wycliffe attended Oxford University, where he received the degree of doctor of theology and became professor of theology. His eminence in civil and canon law was unchallenged, and he was known as "the gospel doctor" because of his zeal for the truth of the Bible.

As a result of his learning and fearless advocacy of Biblical truths and national rights, he became chaplain to the king, and a valued adviser to, and possibly a member of, the Parliament of 1366, which refused to pay arrears of feudal dues levied on King John. At one time he headed Balliol College, and as a lecturer and preacher he was termed brilliant. Any way one wishes to classify him, he stands as one of the leading men of his day.

Because of his untiring work as a writer, and also because he translated the Bible into the English tongue, he is considered by some authorities to be the first great master of English prose. He stands with Chaucer, if not in creating English literature, at least in giving form and beauty to it. It has been said that his efforts in bringing about two translations of the Bible did more to liberate England than was accomplished in any war. His serious mind and involved reasoning left his scholarly writing extremely intricate and completely without a trace of humor. An undeviating spirit, a caustic style, and a conduct void of blunders in behavior characterize both his writings and his life.

In features and form little remains to draw an acceptable likeness of this great Reformer, for the available portraits consist, so it is said, of figments of someone's imagination. From fragmentary references he has been described as gaunt, lean to the point of emaciation, and with little bodily strength. His opponents were wont to say that his asceticism was used as a cloak to impress others with his piety. Lewis Sergeant, in his *John Wycliffe,* quotes others as stating that to this charge Wycliffe countered:

"I eat frequently, greedily, and delicately, leading a social life; and if I were to try like a hypocrite to make false pretense in this regard, they who sit with me at tables would bear witness against me."—Page 12.

He never seemed to be in good health; but, in spite of appearances, he was hospitable, pleasant, and energetic, possessing an iron will with no apparent sign of timidity.

His friends saw in him a man deeply devoted to the word of God. To him the Bible was the way of life. In his estimation society was in a chaotic state, for which the greatest need was the love of justice.

"He was the champion," says Lewis Sergeant, "of the university against pope and hierarchy, . . . of the nation against the papacy, of the new truth as he had seen it against friars, bishops, and bulls. Men of all classes, from peasant to Parliament and kings, looked to him at one time or another for strength, inspiration, or protection, and they did not look in vain."—*Ibid.*, p. 100.

Wycliffe did not make his debut into national prominence over a controversy about creed, as might be supposed. His first open clash with the papacy found its basis in a national issue growing out of his views on the relative status of church and state. The papacy had requested the English Parliament to pay the money in arrears from the time King John had recognized the pope as overlord of England. Wycliffe's opinion denied the rights of all papal claims concerning taxation. His logic and thoroughness aligned Parliament against the papacy, and his position won him many friends and apparently as many enemies among the proponents of the papal hierarchy.

This incident seems to have marked a turning point in his life, for, not long after, he advocated a ban on the export of all precious metals to Rome and also proposed that the church hold a subordinate status to the English government. His logic led him to the conclusion that revelation and reason denied the papal claim of having authority over all secular rulers. From the results of his analysis of the situation he found no reason why the pope, under his allegation as the vicar of Christ, could be, in feudal terminology, an overlord of a country. Such a pretension, Wycliffe asserted, had no authority in Scripture.

Naturally, once having opposed the papacy on one matter, his thoroughness of scholarship and devotion to the study of the Bible, a book which he called "a charter written by God" and "the marrow of all laws," led him into conflict with the various religious views of the church. He maintained that the evils in the church developed from her wealth and temporal power, that such a condition was tantamount to idolatry, and that the church, in order to satisfy its pristine objective, needed to return to the simplicity of apostolic teaching.

True religion, he further averred, depended on a personal relationship between God and the individual, in which relationship the individual ought to be free from the control of priests, whom he at one time designated as "fiends of hell." He denied that the pope had any Scriptural or historic right to set himself up as head of all Christendom. Had Wycliffe had his way, the entire monastic system would have been abolished, for he felt it to be evil in intent and results. The whole idea of monasticism, according to his views, constituted a deterrent to England's greatness.

As time went on, he began to attack the entire papal organization. Any doctrine which emphasized externals to the loss of personal devotion to God, he condemned. Every sacrament, except marriage, received his rebuke.

The natural outcome of such an attitude was an open break with the church, a consummation which apparently was not his original intent. But it remained for his attack on the validity of the sacrament of transubstantiation, the supposed transforming of the bread and the wine of the eucharist into the body and blood of Christ, to catapult him into his most serious altercation with the hierarchical system. He maintained that the doctrine of transubstantiation constituted a heresy brought into the church with the purpose of keeping the laity in blind subjection to the priesthood. Even his refusal to accept the veneration of saints, relics, and pilgrimages as valid presentation to heaven for justification was secondary to his attack on the doctrine of transubstantiation. Soon he repudiated the supreme authority of popes and ecclesiastical councils and refused to come to terms with the papacy.

As Wycliffe's unalterable opposition to the church developed and people in most walks of life began to champion him and his views, the papal hierarchy had no recourse but to attempt to silence this "voice in the wilderness." Doubtless his high standing in the government and his status as an intellectual and spiritual leader kept him from earlier effective papal attacks. A man who held the position of king's chaplain, who was an intimate adviser to Parliament, and who stood in high esteem with the princess of Wales could not be cowed easily or attacked even by a church which claimed supremacy in religious and secular affairs.

But gradually the situation changed. His inflexible attitude and the shift in governmental personnel gave the papacy its opportunity to take effective steps to quiet this "greatest of Reformers before the Reformation."

The papacy instituted two trials against Wycliffe, one in 1377 and one the following year. At this time he still stood in too high esteem to be either greatly awed or severely hindered in his on-slaughts against the church, but his friends advised moderation. The fact that the papacy sent five bulls containing nineteen charges against Wycliffe shows the determination of the church to curtail his work. One of these bulls reached the king, one arrived at the University of Oxford, and the other three were addressed jointly to the archbishop of Canterbury and the bishop of London. Records are at variance as to the actual number of heresies charged against Wycliffe, but they range all the way from the nineteen listed in the five bulls to the three hundred three enumerated by his opponents.

His body, always weak, had in the meantime been attacked by illness. At one time, when rumor spread that he lay dying, a few zealous friars hurried to his bedside to hear what they thought would be his recantation. Instead they heard themselves denounced and threatened with the exposure of their misdeeds.

By 1382, papal pressure grew sufficiently strong to cause his expulsion from Oxford, a departure which marked for that institu-tion the beginning of a considerable decrease in freedom of thought and for more than a century a progressive degeneration of religion, morals, and learning.

Wycliffe spent his few remaining years in charge of the Lutter-worth church in Leicestershire. On December 28, 1384, a final paralytic attack came while he was attending to his duties. He died on New Year's Eve of the same year.

While Wycliffe was alive, the papal hierarchy had never been able to force his excommunication as a heretic; therefore apparently to vent its spleen or to demonstrate its frustration, or possibly both, the Council of Constance ordered, on May 4, 1415, that Wycliffe's body be disinterred and burned. This order reached fulfillment in 1428 with the consuming of his bones and the scattering of his ashes in the river Swift.

The evaluation placed on the influence and prestige of this man, who has been called the Morning Star of the Reformation, is out-standing and phenomenal. Apparently, apart from time, there is little that differentiates him from the Reformers of the sixteenth century. His influence remained high as late as the time of Luther.

In many ways he outlined the basic doctrinal views propounded by the later Reformers. As the first great scholarly opponent of the medieval papacy, he exerted an immortal influence. In fullness of outlook he stood above many of the Reformers of a century later, and from the time of his first abortive trial in 1377 to his death he stands as the most important religious personage in England. The heart of his teaching, by which he won practically half of England, consists of the infallibility of the Scriptures and salvation through faith in Christ. His two great services to his country have been defined as providing the inspiration for a religious revival and the writing of the first English translation of the Bible.

Charles Bigg, in his *Wayside Sketches in Ecclesiastical History,* says of Wycliffe, "The courage which he displayed, if we consider the forces arrayed against him, was extraordinary, and his intellectual moderation and good sense are hardly less so."—Page 131.

Ellen G. White gives the following summation of the man and his work: "In breadth of intellect, in clearness of thought, in firmness to maintain the truth, and boldness to defend it, he was equaled by few who came after him. Purity of life, unwearying diligence in study and in labor, incorruptible integrity, and Christlike love and faithfulness in his ministry, characterized the first of the Reformers. And this notwithstanding the intellectual darkness and moral corruption of the age from which he emerged."—*The Great Controversy,* page 93.

LOUIS DE BERQUIN

The Luther of France

LOUIS DE BERQUIN, a member of the noble family of Artois, and a Huguenot at the court of Francis I, was three times charged with heresy and imprisoned. Finally he was burned at the stake, to become France's first Protestant martyr.

Before Luther came to the forefront as a Reformer, Berquin had already caught the vision of the gospel from Erasmus, and from Lefèvre at the University of Paris. He had also met Margaret of Angouleme, sister of Francis I. Through this woman, who was sympathetic to Protestantism, he gained the king's favor and became his counselor.

Pure in life, open in disposition, tender in his care for the unfortunate, and devoted to his friends, Berquin appeared in France's wicked court like a lily rising out of a fetid swamp.

As a devout disciple of Erasmus he translated into French many of Erasmus's works, as well as some from Luther and Melanchthon. He has been termed "the most formidable champion of the new opinions," performing his work largely by translating other men's writings, a task he did admirably well. Besides this, he wrote original works on the subject of religious reform. These he had printed at his own expense and circulated among his friends at court and elsewhere. He despised the ignorance of the monks, and it is said that he "let no opportunity pass of assailing the theologians and monks, and unmasking their fanaticism."

Part of the time he lived in Paris, and part of the time at his estate near Abbeville. At both places he propounded the new doctrines "with all the zeal of a new convert." He wished that the gospel that had changed his heart might also change the hearts of others. As a layman with the Bible in his hands, he visited the homes surrounding his estate, as well as those in the towns of Picardy and Artois, the place near which he had been born, in 1490. Everywhere he went he taught the people the new faith.

Some of Berquin's hearers reported what they saw and heard to the bishop of Amiens, who reported him to Beda, the sleuthhound of the Sorbonne. Beda immediately became active in persecuting Berquin, for in some of his books Beda had read, "The Virgin Mary is improperly invoked instead of the Holy Ghost." "Faith alone justifies." "Neither the gates of hell, nor Satan, nor sin can do anything against him who has faith in God."

Berquin was arrested, imprisoned, and denounced as a heretic at his trial, May 13, 1523, before parliament. His library was seized, and seven of his own writings and one each of his translations of Luther and Melanchthon were burned August 8 in front of Notre Dame.

The Reformer was asked to retract his errors, but since he absolutely refused to do this, he was taken back to prison to await execution. Margaret, an angel of mercy to hundreds of persecuted Protestants in France, interceded for him with her brother, the king, and he was immediately set at liberty. Of Margaret it was said that she "took wondrous pains to save those who were in danger, and that she alone prevented the Reformation from being stifled in the cradle."

After obtaining his liberty, Berquin returned to Artois and continued to preach from the Scriptures the doctrine of salvation by Christ alone. He condemned the celibacy of the priesthood as contrary to Biblical teachings. At one time he remarked, "You will often meet with these words in Holy Scripture: *honorable marriage, undefiled bed, but of celibacy* you will not find a syllable." At another time he said, "We must teach the Lord's flock to pray with understanding, that they may no longer be content to gabble with their lips like ducks with their bills, without comprehending what they say."

From 1523 to 1526 France was filled with troubles, the greatest of which was the loss of the Battle of Pavia, with the resulting imprisonment of Francis I at Madrid. These episodes gave respite to the Protestants, as a period of tolerance set in, but not for long.

In the meantime the queen mother and regent, Louise of Savoy, felt she needed to conciliate parliament and the Sorbonne. She recognized the feeling of French society that her son's capture and imprisonment were a direct punishment for his leniency toward the Protestants; and since her religious sentiments were usually swayed by the best political policy of the moment, she aided the Sorbonne and parliament in their efforts to track down heretics. With royal power now in her hands she issued an edict that all sympathizers with the new doctrine should be handed over for trial to a group of selected bishops, "an extraordinary court to judge the heretics."

Berquin became one of the earliest victims under the decree. For the second time, in January, 1526, he was thrown into prison, this time at Louise's behest, and again condemned to the stake.

Margaret pleaded unsuccessfully with her mother for Berquin's release, for Louise thought that by burning and torturing the Reformers she was buying papal support for Francis and possibly preventing an internal insurrection against herself and her son in France.

Then Margaret appealed to her brother in his Spanish prison, and on the day of his return to Paris, March 17, he sent word to parliament to release the prisoner. After considerable delay, Berquin was again granted his freedom.

Berquin, with Margaret's help, had won his second round with the papists; and this gave him courage far beyond what the times warranted. He believed that Francis was truly on the Protestant side and would protect and help him; for, to convert all France to Protestantism had now become a holy obsession with Berquin.

With indomitable courage and energy he formed a daring plan whereby all France would be liberated from the pope's domination. It was his conviction that if he and the king, and his old mentor Erasmus, would strike unitedly their strategy could not fail; but he felt that he could never be successful without the king's sanction. He thought that Francis would not oppose. Had not the king twice set him free? Had he not allowed the return of the Meaux preachers who had been exiled in Strasbourg since Louise's edict? Had not Lefèvre become a tutor to the king's youngest son? All these things seemed to indicate the king's favor.

Before he proceeded further, Berquin wished to enlist the aid of Erasmus. To him he wrote, "Under the cloak of religion the priests hide the vilest passions, the most corrupt manners, the most scandalous unbelief. We must tear off the veil that conceals this hideous mystery, and boldly brand the Sorbonne, Rome, and all their hirelings, with impiety."

Erasmus advised him to keep silent and to retire, but that, if he must attack Rome, he should obtain a power of attorney from the king. "Think, dear Berquin, think constantly what a hydra you are attacking, and by how many mouths it spits its venom."

That his old friend and teacher should advise such caution grieved Berquin. However, he received courage for his undertaking from another source. Francis, as a patron of learning and a pupil of Erasmus, had imprisoned Beda for publishing a refutation of Erasmus's *Paraphrases and Annotations*.

From Beda's writings Berquin now took twelve propositions, "manifestly impious and blasphemous," and took them to Francis, who promised that the Sorbonne would examine them.

This raised Berquin's spirits to the highest point as he thought of the king's acting the part of another elector of Saxony. "I will follow these redoubtable hornets into their holes; I will fall upon these insensate blabbers, and scourge them," he said.

Francis kept his promise and presented the propositions to the bishop of Bazas, requesting him to give them to the rector of the university for the purpose of examination by four assembled faculties.

Erasmus tried once more to stop Berquin in what he considered his "mad" venture, for he was certain it could lead only to one place —the stake. "Even should your cause be holier than that of Christ Himself," he wrote him, "your enemies have resolved to put you to death."

Berquin could see no failure ahead; if only he, Francis, and Erasmus could act in unison, then all France would become Protestant. But "just as Francis I stretches out his hand, the scholar of Rotterdam draws back."

Francis, too, was caught in a dilemma. In need of money to pay the heavy fine at Madrid, he appealed to the bishops, who suggested the extermination of the Lutherans in exchange for Catholic gifts or loans of money.

In 1529 the great French Council of Sens met to redeclare the position of the church on infallibility, its right to make canonical regulations, and its various fasts, sacraments, mass, and adoration of the saints. It also asked that the secular arm enforce their sentences upon heretics.

Before the council disbanded, the news circulated that the most sacred image in Paris, the statue of the Blessed Virgin and Child, located in the Quartier St. Antoine, had been desecrated by beheading and mutilation. The council, the king, and all Paris were enraged.

As the Sorbonne got the upper hand, Berquin's friends urged him to flee, but he considered flight an act of cowardice. The Sorbonne considered Berquin the instigator of the outrage on the image; consequently they asked that Berquin be delivered to them. And the king consented that an inquiry be made concerning him.

Berquin was imprisoned once more, and the doctors of the Sorbonne determined to make the pupil pay the penalty they were powerless to impose upon his master, Erasmus. Duprat, Louise of Savoy, and Montmorency all agreed with the university; and twelve judges were appointed to try Berquin.

These judges had a great deal of respect for Berquin. They knew his holy life, his irreproachable character, and the esteem in which he was generally held; and they were of no mind to persecute him.

The Reformer saw his opportunity and resolved to appeal to the king once more by means of Margaret's intercession. She wrote her brother a letter, and Berquin had an interview with Francis. For a time it seemed that Berquin would go free again, but a letter he had written to a friend asking him to burn some books he had left behind, betrayed him to Beda.

At the close of his trial he was told that he had been convicted of belonging to the sect of Luther and of writing wicked books. He was requested to bear a lighted taper in the great court of the palace and to ask the pardon of the king and of God. "You will then be taken, bareheaded and on foot, to the Greve, where you shall see your books burnt," his persecutors told him. "After doing penance at Notre Dame, you shall have your tongue pierced—that instrument of unrighteousness by which you have so grievously sinned. Lastly you shall be taken to the prison of Monsieur de Paris [the bishop], and be shut up there all your life between four walls of stone; and we forbid that you be supplied either with books to read, or pen or ink to write."

After hearing his sentence Berquin was sent back to prison, and Margaret wrote the following prayer:

Thou, God, alone canst say:
Touch not my son, take not his life away.
Thou only canst Thy sovereign hand outstretch
To ward the blow.

At this time Budé, one of France's great scholars, who had allied himself with the Protestants at Meaux, pleaded with Berquin to accept his sentence, but Berquin said he would make another appeal to the king. Francis, however, now at Blois, gave no sign of recognition. For a moment Berquin was almost persuaded to recant, but when Budé returned a short time after, the condemned man said, "I would rather die than by my silence countenance the condemnation of truth."

By an extraordinary assumption of authority, the judges changed their sentence to that of strangling and burning; and Beda commanded haste in its execution, lest the king return and change his mind.

For his death, Berquin put on his finest clothes, for he said that "the King of heaven had invited him to the wedding." "He wore a cloak of velvet, a doublet of satin and damask, and golden hose, and the calmness of a good conscience was visible in every feature," a biographer has written.

One author reports that more than twenty thousand people came, April 17, 1529, to see him executed by strangling, and then to see his body burned at the stake. Théodore Beza later remarked: "He might have been the Luther of France had Francis been a Frederick of Saxony."

GASPARD DE COLIGNY

Hero of the Huguenots

"I TOLD all the captains that if they heard me employ language which breathed surrender, I begged them to throw me over the wall into the fosse; and if anyone proposed it to me, I would do no less to him."—Quoted by A. W. Whitehead in *Gaspard de Coligny*, page 56.

These words, spoken at the battle of Saint-Quentin by the Comte Gaspard de Chatillon Coligny, characterized the man who never evaded a difficulty, and of whom it was later said that he was "the first and greatest leader of the Huguenots" and "the wisest statesman in France." In him, historians have said, "the reform found its best representative whether as a social, political, or spiritual force; who was recognized at home and abroad as its head and its heart, at whom all its enemies struck, in whom all its friends confided, and who was the first and most prominent victim in the St. Bartholomew Massacre, which annihilated the power, though it could not crush the spirit, of the Reformed Church of France."—S. E. Herrick, *Some Heretics of Yesterday*, page 246.

Coligny, scion of a noble French family with a five-century record of participation in national movements, was born in 1519 at Chatillon-sur-Loing. His mother laid claim to the honorable name of Montmorency, likewise a ranking family of the old French nobility.

The father died when Coligny was a lad of five, and his mother supervised his training, along with that of his two brothers, Odet, later bishop of Beauvais and peer of France, and Francis, both of whom won distinction in the Protestant cause. Of the mother the record states that she was among the few women of high rank at the court possessing pure hearts and scandal-free lives.

Nurturing an interest in the developing religious reform, she transmitted it to her children through their instructors. Berauld, an associate of French humanists and a friend of Erasmus, became Gaspard's tutor. This parent-tutor guidance developed in the young man, according to a biographer, "the fine combination of the heroic, the courtly, the scholarly, and the spiritual, and in Gaspard the balance of these seems to have been as nearly perfect as in any character that greets us from the pages of history."—*Ibid.*, pp. 247, 248.

He remained with his mother at Chatillon-sur-Loing until he was eleven, when she became lady in waiting to the new Queen Eleanor, wife of Francis I, at the court of France. Here the lad soon distinguished himself for his scholarly interests. When he was fifteen the study of Cicero and Ptolemy had a greater interest for him than the opportunity of joining the king's hunting parties. His love of reading and his study in solitude developed in him an excellent knowledge of Latin and of politics, and an admiration for honor, virtue, bravery, and sagacity that kept him above the intrigues of a court famous for its sensuality and pleasure seeking.

By 1545 he had been presented at the court and in its inner circle had become the recognized leader of the Coligny family. At this time he had also risen to the acknowledged status of an experienced cavalryman, a soldier statesman, and a favorite of the dauphin. His courage and leadership had made him a respected officer on the military expeditions against Emperor Charles V in northern France, Italy, Lorraine, and Flanders, where he was described as being "always loyal, and never weighing his life against the interests of the king."—*Ibid.*, p. 249.

As a result of his military ability he became the colonel general in full charge of the French infantry in 1547, the year of the death of Francis I and the accession of Henry II. As such, he was the first among army officials to institute military reforms, called "ordinances." Within his command and among the foreign troops employed by the king he stopped the looting, dueling, swearing, and raping by armed men, and turned these men into a respectable, orderly body of soldiers who gave deference to the lives of nonbelligerents, to property, and to the honor of women. Under his command the uniform of a soldier came to denote honor and distinction.

Coligny's elevation to colonel general also resulted in his becoming a knight in the Order of St. Michael, also known as the Order of the King. In the same year he married Charlotte de Laval, daughter of Count Guy, an event which brought out the king with his entire court. Its festivities included many sports and masquerade balls, and concluded with four more days of revelry at the home of the cardinal of Ferrara. Three sons and two daughters were born of this marriage.

His wife died in 1568, and three years later he married Jacqueline, countess of Montlul and Entremont, "a young, beautiful, intelligent, and pious lady of Savoy," later to become a victim of the St. Bartholomew Massacre.

In 1552 Coligny was made admiral of France, a title by which he is generally known. It was purely an honorary title, for it had no connection with the French navy. The governorship of Picardy came into his hands in 1555, and in the same year he began his colonizing endeavors in the New World in behalf of the persecuted Huguenots, although he himself had not yet become one of them.

Although unsuccessful in its immediate purpose, the plan encompassed three separate attempts and historically established the opening of an era which led Quakers, Catholics, and Puritans to the Western Hemisphere in quest of religious liberty.

The first Huguenot colony was established in Brazil, but Villegagnon, the leader selected by Coligny for the expedition, joined the Catholic Church soon after reaching South America and thus left the Protestants a prey to the Portuguese.

The second contingent, under Jean Ribault, reached South Carolina; and the third, under René de Laudonnière, was sent to assist the second. Upon the arrival of the latter no settlers of the second colony were found; consequently Laudonnière continued southward and began a colony in Florida in 1564. The pioneers of this ill-fated adventure were massacred the following year by the forces of the Spaniard, Menéndez de Avilés, who is purported to have said, "I do this not as to Frenchmen, but as to Lutherans."

In the days of religious and national hatreds this episode did not conclude the matter. In 1568 Dominique de Gourges arrived in Florida to seek revenge on the Spanish. He in turn massacred the garrison, and the following remark is attributed to him: "I do this not as to Spaniards, nor as to mariners, but as to traitors, robbers, and murderers."—Quoted in *Ploetz' Epitome of History*, pages 288, 289.

An example of Coligny's statesmanship and diplomacy appeared in his negotiation of the truce of Vaucelles, in 1556, with Philip II of Spain, which resulted in a cessation of hostilities during the intermittent wars of the time. Henry II of France broke the truce, however, much against Coligny's counsel, and this brought the combined strength of Spain and England against the French. The strategy developed to counteract the encroachments of these united forces placed the defense of Saint-Quentin on the Somme under the command of Coligny in 1557. Here he spoke the opening words of this chapter, indicative of his direct and masterful nature.

His defense of Saint-Quentin, although unsuccessful, was possibly among his outstanding military achievements, for it delayed by seventeen days the advance of an overwhelming enemy and gave the French an opportunity to concentrate their forces for the protection of Paris.

With the capitulation of Saint-Quentin, Coligny became a prisoner of the Spanish in the Netherlands, where he remained until after the peace of Château-Cambresis in 1559, when he was released upon payment of a ransom of 50,000 crowns. A report of the defense of Saint-Quentin is found among his memoirs.

Following his release, he stepped into full and open championship of the Huguenot cause. The specific time, however, of his mental abjuration of Catholicism is vague. Doubtless his mother's attitude toward the new faith, and the type of teachers she procured for him, bore fruit, first in humanistic ideas and then in the acceptance of the principles of Protestantism. His consideration of the Huguenots also pointed toward Protestant sympathies. His severance from Romanism became unmistakably clear during his imprisonment in the Netherlands.

One chronicler states that during this time he requested that a Bible be provided—"to ease the griefe and sorrowe of his minde with reading it. And he studied so much upon it, that he began from thensforth to have a taste of the pure religion and trew godliness, and to learne the right maner of calling uppon God."—Quoted by A. W. Whitehead in *Gaspard de Coligny*, page 69.

During this period he also received books from his brother and letters from Calvin, all tending to give him a deeper understanding of the basic issues of the Reformation. Like many others, he had maintained that the church could be changed from within, but eventually he, too, gave up that idea as improbable of fulfillment.

Upon his liberation he also found his political and military status changed, for King Henry II, his friend, had died that same year, 1559, from a wound received in a tourney; and his enemies, the Guises, dominated the court under the new king Francis II, husband of Mary, later Queen of Scots.

For a period the admiral retired to the comforts and quiet of Châtillon, where he owned one of France's most beautiful homes, which, as an art collector, he had filled with the finest masterpieces. There, too, he had established a college and employed a staff of Latin, Greek, and Hebrew scholars. He also demonstrated his faith in liberty of conscience by recognizing the rights of Catholics and Protestants alike, and permitted the priests a great degree of freedom.

His public profession of faith may have been delayed by fear of the possible consequences to his family, for he recognized the dangers to which the Huguenots were subjected. But when once his wife assured him that she would rather endure any type of hardship or torture than to see him turn from Christ, he forthwith made arrangements for a Protestant chaplain for the castle and the town. Shortly after this he celebrated the Lord's Supper with the little Huguenot congregation close by, and automatically stepped into national leadership of that sect, along with their head, the Bourbon Louis, prince of Condé. Opposed to them was the powerful Catholic party, headed by Francis, duke of Guise.

The addition of such strong leadership from the nobility was most fortunate for the Huguenots, for Protestantism in France was at that moment entering upon a period of acute danger. To their aid Coligny brought the greatness of his political stature and turned them into a politico-religious party sufficiently strong to be virtually a government within a government. The Huguenots hailed Coligny as their deliverer, and Calvin remarked, "There is one among the chiefs who acts wisely."—*Ibid.*, p. 93.

Time after time through the ensuing years of colloquies, wars and massacres, Coligny's astuteness at the conference table and his experience in military tactics saved the Huguenot cause.

At the Assembly of Notables called by Catherine de' Medici at Fontainebleau in August, 1560, he petitioned that Huguenot persecutions cease. At a time when it meant death to champion the cause of these people, he asked that they be permitted to worship God according to their interpretation of the Scriptures and that "temples" be provided for them. He presented a written copy of his request to the king, but his appeal was unsuccessful.

In March of that year the Bourbons had laid an unwise plot to seize the king and put the power now in the hands of the Guises back into their own. The scheme, known as the Conspiracy of Amboise, failed; and the Catholic Guises called for a wholesale massacre of the Huguenots, as well as for the death of their leader, the prince of Condé.

But at that moment the king, Francis II, died, and the 11-year-old son of Catherine, Charles IX, came to the throne. Of this timely demise Calvin wrote to Sturm, "Did you ever read or hear of anything more opportune than the death of the king? The evils had reached an extremity for which there was no remedy, when suddenly God shows Himself from heaven. He who pierced the eye of the father has stricken the ear of the son."—Quoted by Thomas M. Lindsay in *A History of the Reformation*, vol. 2, p. 178. The head of the prince of Condé was saved, but not yet the lives of the Huguenots; their slaughter continued, although at a somewhat decreased tempo.

Coligny again pleaded the cause of his coreligionists at the Assembly of the States General at Orleans in December, 1560. This time he was successful; persecution ended, and a mutual spirit of toleration became apparent. Peace seemed near, and refugees returned from Switzerland, England, and Germany. The next year came the conference at Poissy, attended by Catholic and Protestant celebrities alike, resulting in the proclamation of an edict of toleration. But this was shattered the next year by the massacre at Vassay, inspired by the duke of Guise. In the succeeding years, as the Huguenots and the Catholics fought it out on the field of battle, Coligny repeatedly saved the remnants of the defeated Protestant army.

Two months after the Vassay massacre the duke of Guise was assassinated, and Coligny was accused of instigating the murder, a charge which he denied and of which he was later proved innocent.

Coligny realized that in order to attain his purpose, namely, that of making France a Protestant nation, he would need to win the friendship and confidence of the able and unscrupulous Catherine de' Medici, who constantly played the Catholics against the Protestants to maintain a balance of power and gain her own ends. He would likewise need to ingratiate himself with the young king, her son. He set himself at once to his diplomatic task.

The prince of Condé was slain at the battle of Jarnac in 1569, leaving Coligny the only great leader of the Huguenot party. The peace of Saint-Germain-en-Laye, in 1570, brought a respite from fighting, and during this pause Coligny was well received at court. He stepped into kingly favor by advocating a war against Spain by which, he believed, all religious differences could be wiped out; and a united France, shorn of Spanish predominance, might rise to international renown.

In this connection the Protestant and Catholic factions were to be drawn together through the marriage of the French king's sister, Margaret of Valois, with Henry, prince of Navarre and later to become Henry IV of France. The bridegroom was the son of the late Antoine de Bourbon and his Protestant queen, Jeanne d'Albret.

For his part in the successful wedding negotiations Coligny was showered with tokens of the royal family's good will. His friends, however, feared for his safety in the Catholic court and warned him of his danger, a peril which arose as soon as Catherine realized Coligny's growing influence over her son. Her jealousy, urged on to fever pitch by the Guise hatred of Coligny, and led by the son of the murdered duke, outran her reputation for resourceful capability; and she, with the Catholic Guises, began to plan Coligny's assassination.

As the admiral was walking leisurely homeward on August 22, 1572, four days after the wedding of Henry and Margaret, a shot, fired by a hidden assailant, severed the index finger of his right hand and broke his left arm. The next day the king and the queen mother called on Coligny, and after the visit the king confided to his mother that the admiral had urged him to reign without interference from her.

Catherine's plan to be rid of the Huguenot leader now took on expanded proportions, to include as many of his followers as possible. Quickly, but secretly, she summoned her advisers, who agreed to Coligny's immediate death and also to the wholesale massacre of the Huguenots.

Early Sunday morning, August 24, 1572, a few men entered his room and brutally killed him. His body was tossed from the window to the courtyard below, where the young Guise turned it over to make sure it was his enemy. With head severed, Coligny's torso was dragged through the streets and hung by the heels from the gallows of Montfaucon. This was the signal for the infamous massacre to begin, the "blackest in the black catalogue of crime, most horrible among the fiendish deeds of all the dreadful centuries."— Ellen G. White, *The Great Controversy*, page 272.

Huguenots everywhere who had trusted the promise of their king were betrayed. The Huguenot nobles were brought from the Louvre to be butchered in the courtyard. Eight hundred noblemen and gentlemen who had accompanied Henry of Navarre to the wedding were killed. Thousands were aroused from their beds and slain. Day after day the bath of blood continued throughout the city, into the suburbs, and then to all of France. Estimates of the toll of dead ranged from 20,000 to 100,000.

The unutterable grief that hung over France and plunged thousands of homes into bleakest despair transformed Rome into scenes of festive joy, followed by a proclamation of a solemn jubilee. The information of the treacherous slaying of Coligny and the rank butchery of the Huguenots caused Pope Gregory XIII to have the *Te Deum* sung and thirty-three pontifically clad cardinals and state dignitaries to go to the French Church of St. Louis. The painter Vasari was employed to paint frescoes of the massacre on the walls of the Vatican. Nothing could have been more significant of, nor a greater tribute to, the position which the Huguenots had gained in France.

After a few days Coligny's body was removed from the gallows and buried. Later it was reinterred in his ancestral castle wall, which was destroyed during the French Revolution.

Following his death his papers, including his *History of the Wars of Religion in France,* were seized and burned by command of the queen dowager. His furniture, consisting of eighty wagonloads, was sold at public auction in Paris, and his village was razed.

JACQUES LEFEVRE

He Loved His Saviour

JACQUES LEFEVRE occupies a peculiar status as both a Humanist and a Reformer who bridged the gap between the past and the present. He became the steppingstone from the theology of the medieval period to the religious thinking of modern times. One historian called him, "A man on the threshold of a new era who refused to enter it."—Thomas M. Lindsay, *A History of the Reformation*, vol. 2, p. 143.

Lefèvre was deeply attached to the dogma, rituals, and worship of the church; yet he showed alarm regarding the moral corruption of the clergy as he voiced his objection to a priesthood which drank, gambled, and frequented bawdyhouses. Nor did he feel that the doctrines were above correction.

The Scriptures were supremely important to him; whereas works and pilgrimages had little value. Faith did more than anything else to justify one in God's eyes. Even before Luther began his work, Lefèvre preached doctrines identical to those of the German Reformer.

Although not classified as a Reformer in the sense of his pupil William Farel or his compatriot Calvin, he certainly played a comparable part to that of Erasmus in arousing people to think. Like that great humanist, he believed that reason and the study of the word of God would break through the all-pervading darkness of the times.

Like many other Humanists of that period who aided in the success of the Reformation, he was a schoolman of the first rank. Early in his career at the University of Paris, where he taught mathematics and physics, he became dissatisfied with the methods of scholasticism. His teaching was soon characterized by a lucidity unknown at the time. He aimed to reintroduce the study of antiquity and languages; other Humanists regarded him as having reinstated science and philosophy at the university.

Not content with routine teaching, he wrote and published many works on Aristotle, whom he studied in the original, treatises on ancient mathematics, writings of the Fathers, and other productions dealing with the mysticism of the Middle Ages.

Gradually the depravity of the times brought to him the conviction that a better day would appear if the Bible were studied and preached by a clergy that knew the Scriptures. This "notably diminutive figure" with his gentility, piety, and scholarly achievements, "bent over by much study," possessing an earnest, gentle, and beautiful face, became "the first of the French Humanists who led the way to heresy."

The keynote of his life lay in his love for Christ. Through humble submission this love, he believed, would guide, elevate, and make the seeker one with the divine personality of the Christ. "His eloquence, his candor, his amiability, captivated all hearts. . . . His lessons and the zeal of his disciples formed the most striking contrast to the scholastic teaching of the majority of the doctors, and the irregular and frivolous lives of most of the students."—J. H. Merle d'Aubigné, *History of the Reformation of the Sixteenth Century*, vol. 3, pp. 382, 388.

Soon he developed a clear procedure of Biblical interpretation which in time was followed by other Reformers, ultimately reaching the Lutherans, Anglicans, Calvinists, and others. Thomas More said that English students of the period were indebted to him, Luther in his early lectures used Lefèvre's text, and Zwingli listed his commentaries on the Psalms among his favorite books for study.

Some of his greatest achievements lay in the work of the men who were his disciples. Among them may be listed Francois Vatable, the Hebraist and one-time teacher of Calvin; Budé, the distinguished master of classical letters; Farel, the evangelist to Switzerland; Postel, the orientalist; Louis de Berquin, who died as a Protestant martyr; and the bishop of Meaux, who later became a cardinal. Besides these he had many others from different countries. "The scholars who came to learn of him in Paris all loved him, and of the opponents he soon aroused, none seems to have felt anything but respect for the purity and honesty of his life and the natural kindliness of his disposition."—Paul Van Dyke, *The Age of Renascence*, page 270. Under all circumstances and among all classes his dignity held him "at manhood's simple level."

Jacques Lefèvre was born sometime between 1450 and 1455 at Etaples, a village of Picardy. He is also known as Faber Stapulensis, the Latin name applied to him according to the custom of the Humanists.

Of his early education little is known except that it was ordinary. Later, possibly between 1486 and 1492, he seems to have been a pupil in Italy of Pico della Mirandola, who had been a disciple of Savonarola. Before going to Italy he received both his master of arts degree and his doctor's degree. There is also some evidence of his having reached Africa and Asia in his quest for learning. Besides holding professorships at the University of Paris, he also taught mathematics, music, and philosophy at the college of Cardinal Lemoine, perhaps about the middle 1490's.

By 1500 he stood as one of the brilliant intellectuals of the Parisian university circle, as he lectured on justification by faith and the Psalms.

The first Frenchman with sufficient versatility in the Greek to use it effectively, he began after his fiftieth year to study the Bible in the original languages, for he wanted firsthand information. One author says that he wanted "to preach Christ from the sources."—Lindsay, *A History of the Reformation*, page 141. It was not, however, until 1507 that he began to devote all his time to the study of the Scriptures. The next thirteen years he spent in the abbey of St. Germain-des-Pris at Paris where his friend Guillaume Briconnet was abbot. Here Lefèvre studied in the monastery library.

In 1512 he produced the first edition of his commentaries on the Epistles of St. Paul, a work of translation from the Greek to Latin accompanied by a revised version of the Vulgate, which won him the distinction of being "the most skillful commentator of the age."

This work, stressing the doctrine of justification by faith, blasted the subtle arguments of the schoolmen, and set the tongues in the Sorbonne, the Paris theological center, to wagging.

When in 1517, or thereabouts, he published a brochure affirming, contrary to the views of the Sorbonne, that Mary the sister of

Lazarus, Mary Magdalene, and the woman with the alabaster box were three persons, his teachings were pronounced heretical. Yet opposition to him did not become alarmingly vocal until the writings and opinions of Luther were circulated within the university. Up to this time Lefèvre's work had been regarded as the opinions of a mystic rather than the beliefs of a polemicist.

Lefèvre's enemies now began to harass him secretly. This, together with the Sorbonne's charge of heresy, led him to accept the invitation of his friend Briconnet to come to Meaux. Briconnet, who was now the bishop of Meaux, believed about many things as did Lefèvre, and had begun various reforms, among them widespread Bible reading among the people.

Arriving in Meaux, where had gathered a group of kindred religious spirits, sometime during late 1520 or the spring of 1521, Lefèvre soon became known as its venerable Reformer. Here he preached so aggressively that by the autumn of 1521 some members of the Dominican order classified him with Luther, Erasmus, and Reuchlin as one of the four antichrists of the era.

During 1522 Lefèvre completed a Latin commentary of the Gospels, accompanied by an earnest admonition for a return to pristine Christianity. The following year the New Testament in the French language reached the people. It was inferior in scholarship to the work of Luther and Tyndale, but it was, nonetheless, well received by the people.

The Sorbonne seized copies of it and threw them in the fire. Nevertheless, Lefèvre became the vicar-general at Meaux and continued his work. Meaux was rapidly becoming synonymous with Wittenberg. Lefèvre's activity caused Fisher, the bishop of Rochester and one of the eminent prelates of the times, to write against him. Beda, of the Sorbonne, led the open opposition to Lefèvre and the Meaux group.

Notwithstanding this hostility, the Reformers continued Bible reading, preaching, translating, writing. They eliminated from church administration any rituals pertaining to purgatory and holy water. Then in 1525 the Battle of Pavia resulted in the imprisonment of Francis I. Almost immediately repression came to Meaux by way of the parliament of Paris and the university theological faculty with the consent of the queen regent.

11—H.R.

Jean Leclerc, a wool carder, became the first victim. He had declared that the pope was antichrist and had torn Pope Clement VII's bull proclaiming a jubilee from the church doors at Meaux. For this he was captured, branded on the forehead with a hot iron, and banished. He went to Metz, where his zeal again outran his judgment, and here in July, 1525, he was burned at the stake.

Once intolerance gained the upper hand, others became easy prey. The reforming bishop of Meaux had already recanted under duress, and this left the group at Meaux without official support.

Lefèvre became a marked man. Beda had written a book against him, and on August 28, 1525, parliament published a decree condemning nine theses taken from his commentaries. This decree also placed his translation of the Scriptures on the prohibited list. Lefèvre realized that this meant flight or possible torture and death.

He therefore left Meaux and fled to Strasbourg, where he met Farel and other Reformers who received him warmly.

The release of Francis I in March, 1526, from imprisonment in Madrid upset the hopes of the ardent papists. The king suspended the molestations. By his order Lefèvre returned to become the monarch's librarian at Blois and tutor to the royal household. Here he quietly worked on a translation of the Bible at the request of the king and the king's sister Margaret, who later became the wife of the king of Navarre. This Bible, completed in 1535, with the help of Pierre Olivetan, Calvin's cousin, became the translation commonly used by the French Protestants.

But persecution arose again. This time Louis de Berquin, twice rescued from his persecutors by Francis I, paid with his life April 17, 1529. It was said that had Francis I protected Berquin as the elector had Luther, this French nobleman would have successfully completed a French national reformation.

Lefèvre spent his last days at Nérac under the protection of Margaret of Navarre, where he died in 1536.

MARTIN BUCER

He Sought Unity of the Faith

NEXT to Luther and Melanchthon, Martin Bucer is doubtless the most eminent figure in the German Reformation. In fact, some Protestant authors consider him above the other two in his influence upon the theological thinking in Germany, Italy, Belgium, France, and the Netherlands. The Italian Cardinal Contarini considered him the most able and learned theologian among the heretics. Bucer's university lectures, his sermons, and ninety-six published works won for him the designation, "The connecting link between the German and the English Reformation."

Although he played an important role in the development of the Protestant church organization, most of his efforts were directed toward the conciliation of the Lutheran and Zwinglian views, and also, if possible, to bring about a union among all other leading divergent religious groups, including the Catholics.

These endeavors caused him to formulate ambiguous phraseology instead of clear-cut statements of doctrine, which caused his friend Margaret Blaurer to call him, "The dear politicus and fanaticus of union," and the historian Bossuet to name him, "The great architect of subtleties." As a result of this enigmatic language his ability as a theologian and his activity in church organization has been neglected by most church historians.

Bucer was born at Schlettstadt in the vicinity of Strasbourg of humble parentage, November 11, 1491. Divergence of opinion exists concerning his real name, some contending that it was Butzer, others that it was Kuhhorn. According to the custom among scholars he adopted the Greek form by which he is now known.

He attained his early education in an excellent Latin school in his home town. In 1506 he was persuaded to enter the Dominican monastery, apparently against his wishes, and he remained there for eleven years.

In 1517 he went to Heidelberg University where he specialized in Greek, Hebrew, the humanities, and theology under the auspices of the Dominican order. Here he became aware of Luther's opinions as he heard that Reformer debate with the other university doctors. Luther's teachings, together with Erasmus's ideas, caused Bucer to accept the doctrines of the Reformation, at least in theory, in the spring of 1518. And about this time a correspondence developed between him and Luther which increased his desire for liberation from the church.

His interest in Lutheranism, however, led to difficulties with his superiors, and in order to escape persecution he, along with many others, in 1519 took refuge at the castle of Franz von Sickingen, the Ebernberg, near Creuznach.

Once he had broken with the monastery, his learning soon won him consideration among Luther's followers. In 1520 he became the chaplain of Frederick, elector of the Palatine. The same year the archbishop of Speier released him from his Dominican vows on the basis that he had been but a mere boy when he joined the order. But his status as a priest apparently remained unaffected by this liberation.

His loyalty to Luther came to the forefront at the Diet of Worms, as he came from Sickingen's estate to Worms to congratulate the Reformer upon his excellent bearing at the first hearing before the diet. From here on, Bucer's Protestant activities increased in tempo.

In 1522 Sickingen offered him the pastorate at Landstuhl, but when Sickingen suffered defeat at the hands of the elector of Treves, Bucer went to Weissenberg in Lower Alsace. There he advocated Lutheran views and recommended the study of the German Bible, gaining thereby the support of the citizens and the council. His preaching brought forth sharp attacks from the Franciscans and excommunication by the bishop of Speier. Shortly before this ouster he had married a former nun, Elizabeth Silbereisen; he was one of the first priests among the Reformers to renounce the vow of celibacy.

With his wife he escaped to Strasbourg and found a refuge with his father, a citizen of that city. The bishop asked that Bucer be surrendered, but the town council refused because his father's citizenship provided safety for members of his family. Furthermore, the city was full of adherents of, and sympathizers with, the reform movement, a situation which offered additional protection.

Because of his marriage he was at first permitted to preach only in private homes, but erelong he began to lecture on the New Testament in the cathedral. Before the close of 1523 he obtained the appointment, with salary, to lecture daily on the Scriptures, and became one of the seven recognized Strasbourg preachers. Here he also began his long service as professor at the university, and laid the foundation of the Protestant educational system in that area.

In spite of his decisive boldness, he constantly endeavored to avoid divisions on theological issues; he attempted always to maintain a conservative, middle-of-the-road policy between Luther and Zwingli, with the intent of reconciling their views.

During the opening months of 1524 his beliefs on the eucharist still coincided with those of Luther, namely that of consubstantiation, and his attitude toward the use of pictures and images had not yet crystallized. In October of that year he did, however, remove the images and close the miracle-producing grave at the church of St. Aurelia, where he remained pastor for seven years.

While at this post he wrote *Ordnung und Inhalt deutscher Messe*, a work typical of the order and content of worship in the reformed churches. He also attempted by personal interviews to calm the rebelling peasants during this period. In the interest of ecclesiastical discipline he vigorously opposed the Anabaptists and other so-called radical sects.

By 1525 he, along with the other Strasbourg preachers, seemed to place himself on Zwingli's side in the eucharist controversy. They maintained that the Lord's Supper should be stressed for its commemoration of the death of Christ rather than for the composition of its elements, although they agreed and taught that the wine is Christ's blood and the bread His body. Luther, disregarding all efforts at appeasement, made violent attacks on the Strasbourg theologians and maintained the bodily presence of Christ in the Lord's Supper. It was his adamant attitude and harsh censure which caused the Strasbourg group ultimately to favor the Swiss view.

In his role as a peacemaker, Bucer kept on promoting the Reformation in Germany and beyond its borders as he wrote, traveled, corresponded, and visited with church and state officials. He had many fine talents—benevolence, understanding, dignity, zeal, and discernment, with a charming, captivating manner which made him the ideal person for the project he had selected. As his influence expanded and new situations arose, his organizing abilities also came into play. As one of several acts in the reorganization of religious services, he, through the co-operation of secular bodies, abolished the mass at Strasbourg.

At the disputation at Bern, in 1528, he had not yet given up hopes of effecting a solution for the eucharist problem. Regardless of Luther's attacks he still worked for an understanding, and in June of that year he suggested a personal interview between Zwingli and Luther, begging the former to be as conciliatory and lenient as possible. He greatly deplored that religion had become a matter of treaties between cities, and that both Catholic and Protestant disputants were fighting against, not for, God.

The next year came the Marburg Colloquy, arranged for by the landgrave Philip of Hesse in collaboration with Bucer, both of whom considered unity among Protestant groups essential to present a strong front against Rome. The main objective of the colloquy was to resolve the opposing views of the Lord's Supper. The best theological talent appeared for both sides, Zwingli and Bucer for Strasbourg; Constance, Lindau, and Memmingen on the Swiss side; and Luther and Melanchthon for the German. It is said that Bucer demonstrated such keenness of mind and subtleness of argument that he paralleled the ability of scholastic theologians.

Though the conference failed in its chief purpose, it did reveal that substantially the two groups were together, for out of fourteen of the fifteen issues raised, only one, the Lord's Supper, remained unsettled. Had the theological terminology been more clearly defined, the results might have been more satisfactory, but at least a degree of agreement had been accomplished. And Bucer automatically rose to the position of acknowledged leader in further possible negotiations.

As the hair-splitting arguments over the eucharist continued unabated, Bucer's hopes and efforts for union never flagged. At the Diet of Augsburg, 1530, where the proposed confession of faith, later known as the Augsburg Confession, took shape, he showed a spirit of moderation and, in general, agreed with the Lutheran views; although, with others, he did not accede to the confession.

Out of this situation came the *Tetrapolitana*, the confession of the four cities of Strasbourg, Lindau, Constance, and Memmingen, which Bucer and his associate Capito prepared and presented to the emperor in July of the same year. But this document pleased neither the Lutherans nor the inhabitants of Zurich and Basel. It did show, however, Bucer's pacifying spirit, his intermediate position, in that he approached the Lutheran view of the Lord's Supper as nearly as possible by tacitly omitting contradictory statements. By August, expectations for conciliation had fled when Melanchthon, who at Marburg seemed agreeable to union, refused to speak to Bucer and his associates lest he compromise his statements in the Augsburg Confession.

But still Bucer was not discouraged in his efforts to bring about an agreement. In September he met Luther at Coburg, where the latter admitted his longing for union with those who disagreed with him on the sacrament. From this personal conference Bucer wished to draw up a covenant in such an adroit way as to have it appear that Luther had won the others to his own views.

The pressure of a common danger in the form of the emperor aided in drawing the two Protestant groups closer and led to another fruitless effort at Schmalkalden in December. This time, however, the greater share of the blame for failure seemed to rest with the Swiss Reformers.

With the deaths of Zwingli and Oecolampadius in 1531, Bucer became the recognized leader of the south German preachers, and he continued conferences, interviews, and correspondence, all with varying degrees of failure; but by the close of 1534, although a greater feeling of cordiality existed, concurrence of belief became a gradually vanishing fantasy.

Two years later the Wittenberg Concord, aided by a more reasonable and friendly attitude, seemed to give assurance of harmony. It stands among the most successful meetings, having the least recriminations, held up to that time. Yet early in 1537, shortly before Bucer met Calvin at Bern to find themselves in agreement on matters of church discipline, the results of Bucer's intense attempts had all but disintegrated.

In spite of all these discouraging setbacks, he continued making infrequent efforts at understanding, even venturing, between 1541 and 1546, to draw Catholics into the orbit. The most famous of these conferences took place at Regensburg (Ratisbon) in 1541 when Cardinal Contarini and other Catholic theologians appeared to discuss the situation with Bucer and Melanchthon. Bucer returned to Strasbourg from this convention to discover that his wife, three of his children, and his close collaborator, Capito, had died of the plague. Bucer later married Capito's widow.

When the emperor's forces defeated the armies of the Schmalkaldic League at the Battle of Mühlberg in April, 1547, the beginning of the end of all efforts at conciliation and union had arrived. The result of the emperor's victory was the Augsburg Interim, Charles V's "patchwork creed made from snippets from two confessions," to fit Catholics and Protestants alike. It was proclaimed in May, 1548.

This mongrel confession settled nothing, and no one was satisfied, except Charles V perhaps; for it drove at least four hundred Protestant ministers from their homes, among them Bucer, who fled to England. There, by the invitation of Edward VI and Cranmer, he accepted the post of regius professor of divinity at Cambridge rather than a similar position offered him at Copenhagen.

His constant activity in promoting the Reformation and his anxiety to achieve unanimity of faith had begun to affect his health, and not long after his arrival in England his illness increased. Yet his services and counsel were in constant demand. He interested himself in the status of the French and German refugee congregations in London, he gave opinions regarding the ecclesiastical vestment discussion upon the request of Cranmer, and he suggested moderation to Hooper. He recommended revisions to the *Book of Common Prayer* to circumvent Romish doctrines, and by the wish of Edward VI and Somerset he worked on a Latin version of the Scriptures to be translated into English.

The closing year of his life was one of constant activity, despite increasingly poor health. His course of lectures on the Ephesian Epistle, which began in January, 1550, attracted many students who later exerted a worthy influence upon the Anglican Church. To halt the opposition of those English bishops who had not fully emerged from the chrysalis of Rome, he debated at length on the doctrine of justification by faith.

His last work, produced at the request of Edward VI and apparently published posthumously, was his *De regno Christi,* designed to portray the character of God's kingdom and to demonstrate the means whereby it could be realized in a country like England.

His interest in the welfare of the English church, "lest for lack of discipline it be plagued by the same errors that had torn the church in Germany," caused him distress even in his last moments.

He died February 28, 1551, a few days after Cambridge had conferred upon him the degree of doctor of divinity, by order of a royal letter to the university. He was buried in Great St. Mary's Church with high honors in the presence of the whole university and three thousand citizens.

Under Queen Mary his body was exhumed, and, according to the practice of the Inquisition, he was tried as a heretic, his bones burned, and his tomb razed. But under Queen Elizabeth, in 1560, the University of Cambridge reinstated all honors to him.

MARTIN LUTHER

Champion of Truth

AT THE beginning of the sixteenth century all Europe stood in need of a man sufficiently stouthearted and daring to defy the papacy with all its un-Scriptural traditions, its power, its pageantry, and all its anathemas, and to open the Scriptures to show the way to Christ who said, "Thy faith hath made thee whole." Such a leader, in order to be successful, must be respected by all, practical in his outlook, learned in the classics and in the Bible, of sound judgment, and, above all, humble in his walk with God.

For such a time there was born at Eisleben, Saxony, November 10, 1483, Martin Luther, to whom history accords the distinction of overshadowing all other leaders of the Reformation by his courage, clear thinking, originality, and pioneering ability. Taking his battle for spiritual freedom directly to the highest civil and ecclesiastical authorities in the land, he crashed the gates of the emperor, shook off the pontifical yoke, and came away victorious. He was the greatest preacher of his time, and one of the most powerful personalities the world has ever seen.

It seems presumptuous to attempt to encompass in one brief chapter the lifework of a man who inspired the writing of many weighty biographies. So a mere summary of some of the high lights of his career must suffice.

His father, a poor copper miner at the time of Martin's birth, attained a comfortable degree of wealth and local political status while Martin was still a youth. The family removed to Mansfeld shortly after Martin was born, and here he received his early education. Later the boy attended school at Magdeburg and then St. George's high school at Eisenach, where tuition and lodging were free. He earned his board by singing in the streets, an acceptable means in those days of working one's way through school.

At eighteen he matriculated at the University of Erfurt, his father paying the expenses with the intention that Martin prepare for the profession of law. By 1502 he received the bachelor of arts degree, to which he added the master of arts three years later. At this time he stood second in a class of seventeen students. Now, his father thought, his son would surely pursue the study of law.

Before continuing his education much further, Luther visited his home for a few days. On his return trip he was overtaken by a violent electrical storm, during which he promised his patron saint he would become a monk. This he did without further hesitancy, although against his father's wish, on July 16, 1505, when he entered a monastery of the Augustinian order.

It is not quite clear why he took this step, but a reason may be seen in the turmoils of his troubled heart. He did not do it because of any specific sin, but because of a fear that Heaven could not be appeased except by a lifetime of denial and good works. His parents, pious Catholics, had imbued his mind with all the Christian teachings of which they were capable. It must, however, be kept in mind that up to the age of twenty he had not seen a Bible.

The monastery he selected had a high reputation for piety; it stanchly supported the church and all its traditions. In fact, no monastery in all Germany held a comparable rank. Luther began to work zealously to save his soul by daily fasting, prayers, and scourging. Menial tasks became a pleasure for the reason that when they were completed he had access to a Latin translation of the Bible, chained to a desk. This the monks unloosed for his benefit. When he reached the age of twenty-three, his superiors considered him the perfect example of a pious monk, and in 1507 the monastery officials ordained him as a priest.

The following year Dr. Staupitz, head of the Augustinian order in Germany and dean of the theological faculty at Wittenberg University, called Luther to begin his teaching at that institution. This university had been founded in 1502 by Frederick the Wise, elector of Saxony, and hence did not come under church control, a circumstance which helped immeasurably when once the Reformation began.

By 1508 Luther had the distinction of being the most learned man in the Augustinian order, and two years later Wittenberg listed him as its highest trained theologian. Yet his soul had found no rest! Devoutly and intensely he kept on studying the Scriptures, so much so that it was later said of him that he knew from memory every verse in the Bible and also where each was to be found. Gradually the idea of justification by faith, the cornerstone of the Lutheran belief, began to assume meaning.

In October of 1512 the University of Wittenberg conferred upon him the degree of doctor of theology. The year preceding he had made his memorable trip to Rome, where "the terrible corruption, . . . the wholesale lust, cupidity, pomp and vanity, ambition and sacrilege" (quoted by Frantz Funck-Brentano in *Luther,* page 19), filled him with doubt and disappointment. In 1515 he became provincial vicar of Meissen and Thuringia, which entailed, among other duties, the supervision of eleven convents. His capacity and zeal for work seemed to be endless. During Lent in 1517, besides his university lectures, he delivered two sermons daily in which his central theme was that of justification by faith.

The first step leading to an open break with the church was his denouncement of Tetzel's sale of indulgences. Indulgences had been sold for at least two centuries before the Reformation started, but never previously had they been bent to the shameful abuse of money raising. At the moment funds were needed to rebuild St. Peter's Church at Rome. In order to get these funds, the people were promised remission for sins they had not yet committed, their relatives were assured release from purgatory, and divers other equally absurd commitments were made if the people would but buy the indulgences. A couplet perhaps erroneously ascribed to Tetzel summed up his doctrine:

> *Sobald das Geld im Kasten klingt*
> *Die Seele aus dem Fegfeur springt!*

("The moment the money rattles into the box, the soul [for whom it was given] escapes from purgatory.") Quoted and translated by Frantz Funck-Brentano, *Luther,* page 61.

To bring before his university colleagues material for discussion and debate, Luther nailed ninety-five theses on the door of the Castle

Church in Wittenberg, October 31, 1517, an important date in religious history. In these theses Luther questioned the efficacy of indulgences and the authority of the pope, and stated that man is saved by faith and not by works. He had no thought that the pope would ever hear about these topics; they were intended solely as an exercise in polemics.

In a short time these theses had been translated and spread all over the country. Rumor of growing differences of opinion and clashes of argument began to reach Rome and led to the papal request that Luther appear in that city within sixty days of August 7, 1518. Such a summons was tantamount to condemnation without a trial.

The Germans interpreted the demand that Luther recant without a hearing as an example of Rome's tyranny. Then suddenly politics entered the scene, and both the university officials and the elector of Saxony objected to Luther's going to Rome, because, they maintained, Luther should be accorded a hearing, and that on German soil.

Rome, always anxious to get as much money out of German territory as possible, consented to give Luther a hearing at Augsburg by Cardinal Cajetan in October, 1518. Although it was impossible to prove by the Scriptures that what Luther taught was an error, the cardinal told him flatly that either he revoke his position or stay out of his sight. Luther chose to do the latter.

At this time the papacy had not yet awakened to the fact that the cause was not merely Luther's, but that it involved all Germany. The more intensely the quarrel between the papacy and Luther raged, the farther Luther's fame spread. Erasmus is reputed to have said to the elector of Saxony: "Luther has committed two faults: He has touched the Pope on his crown and the monks on their bellies."

During this time Luther's pen never rested. The people were informed of the issues in the struggle, and by 1520 more than one hundred editions of his works had been taken from door to door by colporteurs. Meanwhile the enrollment at the university where Luther taught increased from year to year.

Then came the eight-day debate at Leipzig between Luther, described as "so thin and worn that one could count his bones," and his opponent, Dr. John Eck, theologian from the University of

Ingolstadt. Eck won technically, but it made Luther the focal point of German discontent and served to combine politics and religion in a common aim.

The debate also served to establish Luther in his own views of Biblical truth. Rapidly his three great Reformation brochures, *The Liberty of the Christian Man, To the Christian Nobility of the German Nation Concerning the Reformation of the Christian Commonwealth,* and *On the Babylonish Captivity of the Church,* reached the people.

Quickly and surely Luther was being led to the apex of his quarrel with the church. Dr. Eck had gone to Rome, where he recommended Luther's excommunication. The papal bull, giving Luther six months' grace to recant, was published June 15, 1520, reached Wittenberg October 11, 1520, and was publicly burned by Luther the morning of December 11, before a large and excited crowd of students, townsmen, and university professors.

By this act Luther irrevocably separated himself from Rome, and on January 3, 1521, Pope Leo X published a bull of excommunication against Luther, his works, and all his followers. Charles V, the emperor of the Holy Roman Empire, although urged by the papacy, as well as by his adviser and confessor, Glapio, who had incited the burning of Luther's works, to take drastic action against Luther, refrained from doing so, for his political turn of mind indicated to him whereby he might be able to use the whole case as a bargaining element with the pope.

Finally, Elector Frederick of Saxony received the emperor's promise that Luther would receive a hearing before proceedings would be taken against him, even though he was already under the papal ban. In compliance with this promise Luther received the summons to appear before the Diet of Worms by April 26, 1521. Upon hearing of the emperor's offer to hear him and that he would not be maltreated, Luther stated that should the summons reach him, he would go even if he were so ill he would need to be carried. He felt that if the emperor called him, the call would be from the Lord. Even on the journey to Worms, when he heard that the emperor had given a command that his books be burned, he stated: "I shall go to Worms even if I were to find as many devils there as there are tiles on the roofs!" All along his route of travel distinguished men from all walks of life flocked to see him and to meet him personally if possible.

Entering Worms April 16, 1521, he was accompanied by a retinue of one hundred horsemen, and thousands of people crowded the streets to see him. The trumpet from the top of the cathedral tower announced his arrival. On the next day Luther made his first appearance before the diet, made up of two hundred ten high churchmen and nobles of the land. It is said that Luther spoke in tones so low and hesitating that those close to him could hardly hear what he said. When asked whether he would make a full recantation of his writings he countered by a request for more time, and this was granted him until the next day.

After the first day's session was over, the nobility gathered around him and assured him that he would not meet the fate of John Huss, that "they would with their own bodies make a living wall before they would allow one hair on his head to be touched."

The next day Luther spoke out boldly and without fear, giving a lucid description of his work and position. The statement often attributed to Luther, "Here I stand! I can do nought else! So help me God!" supposedly ended his remark that he could produce evidence that church councils had erred and contradicted themselves.

After the meeting adjourned, Luther is supposed to have said that had he a thousand heads they might all be severed one after another before he would make one revocation.

It soon became evident that Luther would not compromise with the papacy. On April 26 he left Worms under a safe-conduct which was to expire in twenty days. He was forbidden to preach anywhere on the return trip, an injunction he neglected to follow, since he was heaped with honors all along his route. The next month the diet sanctioned full excommunication against him.

By special arrangement the elector of Saxony had provided for Luther's safety by a well-planned "capture," previously revealed to Luther. A band of horsemen took him to the Wartburg Castle, where the keeper greeted him as "Squire George." Here Luther assumed the garb and ways of a knight.

Fearing that Luther had been killed, his friends, and particularly Melanchthon, were grief-stricken. But Luther was soon able by letters to dispel these apprehensions. While at the Wartburg, Luther assisted in directing the national and religious opposition to Rome. It was here that he performed his great lifework, the translating of the New Testament into the German language, thus with the same pen giving to Germany not only the Bible in its native tongue, but also a national book which unified Germany. Heinrich Heine has said, "Luther created the German language, and he did it by translating the Bible."

Differences in points of doctrine began to develop with Luther's absence; in fact, so much so, that he thought it imperative to return to Wittenberg. This he did at least twice, traveling in knight's clothes and each time bringing a semblance of order out of the raging conflicts of opinion. The second time he remained in Wittenberg.

Gradually the teachings of Luther and Melanchthon spread in an ever-widening circle throughout Germany and into other countries. Every aspect pointed to the formation of a German national church. But at this juncture the Peasants' War of 1524 broke out. It had deplorable effects upon the Reformation and upon the welfare of the discontented peasantry.

Luther's apparent responsibility for the uprising has caused many futile discussions. That a relationship existed between his teaching and the revolt, once it had begun, none seem to deny. But the correlation did not necessarily constitute a proof of cause.

Peasant disaffection and periodic outbreaks had been common for many years. The writings of the humanists and the numerous theories favoring economic and political revolutions were factors fully as potent as Luther's activity in starting the peasants' struggle for relief from aggravating social, financial, and political conditions. The revolt was not unexpected; it was its organization, range, and violence which brought consternation and fear.

The Peasants' War did not develop out of religious demands. In the entire sixty-two complaints presented to the lords, the agrarian, not the religious, problems formed the core of grievances. Then, too, the actual outbursts of peasant fury occurred where Luther's teachings had scarcely penetrated.

Wherein then lies the answer to the question of Luther's responsibility for the Peasant's War? It appears in the essence of his teaching, tinged with the democratic theory of the equality of all men. Luther's peasant background prompted his sympathy for them.

He agreed with the righteousness of their cause, but he also warned against recourse to arms. Not until all hopes of averting open violence, and plunder, arson, and promiscuous killing had begun, did he write his unfortunate pamphlet, *Against the Murdering, Thieving Hordes of Peasants.* When frayed tempers possessed rulers and ruled alike, moderation would have been wiser counsel from a man of Luther's intellectual and spiritual caliber than his encouragement to lords and nobles to suppress and annihilate their opponents.

In less than a year from the beginning of the revolt most of Germany had felt the peasants' torch and dagger. Quickly the lords and nobles struck with malevolent savagery. Daily the peasant death toll mounted. Estimates run from 100,000 to 150,000. So effectively did subjugation overwhelm the peasants that historians term them the most victimized European group up to the eighteenth century.

And what did the revolt mean to Luther and his enemies? Luther's doctrine of Christian liberty received a severe blow. When the peasants' reasonable plea for redress of grievances was answered with the death of scores of thousands of their fellows, their faith in Luther and his teachings suffered a deadly wound. The revolt effectively ended the advance of the German Reformation as a national movement and dwarfed it to territorial proportions. To the League of Catholic Princes it brought increased strength in its opposition to the spread of Lutheranism.

In Luther personally the uprising effected several changes. From his position in 1523 that God must be obeyed in preference to men, a year later he swung to the other extreme by asking the civil authorities to punish his papal opponents. Soon he looked upon the temporal princes as bishops of the church. For the lower classes he developed an expanding distrust, and to save the Reformation from possible disintegration he sacrificed the poor powerless peasants to the greedy, powerful princes. By his unwise pronouncements he must carry a portion of the odium of the national enervation and intellectual impotence which pervaded Germany during the closing decades of the sixteenth century.

But in spite of this wretched interlude, Luther did not despair. Though much irreparable damage had been done to Germany and to the cause of the Reformation, he turned aggressively to tasks which were to establish his work for future generations. He advocated that schools be started, and the basic educational ideals he promoted won him distinction as the founder of popular German education.

Luther seemingly never rested. If he was not preaching, he was writing or traveling. As a poet and composer he brought joy and strength to many. His hymns were approved by the people, and his "Ein' Feste Burg ist Unser Gott" ("A Mighty Fortress Is Our God") became the marching song of the German Reformation.

During the years following the Diet of Worms his labors and travels expanded constantly. Disputes and colloquies designed to find a common ground of belief for all Protestants occurred frequently. Luther presented himself at Marburg in 1529, where he and Zwingli debated the merits of the Lord's Supper and each came away with his own ideas intact. He lent his influence to the Diet of Augsburg in 1530, where the Lutherans presented their basic creed in the Augsburg Confession written by Melanchthon, and to the League of Schmalkalden, an alliance of German princes against the empire in 1531.

All the while, Luther's writings, showing an undeviating antipathy toward the Catholic Church, continued to flow from his pen unabated, as he dealt with every known doctrine of the age and lashed right and left at everything he thought stood in the way of the Reformation's success. His *Greater Catechism* and the *Little Catechism* followed in turn, and the German Bible, both the Old and the New Testament, was printed in 1534. In all he produced 294 works in German and 71 in Latin, not to mention his letters, which run into the thousands.

In 1526 he married Catherine von Bora, a young woman who had fled from a convent in 1523. From all accounts he was a loyal husband and father, and she a devoted wife and mother to their six children. Their union furnished the Christian church in future centuries with the example of what a pastor's family life should be.

For several years before the end his health had been failing, and he often spoke of his death, for which he seemed to long. He died at Eisleben, the town of his birth, February 18, 1546, and was buried in the Castle Church in Wittenberg.

PHILIPP MELANCHTHON

Author of the Augsburg Confession

M ANY biographies of the world's worthies tell of the struggles and difficulties until the hero at last reaches a coveted position in life, or after years of toil produces an outstanding contribution to civilization. But in the case of Philipp Schwartzerd, later to be known as Philipp Melanchthon, the scholar of the Reformation, the ascent to fame was unusually rapid. Of this almost miraculous speed in gaining renown, James William Richard in his *Philipp Melanchthon* wrote:

"Melanchthon, though but a boy in years, had taken rank among the learned, and . . . his associates were of that new generation which had risen to herald the coming of a brighter and better day for science and religion in Germany. Indeed he now stood on the dividing line between the Middle Ages and the modern era. But the day dawned so speedily, and the sun shot up toward the zenith so rapidly, that before Melanchthon had passed the meridian of his life, he had witnessed, and had acted a large part in effecting, one of the mightiest revolutions in culture, and one of the most beneficial reformations of religion, that the Christian world has ever known."—Page 17.

This man, who played such a conspicuous role in the religious and educational life of the sixteenth century, was born at Bretten, in Baden, Germany, February 16, 1497, to George and Barbara Schwartzerd. His father achieved the distinction of making such fine armor that his services were in demand by many rulers of the time. Yet he had less pride in forging excellent accouterments of war than he had in giving his children a good education.

Philipp's grandfather and later his grandmother supervised his education. Melanchthon was sent to a famous school of the time located at Phorzheim, where, as one of a select group, he received instruction in Greek. Biographers state that at the age of twelve he presented himself at the University of Heidelberg for admittance. After two years of diligent study, when not yet fifteen years of age, he attained the degree of bachelor of liberal arts.

Always intent on learning more, he now hoped to be admitted as a candidate for the master's degree and studied more zealously than ever. But he was sorely disappointed when the university denied his application on the grounds that he looked too young, rather than because he lacked the strength of intellect or sufficient learning.

Although he was smarting under the slight, his courageous heart led him to ask for permission to enter the University of Tübingen. Here he entered September, 1512, and here at the age of seventeen he attained the coveted master's degree. The only other degree he received was that of bachelor of theology granted by the University of Wittenberg, in 1519, a year after he began his career there as professor of Greek.

The following statement attributed to Erasmus regarding Melanchthon may appear too flattering; but as one reviews Melanchthon's work, one must admit that the young Reformer was no ordinary man:

"What promise does not that youth, or boy, as we might term him, Philipp Melanchthon, hold out? He is about equally eminent in Latin and Greek. What acuteness in argument! What quickness of invention! What purity of diction! What modesty and gracefulness of behavior! And what a princely mind!"

So much for the man's abilities; now what of his personal appearance? Here the verdict was less favorable. Melanchthon has been variously described as little of stature, insignificant and boyish, of delicate frame, a frail body, awkward, stammering. In fact, when he arrived at the university, there was fear lest this man would not measure up to his responsibilities.

But a judgment based on outward appearances alone cannot be a just one. For with his opening address, as professor of Greek, he dispelled all doubts as to his ability. Luther, it was reported, was in ecstasy and wrote to his friend Spalatin: "We quickly retracted the opinion which we had formed when we first saw him."

Students, townsmen, other professors, and visiting dignitaries came voluntarily to his lecture room to hear him. Erelong Melanchthon was described as warmhearted, generous, thoughtful with clear eyes and high forehead, judicial and calm, a man having comprehension, vision, and a profundity of scholarship. The rise in university enrollment reflected the rapidity with which he made his way to popularity. When he arrived, the university boasted but one hundred twenty students. Two years later six hundred were attending his classes, and some records tell of two thousand listening to his lectures.

Melanchthon has been termed the second greatest humanist, Erasmus being the first; he has also been termed Europe's greatest linguist, as well as Germany's most illustrious scholar and teacher. He, like Bacon in the seventeenth century, took the whole world for his field of learning and sought to know everything and to be a master in every science. Fortunately he regarded theology as "the crown of sciences."

As Melanchthon and Luther joined their efforts on the faculty of Wittenberg in behalf of the Reformation, the one impressed the other. It was somewhat of a father-son relationship, with the son, Melanchthon, charming the father with his superior learning and gentle manners, and the father, Luther, filling the son with wonder and reverence at the father's heroism and courage.

Melanchthon's determination to do the right thing gave him opportunity to work for conciliation on disputed points of doctrine, but never did his wish for peace cause him to waver in his conviction that the Bible rather than the papacy was to be man's spiritual guide. His strength of character, combined with deep scholarship and a love for logical order, often modified Luther's opinions, the younger man's winsome manners frequently charming Luther into milder conduct and belief.

Among Melanchthon's greatest contributions to the Reformation stands his ability to win the support of the learned by high scholarship and logical presentation of arguments, which were softened by moderation and sincerity.

Because so much of Melanchthon's teaching and writing was done in the field of religion, he has frequently been thought of as a clergyman, but he never received ordination. Yet as a theologian he holds an honored place. During the early days of the Reformation, before much religious literature had been prepared, Melanch-thon worked almost ceaselessly, day and night, to supply the need, so that his friends frequently despaired of his health. His second year at Wittenberg found him almost regularly beginning his day's work at two o'clock in the morning. In preparing the first edition of Luther's New Testament, Melanchthon worked untiringly.

It is to him also that much of the actual organization of the German churches of the Reformation is ascribed. From his ready pen came a guide in 1528 for the German pastors. It was filled with wise counsel and a liberal spirit rarely found in that period of religious upheaval.

He openly opposed many of the basic teachings of the Catholic Church. He asserted that both the bread and the wine should be given to the laity, that celibacy should not be enjoined upon the priesthood, that the mass should be abolished because it destroyed the souls of men, and that man is justified by faith and not by works.

Doubtless his greatest gift to the German Reformation was the Augsburg Confession. He spared no effort to make this production monumental, for it was to be read before the Emperor Charles V as the basic creed of the German Protestants. At least five German princes and the official representatives of two cities, Nuremberg and Reutlingen, gave their written assent to its acceptance. The effect of the Confession upon the emperor and others at the court is described in these words:

"Would that such doctrine were preached throughout the whole world," the emperor is said to have exclaimed. Duke William of Bavaria said to the elector, "Heretofore we have not been so informed of this matter and doctrine;" and to Eck, "You have assured us that the Lutherans could easily be refuted. How is it now?" Eck answered, "With the Fathers it can be done, but not with the Scriptures." "Then," said the duke, "I understand that the Lutherans stand on the Scriptures, and we Catholics outside of them."—Richard, *Philipp Melanchthon,* pages 202, 203.

In the original draft of the Augsburg Confession, before it underwent its many changes, Melanchthon made mention of the power claimed by the church to introduce ceremonies, fast days, and holy days. He called attention to the authority the Catholic Church appropriated to itself to change Sabbath to Sunday.

"So zieht man auch das an, das der Sabbath in Sonntag ist ver-
wandelt worden wider die zehen Gebote, dafür sie es achten, und
wird kein Exempel so hoch getrieben und angezogen, als die Ver-
wandlung des Sabbaths, und wollen damit erhalten, dasz die Gewalt
der Kirche grosz sei, dieweil sie mit den zehen Geboten dispensirt
und etwas daran verändert hat."—*Kirchen-Gesangbuch für Evangelisch-Lutherische Gemeinden,* Lutherischer Concordia Verlag, St.
Louis, Missouri, 1886.

(So one may also observe, that the Sabbath was changed to Sunday against the Ten Commandments, for which they consider it,
and no example is held so high and vaunted so much, as the change
of the Sabbath, and wish therewith to maintain the significance of
the power of the church because it has tampered with the Ten
Commandments and changed something therein.) Translation
ours.

Melanchthon took the position, however, that Sunday should
be kept for the sake of expediency so that church order might be
maintained.

By 1541 the Reformation had developed to the place where the
Catholic Church considered that Germany was lost to its power.
And yet the mounting antagonism between the papacy and the
empire on the one hand and the German Protestant princes on the
other finally resulted in war which almost ruined the chances of
Protestantism to survive.

Melanchthon with his wife and children moved from place to
place when Wittenberg fell into the hands of enemy troops, but he
returned when peace again came to the land.

All efforts at bringing division and schism into the ranks of
Lutheranism were only partially successful, thanks to Melanchthon's steadfastness as he carried on the work for fourteen years after
Luther's death. Ultimate help came to the German Protestants by
the dissensions among the emperor's forces. By August, 1552, this
discord assured the Protestants of the cessation of oppression.

As one views the entire period of a growing church with its
accompanying strife and recriminations, in which Melanchthon
stood loyally at Luther's side and after Luther's death carried on as
the leader, it is easy to lose sight of an individual's parallel activities
which are also worthy of consideration.

Melanchthon the religionist must not hide Melanchthon the educator. Besides his status as professor of Greek at the University of Wittenberg, where he served for forty-two years, he influenced the course of education in many areas of Germany. He assisted Luther in the development of the famous university preparatory schools, which continued with few changes until the nineteenth century. Few schools were established or new educational leaders appointed without Melanchthon's counsel. Burdened with countless duties growing out of the Reformation, including the necessity of voluminous writing, he still found time to produce textbooks covering practically every subject in the schools. For his outstanding work as an educator he was called "The Creator of the Protestant Educational System in Germany" and "The Preceptor of Germany."

A man of such high intellectual ability and varied talents gathers many friends and some enemies, and Philipp Melanchthon was no exception. After Luther's death those who opposed him within the Reformation circles maintained that he had attempted to change or weaken Luther's teaching. Of this charge he has been cleared by the action of the Lutheran Church itself, in which he has been considered a consistent power for good and honored as a worthy companion of Luther. To his genius stands ascribed the honor of making the Humanists' revival of learning serve the reformation of religion in a way not attained by his contemporaries.

But even to the strong must come a cessation of labor. His body, never robust, gradually grew weaker. At different times he suffered much bodily discomfort. In 1541 he sprained an arm when a carriage overturned, and this caused him much pain the rest of his life. A cold contracted in the spring of 1560 resulted in his death April 19 of the same year. An attendant asked him as death drew near whether there was anything he wished. He replied, "Nothing—but heaven!" By the side of Luther in the Castle Church at Wittenberg lie his remains. He was loved by his friends and respected by his enemies.

MENNO SIMONS

Believer in Godly Living

MENNO SIMONS, or Simon Menno, was a Reformer whose apostolic spirit and labors have not received the recognition they deserve. Doubtless this lack of regard has been due to his connection with the Anabaptists, meaning rebaptizers, *wiedertäufer,* derisively so called by their opponents, over whom there has hung a smog of calumny ever since the attempt of a fanatical offshoot to establish at Münster in 1534 a holy city on earth.

"No innovator, no great theologian, no great organizer," he has, nonetheless, been appraised as "one of the great religious leaders of his day and land, perhaps the most outstanding religious leader of the Netherlands of his time."

Performing the work of a Luther in the Low Countries, he founded the later school of Anabaptists in Holland and brought spirit, life, and order into their ranks following the Münster debacle. The Mennonites named themselves after him.

Menno's birth is variously given from 1492 to 1505, at Witmarsum, in Friesland. He was reared under the influence of the church, took orders as a priest, and for five years, from 1531 to 1536, he served as pastor in his native town, where he attained considerable popularity.

As he was slowly converted to Protestantism, his coreligionists accused him of imbibing heretical tendencies from his associations with the Anabaptists, but Menno asserted, "By the gracious favor of God I have acquired my knowledge, as well of baptism as of the Lord's Supper, through the enlightening of the Holy Spirit, attendant on my much reading and contemplating the Scriptures, and not through the efforts and means of seducing sects, as I am accused."

—McClintock and Strong, *Cyclopedia of Biblical, Theological, and Ecclesiastical Literature,* article, "Menno, Simon."

He renounced one Roman Catholic doctrine after another as he continued to study the New Testament in his attempt to save his own church members who were dissatisfied with the Catholic Church from falling into the errors of the Münsterites. "The great and gracious Lord," he said, "extended to me His Fatherly Spirit, help, and mighty hand, so that I freely abandoned at once my character, honor, and fame, which I had among men, as also my antichristian abominations, mass, infant baptism, loose and careless life, and all, and put myself willingly in all trouble and poverty under the pressing cross of Christ my Lord."—*Ibid.*

For a time he attempted to preach his new doctrines from the Catholic pulpit, but finding that impossible, he voluntarily relinquished his parish at Witmarsum, and about a year later some Anabaptists at Groningen invited him to become their public teacher.

In order to understand better Menno's relationship to that sect, a brief account of their history may be in place, although they are deserving of a far more amplified one than can here be given. First it should be stated that it is somewhat difficult to arrive at truth about them, for much of what has been written concerning the members comes from prejudiced sources. Nearly all historians permit their annals of the Anabaptists to be tainted by the actions of the Münsterites.

During the sixteenth century there existed as many as five different varieties of Anabaptists, and some say eleven; but for the present purpose two divisions will suffice, the moderate and the fanatical.

The moderate, or sensible, type maintained that they were the lineal descendants of the medieval Waldenses, an assertion which is probably correct; it is also possible that their immediate origin was the fruit of Zwingli's early efforts in Switzerland, when that Reformer, along with Luther and others, taught that nothing was to be accepted as Christian doctrine but what was found in the Bible. At the time some of his hearers in Zurich asked Zwingli for a Scripture text authorizing infant baptism.

At first Zwingli temporized, but finally he estranged himself from the group. Concerning the doctrine of infant baptism, one historian reports, "Nearly all of the leading Reformers were for a time brought face to face with the fact that infant baptism is without clear, Scriptural authorization, but were ultimately led to defend it as a practical necessity."—Albert H. Newman, *A Manual of Church History*, vol. 2, p. 153. Charles Beard remarked, "Baptism of the believing individual was the logical outcome of justification by faith."—*The Reformation of the Sixteenth Century in Its Relation to Modern Thought and Knowledge*, page 189.

The group at Münster represented the fanatical fringe. They taught that the millennium would soon appear, and with John of Leyden at their head they attempted to set up God's kingdom on earth. After they gained control of the city they proceeded to cast out the magistrates and slaughter the ungodly, probably in retaliation for the murdering in cold blood by the Catholics of numerous Anabaptists. Lutherans and Catholics alike fled the city. Münster was now termed the New Jerusalem. It is incontrovertibly true that polygamy was declared by John of Leyden to be the law of the kingdom, "the one dark stain on the Anabaptists of Münster." (See Thomas M. Lindsay, *A History of the Reformation*, vol. 2, pp. 430-469, for an account of the Münsterites.) One may here be tempted to draw a parallel between the polygamy of John of Leyden and the bigamy of the Lutheran prince Philip of Hesse, the latter's violation of marital sanctity condoned by Luther, Melanchthon, and Bucer.

The city was besieged, but more than a year elapsed before it fell, to be followed by a horrible massacre which spread to the whole territory of Anabaptists, all doubtless innocent of the sins committed within the city. Thousands were executed, many by drowning, which was considered to be a fitting punishment for their heresy of "believers'" baptism.

From that time to the present the stigma attached to the Münsterites has been affixed to all Anabaptists, regardless of how mild-mannered or soundly Biblical they might be, so much so as to make present-day Baptists deny any connection with them, although they are reputed to be their direct lineal descendants.

A few authors have, however, come to the defense of the sober Anabaptists and of the doctrines they taught. Beard stated, "They had a grasp of principles which, as time advances, are destined to play an ever-greater part in the development of religious thought and life. Theirs were the truths which the Reformation neglected and cast out, but which it must again reconcile with itself if it is ever to complete the work."—*Op. cit.,* p. 187. Another historian remarked, "That they were as a party guilty of the charges brought against them, . . . is untrue. As a class they were as holy in life as their persecutors; and their leaders, in Biblical knowledge and theological acumen, were no mean antagonists. . . . The fanatical Anabaptists were universally taken as typical, and to this day when Anabaptism is mentioned it is supposed to be equivalent of absurd interpretation of Scripture, blasphemous assumption, and riotous indecency. Münster was, however, only the culminating point of fanaticism engendered by persecution, and Anabaptism in itself, strictly interpreted, is not responsible for it."—*The New Schaff-Herzog Encyclopedia of Religious Knowledge,* article, "Anabaptists."

Menno regarded unsympathetically the state of affairs at Münster; in fact, in a written statement he censured John of Leyden severely for his outlandish beliefs and vile practices.

Convinced that the group that had called him to preach at Groningen was free from the fanaticism of the Münsterites, Menno accepted their invitation. He was rebaptized at Leeuwarden. About this time he also married and later became the father of several children. At Groningen he was ordained as an elder, or bishop, in the Old Evangelical, or Waldensian, church. He was recognized as their leader from the time of the Bockholt Congress in 1536, and from that date the moderate group assumed the name of Mennonites.

Not content to live a life of ease and seclusion, he took as his great aim the organization of the scattered members of Anabaptists into one body. Now began the most eventful part of his career. He spent much time traveling, and for twenty-five years after he renounced the priesthood he worked indefatigably, anxious to make converts. He crisscrossed the Netherlands repeatedly and traveled over Germany. His success was phenomenal as he gathered a vast number of followers, who assembled by the thousands in East Friesland, under the regency of the Protestant-sympathizing Countess Anna, practically the only spot left on the European continent where the Anabaptists were not persecuted.

From 1543 to 1545 Menno had his headquarters at Cologne, where he received the protection of the elector, Hermann von Wied; but with the elector's overthrow Menno was forced to seek other quarters. He removed to Wismar, where he remained for nine years, working in the East Sea area. Finally he settled at Oldesloe, Holstein, where he succeeded in establishing a printing press for the dissemination of his views.

About his work Menno wrote, "Through our feeble service, teaching, and simple writing, with the careful deportment, labor, and help of our faithful brethren, the great and mighty God has made so known and public, in many cities and lands, the word of true repentance, the word of His grace and power, together with the wholesome use of His holy sacraments, and has given such growth to His churches, and endued them with such invincible strength, that not only many proud, stout hearts have become humble, the impure chaste, the drunken temperate, the covetous liberal, the cruel kind, the godless godly, but also, for the testimony which they bear, they faithfully give up their property to confiscation, and their bodies to torture and to death; as has occurred again and again to the present hour."—McClintock and Strong, *Cyclopedia*, article, "Menno, Simon."

Menno complained bitterly that it was his lot, along with his followers, to be persecuted, to stand in constant jeopardy of his life, while the priests took their ease, made themselves merry, and enjoyed the weddings and the baptisms. He said, "Instead of being greeted by all as doctors and masters, we must be called Anabaptists, clandestine holders-forth, deceivers, and heretics. In short, while for their services they are rewarded in princely style, with great emoluments and good days, our reward and portion must be fire, sword, and death."—*Ibid.*

The Anabaptists had more martyrs than had any other sect. Lindsay reported that they "were subjected to persecutions, especially from the Romanists and the Lutherans, much more harsh than befell any of the religious parties of the sixteenth century."—*Op. cit.*, p. 445.

Menno spent the close of his life under the patronage of Baron von Ahlefeldt, and he died in peace at Oldesloe, sometime between 1559 and 1561, after having found time to amass a considerable fortune as well as a prodigious following.

The key doctrine of the Anabaptists is that baptism should be administered only to those who had expressed their faith in Christ as their Redeemer. Naturally this eliminated infant baptism. But baptism of believers was not necessarily observed by immersion; they practiced sprinkling, immersion, and pouring, the last method primarily advocated by Menno. That is the method followed by the Mennonites to this day. Concerning this rite Menno taught: "We are not regenerated because we have been baptized, . . . but we are baptized because we have been regenerated by faith and the word of God."—Quoted in *The Converted Catholic Magazine*, January, 1949.

Other tenets included unlawfulness of oaths, wars, lawsuits, capital punishment, and divorce, except for adultery. They excluded magistrates from the church and discouraged holding public office, but the civil government was to be obeyed in all things except that especially forbidden by Scriptural teaching. They believed that Christ would reign personally for a thousand years at the millennium. To them human science was useless, if not harmful, to the Christian, and they were the first to advocate separation of church and state so that there might be complete religious freedom.

Another phase of their practices included communion of goods, at least to the extent where they considered their belongings subject to Christian generosity. The churches were composed exclusively of professed believers, the truly regenerate, whom only they admitted to the Lord's Supper. They followed the practice of foot washing as Christ washed His disciples' feet.

They also believed in "soul sleep," that is, the doctrine that the dead know not anything from the time of death until the judgment. Insisting on the freedom of the will, the necessity of good works as the fruits of faith, they emphasized following Christ's pattern of life, His work and suffering. On the holiness of the Christian life Menno wrote, "True evangelical faith is of such a nature that it cannot be workless or idle; it ever manifests its powers. For as it is the nature of fire to produce nothing but heat and flame, of the sun nothing but light and heat, of water moisture, and a good tree fruit after its natural properties, so also true evangelical faith brings forth true evangelical fruit, in accordance with its true, good, evangelical nature."—*Ibid*.

They laid even more stress on discipline than on doctrine. Luxurious living, earthly comfort, personal adornment, social enjoyment, amassing possessions—all these they condemned. They walked circumspectly before God and men and succeeded in gaining the good will of at least some of the civil authorities.

Menno's strong characteristic was his insistence upon discipline. He forbade his followers from associating with members of other churches and insisted upon excommunicating those who listened to sermons by Lutheran ministers. He contended that the marriage bonds be dissolved when one of the marital parties was an unbeliever, and meted out excommunication if any departed, even in a slight degree, from principles of dress as laid down by the church.

Such strictness led to dissension and division among the ranks, as did his finespun theory concerning the incarnation. He taught that Christ was born *in* but not *of* Mary, thereby negating the human nature of the Son of God. He spent much time in controversy, and his insistence upon expulsion of all who were guilty of disobedience, however slight, led to at least two divisions, *"die Groben"* and *"die Feinen,"* and perhaps three: the most liberal, intermediate, and the least liberal.

As the result of this disagreement a great conference of German Anabaptists was held in 1555, in Strasbourg, where to Menno's sorrow and chagrin this conclave disapproved of his doctrine of incarnation and his disciplinary measures, but he would not be turned aside from his purpose.

That Menno was a mild-mannered, modest, pious man is attested to by the fact that when John Laski, determined to make a Reformed church member of him, engaged him in a three-to-four-day public controversy on infant baptism, Christ's humanity, and the function of the ministry, Menno's Christlike spirit convinced Laski that Menno was a really pious man; and the two separated in peace with promises of good will toward each other.

Menno's influence upon the Reformation, as well as that of his followers, came not so much as the result of any doctrines he propounded but rather from the principle of godly living they set before the world. He "gave birth to the ideal of separation of church and state, of toleration and freedom of conscience, of high moral and social ideals, of the preaching and practice of peace, of the supreme sovereignty of Christ over His own in this worldly world of ours—all ideals far in advance of their day."—*Ibid.*

PETER MARTYR

A Voice of Reform in Italy

ITALY numbered among her Reformers many intellectual and aristocratic men and women who were high in ecclesiastical and court circles. But as soon as they had been given a new birth of religion, they became objects of the wrath of the church; and she trampled them underfoot or drove them out of the land. This had the effect of greatly enriching the Protestant movement in other countries when those who wished to escape the Inquisition left her borders and hastened on to areas of safety.

Among the most renowned to leave her boundaries to bring dignity and learning to the cause of the gospel in foreign lands, when he once became a refugee of the Inquisition in his own, was Pietro Martire Vermigli, commonly known as Peter Martyr (the younger).

He was born in Florence in 1500 to well-to-do parents, Stephen Vermigli, a follower of Savonarola, and Maria Fumantina. The name of Martyr was given him because his father vowed, after a number of his children died in infancy, that any who survived would be dedicated to the thirteenth-century Dominican saint, Peter Martyr.

After attending the public schools in Florence, young Martyr, at sixteen, entered an Augustinian monastery near Fiesole, much against the wishes of his father, who wanted him to enter the services of the state, and who consequently disinherited his son. But this made no change in the lad's course of action.

The monastary had a fine library, and he learned much about the Bible from the Austin canons. It is recorded of him that he "was distinguished for the quickness of his understanding, the extent of his powers, the strength of his memory, and above all by such a thirst for learning that no difficulties could stop him. . . . Peter Martyr possessed solidity of judgment and depth of mind."—J. H. Merle d'Aubigné, *History of the Reformation in Europe in the Time of Calvin*, vol. 4, p. 433.

When nineteen he went to the University of Padua, where he studied for eight years and attained the degree of doctor of divinity, about 1527. Here he made the acquaintance of the future Cardinal Pole. As a student he maintained an attitude of respect toward his superiors, and he applied himself with all diligence to his studies. In thought he was chaste and in conduct pure. But he could no longer believe the religious teachings of his professors. Disgusted with their sophistries and perversions, he determined to study for himself and soon perceived "that the theology of primitive Catholicism was quite different from that of the papacy."—*Ibid.*, p. 434.

Shortly after attaining his degree he became a public preacher, and large congregations in Brescia, Pisa, Mantua, Vercelli, Venice, Rome, and elsewhere came to hear him. Between preaching seasons (Lent and Christmas) he presented Biblical lectures at the various Augustinian convents, where he also taught philosophy and literature, especially Homer; and during leisure moments he studied Greek and Hebrew. He became one of the most learned and capable men of his age.

Received with acclaim wherever he went, he also had several honors bestowed upon him. In 1530 he was elected abbot of the Augustinian monastery at Spoleto, and three years later he was made prior of the convent of St. Peter *ad Aram* at Naples, a highly important post.

Here he came under the influence of Valdés and joined his highly spiritual circle of illustrious notables. He also read the writings of Zwingli, Luther, and Bucer. For a time he attempted to conceal his new-found faith, but further study convinced him of the error of the Roman Catholic Church.

As his preaching began to reflect his views, he was accused of heretical doctrines, especially concerning the nonexistence of purgatory. The viceroy of Naples stopped his sermons, but an appeal to Rome brought a reversal of the restriction, by influence of Martyr's many friends among the cardinals, including Pole and Contarini.

Suffering from malaria, he decided to go to Lucca, in 1541,

where he became prior of St. Frediano. His duties also included that of visitor general for his order. His preaching continued to draw large crowds; among his listeners were teachers of Latin, Greek, and Hebrew, university professors, bishops and cardinals, and members of the nobility, as he exhorted his hearers to obtain a greater understanding of the Scriptures and told them that the Lord's Supper was merely emblematical, a memorial of Christ's suffering.

At Lucca, where the prior had quasi-episcopal authority over half the city, he organized a school of theology. Influenced by Valdés, he gathered about him some of the most renowned scholars in Italy, who were likewise affected by Protestant views, as professors in his academy. Latin, Greek, Hebrew, literature, and theology formed the basic curriculum, and Martyr himself expounded on St. Paul's epistles and upon the Psalms.

Many of the nobles and the leading citizens in the city shared his plan of study, and the evangelical movement became distinctly popular. Reports of this movement spread throughout all Italy.

About this time Martyr published his first evangelical tract, and for this he was cited to appear in Geneva before the chapter of his order. At this time the papal injunction had gone forth to the city fathers in Lucca to take into custody all teachers of heresy and send them to Rome.

Martyr decided that the time had come when it was no longer safe for him to reside in Italy and live his faith. With some companions he fled from Lucca, remained in hiding a short time in Pisa, during August, 1542, where he celebrated the Lord's Supper after the Christian manner, and went to Florence to join Bernardino Ochino. Both determined to leave for Switzerland.

The Italian Inquisition was now hot on the trail of heretics. "Within a single year no less than eighteen members of his [Martyr's] order left Lucca and put themselves in safety beyond the Alps." —Edward Maslin Hulme, *The Renaissance, the Protestant Revolution, and the Catholic Reformation*, page 330.

From Pisa, Martyr wrote to his friends in Lucca and also to Cardinal Pole, giving them the reasons for his flight, namely, the abuses and errors in the church and the ill will of his enemies.

On his way to Switzerland he went by way of Bologna and Ferrara, and then on to Zurich. Finding no opening there, he proceeded to Basel, with no better success, and then to Strasbourg, where the vacancy created the preceding year by the death of the Reformer Capito, associate of Bucer, remained unfilled. Martyr, with Bucer's support, received the senate's appointment as Capito's successor.

For five years he remained in this city as professor of theology and associate pastor to Bucer. In his learning and eloquence he remained as capable as ever, and his listeners greatly appreciated his public lectures as he opened before them whole books of the Bible, encompassing most of the Old and New Testaments, as was the custom among Reformers.

While at Strasbourg Martyr married a Frenchwoman from Metz, who was a converted nun and also a refugee for religious reasons.

With the accession of Edward VI to the English throne in 1547, Cranmer, at the behest of the king, called a number of leading Reformers to England, Martyr and Ochino among them. Cranmer who was anxious that an adequate library be at hand, requested them to bring as many books as they possibly could. In compliance the two packed their volumes together at Basel and transported them by water through Antwerp, Martyr shipping 13½ guilders' worth of Basel editions of Augustine, Cyprian, and Epiphamus, and Ochino 40½ guilders' worth of similar editions.

In England Edward VI had appointed Martyr regius professor of divinity at Oxford, and he was a popular lecturer, the fame of his learning having preceded him. Huge crowds attended his discourses on Biblical topics; even the Romanists listened.

All went well "till he came to handle the doctrine of the Lord's Supper. Then they began to break forth into outrages, to disturb him in his lectures, to fix up malicious and scandalous schedules against him, and to challenge him to disputes; which challenges he did not disdain to accept."—McClintock and Strong, *Cyclopedia of Biblical, Theological, and Ecclesiastical Literature*, article, "Martyr."

For four days he disputed on the eucharist as he defined his position on the real presence determined by the faith of the one receiving it. Cranmer and Ridley held similar views at that time.

Serious discord arose, and the Romish priests incited the multitude to violence. For a time Martyr's life was in danger, and he retired from London until the storm blew over.

When he returned, the king congratulated him on his escape and made him first canon of Christ Church. Here his wife and the wife of Richard Cox, as the first women ever to reside in an "Oxon hall," aroused considerable indignation among the papists, who resorted to stone throwing and window breaking to torment the women. So uncomfortable did they succeed in making it for the Martyrs, that they were forced to move to the lodgings in the second canonry of Christ Church. At that place Martyr "built in a garden 'a fabric of stone' two stories high, as a study."—*The Dictionary of National Biography*.

Martyr "exercised a great influence at Oxford and in the English episcopacy."—Hulme, *loc. cit.* He made many friends among the foremost Reformers in England. "Hooper and Coverdale attended his lectures, and he saw much of Latimer and Ridley, and other distinguished Reformers."—Christopher Hare, *Men and Women of the Italian Reformation*, page 81. As a stranger in a foreign land he remained a true ambassador for Christ.

It is not known how great a contribution he made to the revision of the *Book of Common Prayer* in 1552, but doubtless as a member of the committee to revise the book he may have made some suggestions which were accepted. It is thought, however, that these ideas were similar to those already propounded by Bucer. He was also placed on a commission of eight for reforming ecclesiastical laws. For this purpose he came up to London as Cranmer's guest in Lambeth house, where he, Cranmer, and Bucer secretly revised the code.

But Martyr's time in England was running out, as was that of the other Protestant Reformers, with the accession of Queen Mary, the Catholic. Since Martyr "had the warrant of the public faith and the law of nations for his safety," he was permitted to leave the country, but not before he had been imprisoned for six weeks in his own house.

He returned to Strasbourg in 1553 alone, his wife, "a most devout and pious woman," having died of a fever earlier the same year. Martyr, too, had suffered severely for months from the same disease. In 1557 the papists disinterred his wife's body and tried her for heresy; but since legal evidence against her was unobtainable, the corpse was thrown on a dunghill in the stable of the dean of Christ's Church, there to rot until sometime during the forepart of Elizabeth's reign, when it was identified, and reinterred in the cathedral with the bones of St. Frideswide to prevent further outrage.

Back in Strasbourg Martyr was appointed by the senate to his former chair of theology, which he held for three years as he continued to teach and preach. He also corresponded with his English friends, and Jewell, later bishop of Salisbury, then a very young man, was among the English exiles in Strasbourg to whom Martyr showed much kindness.

Because he had alienated himself from the Lutheran doctrine on the eucharist it became necessary for Martyr to accept an invitation, in 1556, to the chair of Hebrew in the University of Zurich, where "he lived, beside Ochino, as the most esteemed member of the Italian congregation."—*The New Schaff-Herzog Encyclopedia of Religious Knowledge,* article "Vermigli." In 1557 he was invited to Geneva, and in 1561 back to England, but he refused both invitations.

The greatest event of his later days was the Colloquy of Poissy, a conference held in France, in 1561, between the Protestants and the Catholics at the behest of Catherine de' Medici to determine some basis of understanding between the two faiths. The queen of France, the king of Navarre, the prince of Condé, Beza, and others, all asked Martyr to attend. "Here he distinguished himself as well for his skill as for his prudence and moderation."—McClintock and Strong, *op. cit.* He spoke purposely in Italian to get the attention of Catherine de' Medici, and from her he received a note of acknowledgment, which he took back to Zurich.

But the journey proved too much for him; it undermined his strength. He died on November 12, 1562, in Zurich, of a fever little more than a year after he returned from the colloquy. He passed away "in the midst of his friends, full of years and honors, dearly beloved and deeply regretted."—Hare, *op. cit.*

During his life Martyr wrote a great deal. Most of his books were against the papists, and his *Defense of the Orthodox Doctrine of the Lord's Supper,* against Bishop Gardiner, is considered his best. He also wrote many tracts on divinity, as well as Biblical commentaries, as he took part in the doctrinal arguments of his age.

Martyr has been characterized as possessing greater learning than originality, and it has been said that he was "the least heterodox of the Italian divines who rejected Roman Catholicism," and that he came most nearly to reflect the views of Martin Bucer. Even the Catholics acceded that he was free from the arrogance and vituperativeness usually attributed to the Protestants, and that he was completely upright in character. He has been described as "a man of an able, healthy, big-boned, and well-limbed body, and of a countenance which expressed an inwardly grave and settled turn of mind. His parts and learning were very uncommon; as was also his skill in disputation, which made him as much admired by the Protestants as hated by the papists. He was very sincere and indefatigable in promoting a reformation in the church, yet his zeal was never known to get the better of his judgment. He was always moderate and prudent in his outward behavior, nor even in the conflict of a dispute did he suffer himself to be transported into intemperate warmth or allow unguarded expressions ever to escape him."—McClintock and Strong, *op. cit.*

BERNARDINO OCHINO

A Free and Tolerant Spirit

IN THE past too little consideration has been given to the Protestant Reformation in the Southern European countries. These nations have at times been represented, at least by inference, as though sterile in reform views. By and large, historians and biographers have given their attention to the Lutheran, Calvinistic, and Anglican aspects of the Reformation; and comparatively few have turned their research to the choice materials to be discovered in the Latin areas. Consequently, courses in the Reformation offered in colleges and universities have left much to be desired in presenting an over-all view of the reform movement.

The importance of a Reformer is not to be judged by the amount of space historians have accorded him, for "of many of the greatest men the world knows the least." For Protestantism, Italy produced the finest and most gifted men and women to be found anywhere; their contribution to the Reformation was not inconsiderable. In fact, the impact of their ideas and their numbers in Italy was tremendous, barely exceeded by that of Wittenberg and Geneva.

Foremost on the list, in oratorical and persuasive ability, must be placed Bernardino Ochino, a preacher second only to Savonarola. His pious influence was felt throughout all Italy, and afterward on the Continent and in England, as the Catholic Church forced him to become a wanderer. So great was his following that when the news of his defection from Roman Catholicism became known it rocked all Italy, caused the members of his order to be condemned as "hypocrites and breeders of heresy," created a panic in Rome, and led Cardinal Caraffa, later Pope Paul IV, to compare his fall to that of Lucifer's from heaven.

Ochino was born in Siena, in 1487. Early in life he entered the

Franciscan order, but, disappointed with its laxity, he joined the more austere one of the Capuchins, in 1534, at the age of forty-seven.

At this period he was attempting to save his soul by a series of negations: *"Eat not, touch not, taste not."* "I believe in salvation through works," he said, "through fasting, prayer, mortifications, and vigils. With the help of God's grace we can, by means of these practices, satisfy the justice of God, obtain pardon for our sins, and merit heaven." Yet, dissatisfied after his self-applied scourgings, he would exclaim, "O Christ! if I am not saved now, I know not what I can do more."

As a Capuchin he became a revivalist, an itinerant preacher, exhorting the masses to repentance after the manner of Savonarola, whom he emulated. Large crowds listened to him wherever he went, and he attained the highest honor his order had to bestow. In 1538 he was chosen their vicar-general, and was re-elected in 1541. He also became the father confessor to Pope Paul III.

About the time he joined the Capuchins he came under the influence of Valdés in Naples, as did the other preachers of his order. From him he learned that salvation could not be obtained by works of penance, fasting, and all the mortifications to which he had been subjecting his body, but that it was given as a free gift from God to all who believed in the redeeming power of the blood of His Son, Jesus Christ.

Encouraged by Valdés to take a bold course, he now entered upon a new phase of his life. He turned away from his old superstitions and beliefs and began studying the Holy Scriptures. He gave particular care to the preparation of his sermons, and they took on a new meaning. They became more spiritual; they now contained the purely Biblical doctrine of salvation by faith. " 'He who hath made thee without thine help,' he asked, 'shall He not also save thee without thine aid?' "—Edward Maslin Hulme, *The Renaissance, the Protestant Revolution, and the Catholic Reformation,* page 329. He continued his itinerant preaching, always on foot, and wherever he went the people were attracted to him. "His name filled the peninsula, and when he was expected in any city a multitude of people and even nobles and princes would go out to meet him."

The Biblical topics upon which Valdés and his circle in Naples conversed day after day became the themes for Ochino's sermons, and elsewhere in Italy Peter Martyr was preaching on the same subjects. De Vio, cardinal of Gaeta, who had heard Luther, suspected heresy. Becoming alarmed at the influence of these three, he remarked, "These triumvirs of the republic of Satan are circulating doctrines of startling novelty, and even of detestable impiety about purgatory, the power of the sovereign pontiff, free will, and the justification of the sinner."

But Ochino kept on preaching. His resonant voice, the grace and natural elegance of his style, his exact diction, combined with his imagination and enthusiasm, made him the perfect evangelist. Then, too, his appearance heightened the whole effect to make people want to see and hear him. His emaciated body clad in the coarse garments of his order, his gray hair, his thin, pale face with a beard that fell below his waist, and all that the people had heard about his piety made them regard him as a saint.

But in spite of all the attention showered upon him and the courtesies extended to him, he maintained his humble spirit and simple life. He drank no wine and ate but one plain dish at a meal. And when the magistrates of a city invited him to their gorgeous homes to sleep in their soft beds, he acknowledged their hospitality with a smile and lay down on the floor with his worn mantle beneath him.

Success and applause attended him wherever he went. Whole cities came to hear him, and no church was large enough to hold the crowds, as he preached against purgatory, indulgences, fastings, and ecclesiastical laws, all the while citing the authority of the Scriptures.

So great was his persuasive power that "at Perugia, enemies embraced one another as they left the church, and renounced the family feuds which had been handed down through several generations. At Naples, when he preached for some work of charity, every purse was opened: one day he collected five thousand crowns—an enormous sum."—J. H. Merle d'Aubigné, *The Reformation in Europe in the Time of Calvin,* vol. 4, p. 432.

When Emperor Charles V came to Italy, he, like all the rest, went to hear Ochino preach. He came away with the remark, "That monk would make the very stones weep." Also among his listeners were the beautiful duchess of Trajetto (Giulia di Gonzaga) and the noble Vittoria Colonna.

But he could not keep on indefinitely without being checked in his career. Even as early as 1536 an attempt had been made to stop his preaching. In 1539 he was denounced as a heretic to Cardinal Caraffa, and the publication of his *Seven Dialogues* incurred still further suspicion. The *Dialogues* consisted of a series of conversations on Biblical topics, four of which were between himself and Caterine Cibo, a Reformer in Florence.

The real catastrophe came in 1542 when he publicly criticized the newly formed Inquisition for arresting a friend of his. By order of the papal nuncio Ochino was prevented from preaching, but public clamor caused the ban to be lifted. And then came the real blow. He was commanded to appear at Rome to answer for his faith.

He started out and went to Bologna, where he met the dying Cardinal Contarini. From him he learned that if he went to Rome he would either have to recant or die. Not caring to do either, he proceeded to Florence, where he met Peter Martyr. Working on the principle that "he who fights and runs away will live to fight another day," they resolved to flee to Switzerland.

Before leaving Italy, Ochino wrote a letter, dated August 22, 1542, to Vittoria Colonna, explaining his reasons for flight:

"ILLUSTRIOUS LADY,

"I am now in the outskirts of Florence, in no small anxiety of mind. I have been cited to Rome, and, against all persuasion, I set forth with the intention of going there. But hearing every day fresh accounts of their mode of proceeding (the Inquisition), I have been prevailed upon by Peter Martyr and others, not to go, lest I should be obliged either to deny Christ or be crucified. The first I will not do; for the last I am not willing, through the grace of Christ, but in His own good time. To go willingly to die I have not courage; God when He chooses, can find me wherever I am. . . . Besides, what can I do in Italy? Preach as a suspected person, and preach Christ obscurely, under a mask! . . . For this and other reasons I am compelled to go away; for I see that they would examine me by torture, to make me deny Christ, or else put me to death. If St. Paul were in my place, I think he would act in the same way. . . .

"Your ladyship knows what I am, and my doctrine may be known from those who have heard me. . . . It would have been extremely grateful to me to have your opinion and that of the Rev. Monsignor

Pole, or a letter from you. . . . Pray to God for me; I desire more than ever to serve Him by the help of His grace. I salute you all. . . ."—Quoted by Christopher Hare in *Men and Women of the Italian Reformation*, page 171.

This letter Vittoria never received, for as all the furies of Italy broke loose over Ochino's heresy, Cardinal Pole, who later missed the pope's tiara because he was tainted by "justification," could not endure all the furor and publicity associated with heresy, and commanded Vittoria to send all letters from Ochino to Cardinal Cervini.

On his way to Geneva, Ochino stopped for a few days in Zurich, where Bullinger, Zwingli's successor, was pastor. Ochino made a deep impression upon Bullinger, for he wrote later, "Signor Bernardino of Siena remained here two days, before going on to Geneva, and we had much religious converse. He is celebrated for his sanctity and learning; a venerable man with a tall figure and an imposing appearance. . . . In Italy he was so greatly revered that he was adored almost as a god."—Quoted by Karl Benrath in *Bernardino Ochino*, page 79.

Upon his arrival in Geneva, Calvin gave him a rigorous catechizing, followed by a license to preach. For two years, 1542-1544, Ochino preached to the local Italians in that city. He also published six volumes of tracts, sometimes called sermons, explaining his change in religious views. By means of these and other writings he continued to enlighten his countrymen concerning the Biblical reasons for his departure from the Roman Catholic faith.

But he had difficulty agreeing with Calvin, so he departed for Germany and settled in Augsburg, where for three years he shepherded the Italian believers. He was then already married. When the imperial forces entered Augsburg in 1547 during the Schmalkaldic War, they demanded that the Reformer be delivered to them, but the senate permitted his escape to Strasbourg. There he joined Peter Martyr, and together they made their way to England, upon Cranmer's invitation.

Here he became prebendary of Canterbury and received 100 marks from the crown. He preached to the Italian Protestants who attended the Strangers' Church in London, and enjoyed the favor of both Cranmer and Princess Elizabeth.

His chief writing at this time consisted of a dramatic polemic, *Tragedy or Dialogue of the Unjust Usurped Primacy of the Bishop of Rome,* in which he accused the papacy of having been sired by the prince of evil.

When at Mary's accession, 1553, he with other Protestants had to leave England, he returned to Geneva, but found no permanent asylum there because he protested against Calvin's condemnation of Servetus. His next stop was Zurich, where he once more preached to an Italian congregation.

All this time his pen never remained idle. Among his writings at this period were a volume of *Apologies,* denouncing the pope, the clergy, and the monastic orders; a *Dialogue on Purgatory;* some tracts on the Lord's Supper, concerning which he held the Zwinglian view; the *Labyrinth,* a discussion on free will; and *Thirty Dialogues.* The last contained some unwise statements which theologians interpreted as a rejection of the doctrine of the Trinity and an advocacy of polygamy according to the old dispensation, and the senate at Zurich banished him from the city in 1563.

From that time on Ochino was a marked man, without a resting place. He went to Basel, to Mühlhausen, to Nuremberg, seeking an abode, but found none. "He was tossed about the world hither and thither like a ball."

During a severe winter he fled to Poland, where he received aid from Nicholas Radziwill, a Protestant Polish prince, to whom he had dedicated his *Dialogues.* For a time he preached to the Italian residents in Cracow, but the Roman Catholic power was something to be reckoned with; and in submission to its wishes, Poland, by royal edict August 6, 1564, ejected him from its borders.

He fled to Moravia, where in Slavkov (Austerlitz) shortly after, at nearly seventy-eight years of age, "this man who had been equipped with such exceptional endowments, and had brought the reformed church so much honor," died of the plague in solitude, without friends, and without a country.

Shortly before his death he remarked, "I have had to suffer many things, but that is spared none of Christ's disciples and apostles. But that I have been able to endure all things, shows forth the might of the Lord."—*Bernardino Ochino,* page 84.

Ochino has been bitterly criticized by Protestants and Catholics alike because he had broken with the Calvinists by impugning the doctrine of predestination, alienated the Lutherans by denying the real presence of the Lord's Supper, and made the Catholics hate him by leaving their church. Consequently it appears that his enemies "misrepresented his doctrines and foisted many forgeries upon him."

In an age when tolerance in matters of faith was still at a premium, his sufferings were considered a just retribution for his heterodox views, but they never found anything about his life to condemn; he remained great and good until the end. And his biographer, Benrath, makes the observation, "His thoughts and the standpoint he took, have in the course of time, become commonplaces, but they far transcended the general intellectual of his time. . . . There is something deeply tragic in the fact of his final cruel persecution by the Reformers for his free and tolerant spirit."
—*Ibid.*, p. 83.

AONIO PALEARIO

Orator, Teacher, and Author

ANTONIO DELLA PAGLIA, later Latinized to Aonio Paleario, a highly educated and gifted layman, like Jerome of Prague, "must be viewed as one of the greatest ornaments of the Reformed cause in Italy." He was one of the most renowned orators, teachers, and authors of his day; and as a professor in several Italian universities, a public speaker, and a poet, he frequently lectured on man's attainment of freedom from sin through faith in Christ Jesus, often at great risk to his own personal safety.

He was born in 1500 in Veroli, fifty miles southeast of Rome. His parents, both descendants of the nobility, died when he was a mere boy. Since he was a precocious lad, the bishop of Veroli and Martelli, a friend of Paleario's father, supervised his early education and sought to instill in him right principles of conduct. The youth studied Greek, Latin, philosophy, and divinity.

Dissatisfied with any further education his home city could offer him, he began, when seventeen, to travel to other places in search of the learning he so greatly craved. An eager student of the classics, of Cicero and Aristotle, he sought the acquaintance of famous professors and associated with other illustrious men wherever he went—to Siena, Florence, Ferrara, Padua, Bologna, Perugia—getting from them what knowledge he could.

For some six years he studied in Rome, where he made the lasting friendship of eminent men, such as Cardinal Sadoleto, who is said to have admired the German Reformation.

At the time of Rome's fateful destruction in 1527 by the forces of Charles V, he left the city, and sometime after 1530 he determined to make Siena his permanent home. His great love for country life prompted him to purchase a villa located on the summit of a plateau about three miles from Colle. The home had belonged to a friend of Cicero. Here he met Marietta Guidotti and made her his wife. To them were born four children—two boys and two girls.

The University of Siena made him professor of ancient languages and philosophy in 1534, and his reputation and popularity among the students aroused jealousy among his colleagues, who could not begin to equal his eloquence or brilliance.

At this time he was already interested in Protestant views, as the result of Valdés's teachings, supplemented by his own reading of the Bible, St. Augustine, and other church fathers, as well as the German Reformers. His lectures on moral philosophy, tinctured by liberal thinking, greatly delighted his audiences, but greatly exasperated the papist professors. Cardinal Sadoleto cautioned Paleario, in view of the times, to moderate his statements, or, better yet, turn his attention to clothing Aristotle's ideas in eloquent language, rather than disturb the thinking of the university with his new religious views.

Such advice displeased Paleario, for his devotion to truth was such that his conscience would not permit him to rest if he remained silent. "The freedom with which he censured vain pretenders to learning and religion irritated a class of men who scrupled at no means to oppress and ruin an adversary, and who eagerly seized the opportunity to fasten on him the charge of heresy."—McClintock and Strong, *Cyclopedia of Biblical, Theological, and Ecclesiastical Literature,* article, "Paleario."

Paleario is credited by some historians with having written, in 1542, *The Benefits of Christ's Death,* the greatest piece of religious writing to come out of the Italian Reformation. *The Benefits,* which gave much offense to his enemies, was called the "little golden book," and became the creed of the Italian Reformation. "Nothing," said Vergerio, an eminent Italian jurist and leading Protestant, "was ever printed so entirely pious and simple, or so adapted to teach the weak and ignorant, especially in the matter of 'justification by faith.' "— Quoted by Christopher Hare in *Men and Women of the Italian Reformation,* page 47.

Various other incidents, likewise, made Paleario's circle of enemies expand. His best friend, Antonio Bellantes, president of the council of nine in Siena, had, upon his death, entrusted his mother with money to be held by her for his sons until they became of age. When the mother died, the Capuchin monks hovered around her bed, and when search was later made for the money, it was nowhere to be found. Paleario represented the sons against the monks, who were acquitted; but they, with Otto Melio Cotta a senator, as their leader, swore vengeance against their accuser. Cotta immediately began to devise a plot to catch Paleario in an unguarded act or word which might be construed as heretical.

Furthermore, Paleario had sarcastically ridiculed a certain wealthy priest who refused to pay his debts but who always with grave piety never missed praying before a shrine of a saint. Paleario's irony had bitten deeply into the cleric's sensitivities, and as a result the wrath of the priests had increased against their critic.

Now they sought more than ever to catch him in heresy. One day a group asked him three questions as to what he considered the first, second, and third means to be saved. Unsuspecting, Paleario replied, "Christ," to all the queries. His interrogators thought he should have answered, "Christ," "meritorious works," and "the church." According to their interpretation, his answers constituted heresy, and it was so reported to Cotta.

At his home in Colle, Paleario had attracted the attention of noted scholars and philosophers, as well as other visitors, many of whom he introduced to the new faith. Repeatedly outspoken in his attacks on injustice and fraud, he one day publicly disproved the fraudulent statements and unjust indictments made by a strolling friar, and thus gave rise to a further suspicion of heresy against him.

About this time Paleario accepted an invitation from Cardinal Sadoleto and other friends to come to Rome. Shortly after arriving, he received an anxious letter from Faustus Bellantes, a son of his friend, Antonio, which read, "There is a great agitation in the city; an astounding conspiracy has been formed against you by the most criminal of men."—Quoted by J. H. Merle d'Aubigné in *History of the Reformation in Europe in the Time of Calvin*, vol. 4, pp. 441, 442. In his absence his enemy Cotta had set to work to inform the senate of what he termed Paleario's "monstrous language" and heretical opinions. He also slandered Paleario's character.

Hearing that his wife was spending whole nights in tears over what she feared would be his fate, he had a bad time of it and resolved to return home. His friends advised against his doing so lest he fall into grave difficulties. But he resolved to go to Colle regardless, and Sadoleto assisted him in leaving Rome by way of Viterbo. Traveling by night, Paleario evaded detection and arrived home safely.

He was soon summoned to appear before the senate before twelve judges, all of whom seemingly hated him with the bitterness and contempt born of flouted respect and authority. Paleario derided their wickedness to their faces, calling them wild beasts because they desired him to be burned for what he had written. He denounced Cotta as the fiendish instigator of the charges against him.

With all the eloquence at his command he presented a masterful defense. He told them that the doctrines they accused him of holding were those found in Holy Scriptures and in the church fathers. He praised the German Reformers for bringing the "thoughts which for ages had been obscured by a barbarous style, hidden under the brambles of scholasticism, and sunk into the deepest darkness . . . into the full light of day, placed within the reach of all." He defended them by stating, "As to the passages taken from the commentators, whoever accuses the Germans accuses also Origen, Chrysostom, Cyril, Augustine, and Jerome," and proved his statements by comparing quotations taken from both sources.

He even spoke in behalf of Ochino, who at the height of his Christian service to Italy had been forced to flee from persecution. He did not deny having written a book on Christ's death, but if what he had written in it about Christ's power to save from sin would lead him to be burned, he would say; "No better fortune could befall me! In my opinion, at a time like ours *no Christian should die in his bed!* Accused, imprisoned, scourged, hanged, sewn up in a sack, thrown to the wild beasts, or roasted in the flames—what does it matter, if only by such a death the glorious truth comes evermore to light?"

As he saw his wife in the courtroom, weeping and mourning, he told her to return home to train up their children in the fear of the Lord. "Do not be afraid," he said; "Christ who is thy spouse will be their father."

He also told his judges that his own wants were few: "My books," "a woolen rug as a protection against the cold, a piece of linen to wipe away the sweat from my brow, a bed to rest on, and a simple bench to sit upon—these are all I need." Christ, he said, had taken from him all desire for worldly goods, but had instilled in him a strong determination to speak the truth.

Paleario went free; the senate did not even pass a censure upon him, but his enemies determined that he attain no permanent preferment in their city. He was keenly disappointed at not being appointed to the chair of philology when it became vacant. For three or four years the going was rugged, as his private pupils left him and he was cut off from all respectable employment.

When the city of Lucca extended him an invitation to become professor of eloquence and also orator of the republic, he accepted with alacrity. Sadoleto, who had advised him to take the position, again cautioned him to be prudent and discreet in his statements.

In Lucca he received a warm welcome from the circle who had surrounded Peter Martyr before that reformer fled to Switzerland. Here he wrote to the Council of Trent, 1545, his letter of defense in behalf of the Protestants, which was published at Leipzig in 1606.

But some of the citizens of the city took exception to his religious teachings, and even some of his enemies from Siena followed him to his new abode. The Roman Curia was anxious to trap him, and the senate at Lucca seemed ready to assist. Already Paleario could see the fires of the stake lighted for him.

In 1555 Paleario left Lucca and went to Milan, where he held the professorship of eloquence at a handsome stipend for eleven years. He was again accused of heresy in 1559, but defended himself by means of a tract.

With the election of Pope Pius V in 1566, the Reformers knew that their time had come and that peace and safety for them was at an end. "One by one, distinguished men were summoned to Rome and put to death, after a mere mockery of a trial."—Hare, *op. cit.*, p. 215.

Paleario realized his life was in peril. To assure that his writings be kept intact, he had them sent by friends to Zuinger, a printer in Basel, where they were published in their entirety without the mutilations to which the works of other Italian Reformers were frequently subjected.

In 1568 he was arrested by the Inquisition and imprisoned in Rome in the Torre di Nona, the most wretched of the three prisons the Inquisition had in the city. For more than two years he remained here, frequently tortured to get him to recant.

All the factors entering into his case and supposedly settled more than twenty years before in Siena were once more charged against him. Among these was his book on Christ's life, his defense of Ochino, his rebuttal in his own behalf before the senate in Siena, and the suspicions of heresy he had incurred at both Siena and Lucca. The Inquisition accused him of denying the existence of purgatory, disapproving of burying the dead in the churches, ridiculing the monastic life, and teaching justification by faith.

He was sentenced to be hanged on a gibbet and his body to be burned. The execution took place July 4, 1570, on Ponte St. Angelo. From his prison the day before his martyrdom he wrote two letters to his family—one to his two sons and the other to his wife. They show that he still believed the gospel story, despite all the papists' attempts to get him to renounce Protestantism. Hare quotes the following:

"My Dearest Wife:

"I would not have you be sorrowful at my happiness; . . . the hour is come when I shall pass from this life to my Father in heaven. I go there in joyful humility. . . . Console yourself, my dear wife, for this is the will of God, and to me joy; devote yourself to our children and bring them up in the fear of the Lord. . . . I am already past seventy, and my work is done. May God bless you, and the communion of the Holy Spirit be yours. Rome, 3d July, 1570.

"Your husband, AONIO PALEARIO."

SAVONAROLA

Pioneer of Reform

A REFORMER before the Reformers, a martyr, mystic, prophet, and priest, Girolamo Savonarola was Italy's greatest contribution to the Protestant Reformation. A visionary who professed divine revelation, he reprimanded popes and secular rulers alike, and foretold that Rome would meet terrible destruction if she did not repent.

The third in a family of seven, he was born September 21, 1452, in Ferrara, Italy. This was a city of vice, corruption, and luxury, where, it seemed, almost all decent customs and Christian virtues had been forgotten.

His grandfather, a celebrated scientist from Padua, was the court physician at Ferrara. His father was a spendthrift who sank to the level of a courtier. From his grandfather and his mother, "a woman of lofty sentiments and strong character," Girolamo received an excellent childhood training, the grandfather supervising the youth's studies with the intent of making him a physician.

Early in life a mystic flame burned within him. He loved being alone, and he played at making small altars and other toys having religious significance. In his studies he excelled his classmates.

At the age of twenty he was repulsed in love, and he never loved again, turning his thoughts thenceforth resolutely toward the monastery. Opposed by his family in his desires to become a monk, he secretly left his father's house at the age of twenty-three and went to the monastery of the Dominicans, where he was accepted immediately.

Here he remained seven years studying and teaching. He was devoted to the Bible and to Thomas Aquinas, as well as to Aristotle. It is said that he memorized the entire Bible. As he instructed the novices it was discovered that he had a gift of oratory and preaching. As a result, his superiors sent him back to Ferrara, his home city, to preach the Lenten sermons.

Ferrara had become embroiled in war and gave its native son a cold reception; only his mother, for whom he was to retain a life-long affection, comforted him.

On Savonarola's way back to the monastery he found himself in the midst of a band of blaspheming, uncouth soldiers, whom he reproved and told of Jesus Christ. Eleven of the number fell on their knees and asked pardon for their sins. Thus he obtained the first fruits of his labors.

Now Savonarola was sent to the monastery of San Marco, a center of science and Christian art, in the important city of Florence, which was under the rule of Lorenzo the Magnificent. Here he inveighed against corrupt art and poetry, which profaned religious scenes and degraded the literature of that age.

During Lent, 1482, he preached for the first time in the church of San Lorenzo in Florence, but his congregation did not number more than twenty-five persons. This lack of appreciation for the young priest's sermons was due in large part to his lack of grace in delivery; his voice was stern, and his vocabulary austere in its simplicity.

Anxious for the success of the young monk, the superior of San Marco sent him the next two Lenten seasons to a small mountain village where the folk were pleased to listen, and there he launched his life's program of preaching the theme, "The church will be scourged and then regenerated."

Pope Sixtus IV died in 1484. He was succeeded by Innocent VIII. It was a period of ecclesiastical corruption. The mystic in Savonarola's soul arose. He saw visions. He maintained that he heard mysterious voices. He preached with unsurpassed eloquence against the defects and evils of the clergy and the people of Italy. The people in this mountain village were terrified; their habits and customs changed overnight. From here reform spread to other Italian cities, including pagan Florence.

For a while Savonarola became a wandering preacher, predicting ruthless vengeance and dire chastisements if the people did not reform.

On August 1, 1489, he appeared again in the pulpit at San Marco. This time the audience was immense.

The next year he preached in the Duomo or Santa Maria del Fiore. It is said his popularity was so great that people, old and young, gathered at midnight before the church door and waited joyously through cold and discomfort in order to be on time to get inside when the doors opened in the morning. Once they were inside, all was so quiet that not even a whisper could be heard. "His words were like keen darts which entering the hearts of his hearers ignited in them a blaze of emotion and faith."—Piero Misciattelli, *Savonarola*, page 41. He was one of the greatest preachers of all time.

His chief theme was the purifying of the church and the reconstruction of society on democratic principles. The fulfillment of many of his predictions concerning current events made nearly everyone believe him to be a prophet. They had occasion to remember his prophecy when Rome was sacked in 1527 by Charles V.

His fiery, violent denunciations of priest and prince alike brought him into disfavor with Lorenzo de' Medici, and later with the pope. When the Magnificent's emissaries demanded that he desist from such incriminatory statements, Savonarola replied, "Go, tell Lorenzo de' Medici that although he is a Florentine and the first in the city, and I am only a stranger and a poor friar—yet he will depart, but I shall remain."—*Ibid.*, p. 45.

In 1491 the prophet was elected prior of San Marco. Although the monastery had been enriched by Lorenzo, Savonarola refused to pay him homage. Savonarola immediately set to work to reform the monastery by condemning pride, ambition, concubinage, feasting, malice, and unnecessary ornamentation. He wanted the quiet of the spirit. He lived in a simply furnished cell, was sparing in his diet, and slept only four hours a night. He devoted all his time to preaching, to works of charity, to study of the Bible, to prayer, to duties of office, and to political activities.

It was mainly the corruptions of the church, and only secondarily its dogmas, that he attacked. He maintained that he was submissive to the church, but that if the commands of the superiors were contrary to those of God, then he was not bound to obey. Thus he upheld the infallible authority of the Bible. He also

wanted to lay the foundations of a new political citizenship for the
people of Florence. Patriotism with him was a religious duty.

As the prior of San Marco, he started self-supporting schools
for architecture, painting, sculpture, literature, and foreign languages for lay brethren and monks who were not preachers.

Called in 1490 to the deathbed of Lorenzo the Magnificent,
whose death he had predicted, he left the king without giving
absolution because Lorenzo failed to promise to restore liberty to
Florence. The Magnificent's mantle fell upon Piero de' Medici,
who was to be a weak ruler.

Then followed the death of Pope Innocent VIII, also predicted
by Savonarola. Rodrigo Borgia, as Alexander VI, equally as dissolute, unrighteous, luxury-loving, self-indulgent a man as Innocent
had been, was placed on the papal throne by what historians confirm to have been incredible simony.

At this time Italy was a group of disunited states, each striving
to preserve its own independence and strengthen its own dominion.
It was easy to attack from without; and when Piero fled before
Charles VIII of France and his invading armies, the head of the
anti-Medicean revolution asked Savonarola to act as their ambassador to Charles. The Reformer trusted the unworthy French king
to give Florence a democratic government.

Savonarola was now at the height of his influence. A fly in the
ointment of his popularity was, however, soon to appear. Charles
VIII had failed to carry out the ecclesiastical reforms he had promised for Florence; and the League, of which the pope was a member, had already been formed for the purpose of driving Charles
out of Italy. Florence's refusal to join placed the prophet in line
for the pope's censure. A light discipline followed. The pope
devoutly wished to remove the prophet from Florence. He tried
persuasion, kindness, and an invitation to Savonarola to come to
Rome; but the man remained unmoved, lest by his leaving Florence
all the good he had thus far accomplished would come to nought.

Next came an order that Savonarola abstain from preaching.
The signory, a committee ruling the city after the overthrow of the
Medici, asked that his suspension from preaching be revoked. Consequently he was allowed to preach during Lent. He castigated the
evils about him and prophesied the doom of Rome.

By this time the pope was so desirous of removing the prophet from Florence that he decided to promote him by offering him a cardinal's hat. Savonarola said, directing his gaze at a crucifix, "I desire neither hats nor miters, be they great or small; I desire nought save that which Thou hast given to Thy saints—death—a crimson hat—a hat of blood. Those are all that I desire."—*Misciattelli, op. cit.*, p. 93.

Savonarola maintained that he was subservient to the Catholic Church, and that he had not preached or written any heretical thing. But the situation was becoming more difficult for him and for Florence.

Factions within the city, particularly the Piagnoni, followers of the prophet, and the Arrabbiati, his enemies, were at odds with each other. The prophet's mind, too, took on a subtle change, less lenient than before: he counseled justice, and as a result several conspirators lost their lives. Against the pope he hurled the reproach, "Thou hast made brothels everywhere." He called the church ribald, a shameless harlot, and said that she had made idols of beautiful vestments. "Thou hast made thyself a devil, lower than a beast; thou art a monster of abomination," he said.

Then came a ban of excommunication, June 18, 1497. He tried to escape it by saying that it was based on unjust accusations, and he declared anyone a heretic who regarded his excommunication valid. Political and religious aspects became hopelessly intertwined.

After six months of enforced retirement, during which he wrote his most important work, *The Triumph of the Cross*, as well as several treatises, he returned to the pulpit on February 11, 1498. This was the year of his last triumph. He persuaded the people of the city to bring their veils, perfumes, false hair, mirrors, indecent Latin and Italian books, expensive pictures and pieces of sculpture, and pile these "vanities" on the piazza steps where they were burned in a huge bonfire.

Savonarola's sermons were printed as tracts and distributed throughout Italy. He called the pope "a broken tool." This angered the pope to the extent that he asked again that Savonarola be sent to Rome. The papal brief threatened an interdict on Florence and caused prominent friends, who feared losing trade, to turn against Savonarola. On March 18, 1498, he preached his last sermon.

All Florence turned against him. He undertook, as a desperate measure, to call a council to depose Alexander VI. He wrote letters to all the leading kings and to the emperor stating, "Alexander was an illegal vicar of Christ, because, besides having bought the votes of the cardinals in the conclave, he had also traded in benefices, led an immoral life, and was an unbeliever." None of the letters reached their intended destination, but one reached the pope in short order.

Here was positive proof that Savonarola had instituted a plot to remove the pope from office. Then followed the fiasco of the ordeal by fire. Savonarola was ready; but rumors spread that he had refused, and the faith of his followers was weakened.

Soon afterward the Arrabbiati attacked San Marco. The Piagnoni, unbeknown to Savonarola, had hidden a supply of ammunition in the monastery, and many lives were lost in the battle. Savonarola was heartbroken that so much blood was shed. He and two companions, Dominic and Sylvester, were arrested and thrown into individual cells.

Here the prophet was tortured without cessation from April 19th to the 26th, the chief form of cruelty consisting of hoisting him as he was roped to a pulley and then allowing him to fall with a jerk. This caused a terrible, agonizing pain in all his joints. Fourteen times in one day he was subjected to this treatment.

Finally the signory, composed of Savonarola's bitterest enemies, obtained what some biographers believe to be false depositions, and the pope consented to the prophet's execution. He had been accused, among other things, of teaching free justification through faith, Communion in both kinds, the ineffectiveness of indulgences and pardons, the supreme authority of God—and not the pope—for the church, the giving of the keys to a universal church and not to Peter alone, the sinfulness of worshiping images, and the uselessness of auricular confession. He was also charged with having spoken against the wickedness of the clergy and with having slandered the pope.

Savonarola was hanged between his two companions on a cross-shaped scaffold which stood near the center of the piazza. He died at ten o'clock, May 23, 1498. His body was then burned and the ashes spread on the Arno River.

Savonarola's achievements were many. He was the first to drive a wedge into the block of Roman Catholic evils. Luther attributed much of his success to Savonarola's pioneering. The celebrated Humanists of Florence were his disciples, and it is said that John Colet of England, upon a visit to Italy, caught the spirit of Italian Renaissance from the fervor of the prophet's religious revival.

Savonarola was one of Italy's great men of letters. Moreover, he caused many of the great artists, such as Botticelli, Leonardo da Vinci, Raphael, Lorenzo di Credi, and others, to revive the religious spirit in their paintings. Michelangelo, who often listened to Savonarola's preaching, owed to him the representation of the "Last Judgment."

JUAN DE VALDES

"A Great Soul in a Little Body"

WHEN the Protestant Reformation began in the various European countries, it included Italy, probably the strongest fort of Roman Catholicism, within its scope. Certain conditions foreign to other nations obtained, however, in this country, which made the adoption of the new religious ideas impossible.

One obstacle was the nature of Italy's government. The peninsula, divided into five powers—Venice, Milan, Florence, Naples, and the Papal States—had no central government. These separate realms maintained a finely balanced equilibrium with one another, but they did not possess the benefit of unity to withstand the repeated attacks from their external foes. To remedy this situation the Papal States, the seat of Rome, pursued a policy of craft, ruthlessness, and bloodshed as the popes attempted to extend their sway, both political and spiritual, over all Italy, an incursion naturally resented by the other powers.

Other factors preventing the acceptance of Protestantism were the Latin temperament of the people, the isolation of Italy from the rest of Europe, the solidarity of the Catholic faith, and, most important, the Inquisition. Italy was the motherland of the Roman Church, with all its pomp and glittering splendor ever before her eyes. She could not cast out her child, even though she knew it to be the blackest of black sheep.

There were many in Italian state and church officialdom who recognized the sinister forces at work in the church, and who yearned earnestly for reform. Perhaps nowhere else in Europe was there such a concerted action on the part of its nobles, intellectuals, and ecclesiastical leaders to reform its abuses; bishops and archbishops, princes and university professors, all lent their aid. To one who has been schooled in the idea that Luther was the source from which all new doctrine emanated, the rising tide of Protestantism in Italy which began apart from his influence comes as somewhat of a surprise.

The most influential of those who taught the new faith was Juan de Valdés, who played a significant, even brilliant, role in the movement in Italy. From him that country received her most important reformatory impetus, and not from Calvin in Geneva or Luther at Wittenberg, as some have supposed.

Born in Cuenca, Spain, about 1500, of a wealthy royal family, Juan was the identical twin of the scholarly Alfonso. So alike were the two that no one was able to distinguish the one from the other, and even some of their writings were frequently attributed to the wrong twin. Their family was one of the most ancient and noted in the kingdom of León, an ancestor having founded the city of Cuenca sometime during the twelfth century.

Both brothers were taught by the noted Milanese Humanist Pedro Martir de Angleria (Peter Martyr, the elder), who prepared them for the acceptance of reform. Juan studied Spanish, Hebrew, and Greek. In fact, he became such a proficient Spanish scholar and author that his service to the Spanish language has in some respects been compared to that of Dante's to the Italian.

Alfonso followed the study of jurisprudence and Latin composition. Both were "distinguished by superior minds, intellectual gifts, amiability of character, and blameless lives."—C. A. Wilkens, *Spanish Protestants in the Sixteenth Century*, page 9. Both were educated for public service, and both were attached to the court of Charles V—Alfonso as secretary to the emperor, and Juan as secretary of the Spanish viceroy of the emperor, and later as chamberlain in the imperial service of Pope Clement VII in Rome, Bologna, Naples, and elsewhere. It is said that the pope loved him dearly.

Both of the twins were Humanists. They were friends and disciples of Erasmus, Alfonso to the extent that it is said he "out-Erasmussed" his mentor. Alfonso was present at the Diet of Worms in 1521 and at the Diet of Augsburg in 1530, where he translated the Confession into Spanish for the emperor and mediated between Charles V and the Protestants in the discussions that followed.

Alfonso saw little spiritual value in the Reformation; he supported it rather as a politician because of its attack upon the corruptions of the church. In 1527, at the sack of Rome, he aided the cause of Charles V and freely criticized, in his dialogue called *Lactantius*, the papal abuses of the time. He sharply reprimanded the pope for his worldliness and for his responsibility for bringing about the destruction of Rome, a cataclysm which caused thirteen thousand houses to be burned and thirty thousand inhabitants to lose their lives. He also candidly disapproved of the profiteering, the greediness, and the excesses of the church, including the indulgences, political chicanery, and spurious relics. It is said that this dialogue "marked an epoch in the history of Europe, and in the evolution of religious opinions."—*Ibid.*, p. 11. It aroused the suspicions of the papists, some of whom branded Alfonso a heretic and a Lutheran. He lived at the court of Brussels, but died of the plague in Vienna in 1532.

It was Juan who was convinced of the spiritual efficacy of the Protestant movement. A master of Castilian prose, he wrote his earliest work, *The Dialogue of Mercury and Charon*, probably in 1528, in imitation of Erasmus's *Familiar Colloquies*. With biting satire he ridiculed the abuses of both state and church, derided the immorality and ignorance of the clergy, and lauded the Scriptures and divine grace as having greater efficacy than the worship of images, relics, and the Virgin Mary. Using as a mouthpiece a woman character, resembling, it is said, his maternal grandmother, Juan made known what a boon it is to ordinary people to be able to read the Scriptures for themselves.

"That which my parents left me of greatest value was the ability to read. . . . Such pleasure did I feel in reading Sacred Scripture, that I learnt much of it by heart; and not satisfied with the mere knowledge of it, I endeavored to conform my life and conduct to it, losing no opportunity of instructing those of my female friends and companions who conversed with me in what God had taught me."—Quoted by Henry S. Lucas in *The Renaissance and the Reformation*, page 549.

In his writings the doctrine of justification by faith early manifested itself. He attacked such externals as the burning of candles, the use of indulgences, and the making of pilgrimages. He taught that religious persecution of any kind should find no place among Christians. There also existed a strong mystical strain; he believed he could receive new light through meditation and prayer. This is indicated in a passage from his greatest work, *Hundred and Ten Considerations,* a theological treatise:

"Oftentimes I have studied to understand in what that image and likeness of God properly consists of which Sacred Scripture speaks, when it declares that man was created in the image and likeness of God. So long as I strove to understand it by consulting authors, I made no advance toward its apprehension, because I was led by reading, at one time to entertain one opinion, and at another time another; until gaining the conception of it by reflection, it appeared that I apprehended it, or at least that I began to do so; and I feel certain that the same God who has given me the knowledge I possess, will give me that which I still want."—*Ibid.*

In 1529 the Spanish Inquisition caused Juan to flee, and for five years he wandered from place to place in the service of pope and emperor before settling in Naples, capital of southern Italy, where he died of a fever in 1541 without breaking with the church.

At Naples, it is said, his eminent work began. As a great teacher he became the center of a group of choice and kindred spirits, as Lefèvre of France had been at Meaux. Valdés possessed great personal charm. Small in stature, he was polished and courteous in manners, and attractive and winning in conversation. Of fair and pleasing countenance he possessed a pure character and genuine piety. He never entered into orders. He was a self-taught theologian of the first rank, one who had no need to unlearn the many sophistries and untruths of current religious thinking. In short, his was "a great soul in a little body." Noble and gifted as he was, he drew to himself like-minded individuals, most of whom belonged to the aristocracy. His adherents numbered more than three thousand.

Other cities in Italy—Florence, Venice, Ferrara, Bologna, Lucca, Padua, and Verona—were also centers of Protestant thought. Translations of the writings of Luther, Melanchthon, and Zwingli had been circulated by the thousands of copies, in Venice particularly, because of its being a commercial center. The influx of the Lutheran soldiers into Italy as Charles V and the pope warred with each other had also spread Protestant ideas. At Ferrara, Duchess Renata, a French princess, was an adherent of Calvinism. Here Calvin had repaired in 1536 with the hope of establishing a Protestant stronghold, but he returned to Geneva, disappointed in his desires. The adherents of Lutheranism, however, were said to number into the thousands, so many in fact that Pope Clement VII murmured against "the pestiferous heresy of Luther."

But Naples contained the strongest Protestant circles. Members of it were called Valdesians, after Valdés, and all were ultimately regarded by the church as heretics.

Valdés frequently engaged his disciples in long conversations as together they walked along the Neapolitan bay, their discussions dealing with the themes of God's great love to mankind and salvation by grace rather than by works. "He generally collected his friends together at Chiaja, near Pausilippo and Vergil's tomb, in a villa whose gardens looked over the wide sea, in front of the island of Nisida." There he discoursed with them on topics of grace, faith, and salvation. " 'An honored and brilliant knight of the emperor,' says Curione, 'he was a still more honored and brilliant knight of Jesus Christ.' " In Naples he "committed greater ravages among souls than many thousands of heretic soldiers had done."—J. H. Merle d'Aubigné, *History of the Reformation in Europe in the Time of Calvin,* vol. 4, p. 460.

Little is known concerning Valdés personally. To understand what an influence he exerted upon the Reformation one must sense the part his disciples played in it, especially when the Italian Inquisition, organized after the Spanish fashion, started functioning in 1542. Up to that time none of Valdés's disciples had any thought of breaking with the church, but persecution brought their true Protestantism to light. Valdesianism and Valdesians were arraigned before the Inquisition. Nonetheless, his opinions continued to gain such momentum that it was said hardly a highborn person in Italy existed but who entertained some notion of Valdés's ideas.

Among his most renowned followers to achieve fame and spread reformatory ideas abroad were Peter Martyr and Bernardino Ochino. The papist Antonio Caraccioli called Valdés and these two "the Satanic triumvirate." See *Cambridge Modern History,* vol. 2, p. 390.

Other renowned followers included Vittoria Colonna, an author belonging to one of Italy's greatest families, a friend of Michelangelo, and "perhaps the noblest woman of her age." Undoubtedly his most noteworthy woman convert was Giulia di Gonzaga, a poetess called "the most beautiful woman in Italy." To her he dedicated his manual of Christian living, the *Christian Alphabet*. As "a princess of the Italian Reformation," she remained behind after the dispersion, and, because of her, Valdés's writings were preserved from the flames of the Inquisition.

Galeazzo Caraccioli, a Neapolitan nobleman and nephew of Pope Paul IV, and later a close associate of Calvin in Geneva, and Pietro Carnesecchi, private secretary to Pope Clement VII, were both executed for their Valdesian beliefs. Many others who did not flee were likewise beheaded and burned.

Aside from the work of Valdés's disciples, that which perhaps had the most pronounced and far-reaching influence was a little book entitled *The Benefits of Christ's Death*. It represented the voice of this band of Protestants; it contained the kernel of Valdés's teachings. Authorship has been variously attributed to Benedetto of Mantua, to Aonio Paleario, and even to Valdés himself. It was the most important work of the Italian Reformation, and its popularity was indicated by its wide circulation, hundreds of thousands of copies—forty thousand in Venice alone. It was translated into many languages.

So much did the papacy despise this book that the book police of the Inquisition tracked down almost every copy; not one was to be found until a lone copy appeared in the University of Cambridge in 1855, after which the English Bible Society took steps to circulate it once more in Italy.

JOHN LASKI

Polish Reformer and Leader

$\mathbb{A}$MONG the men of the Reformation few sacrificed so much of wealth and earthly glory as did John Laski, also known as Johannes Alasco. Born to riches and royalty, he gave up the primateship of Poland to become a disciple of the King of kings, "one of the most beautiful examples of moral freedom presented in the sixteenth century."—J. H. Merle d'Aubigné, *History of the Reformation in Europe in the Time of Calvin,* vol. 7, p. 451.

The second of three sons, he was born in 1499 at the castle of Lask, ninety miles from Warsaw, Poland, of John Jaroslaw, baron of Lask, and Suzanna of Bakova-Gora. At the age of eleven, he with his two brothers, later famous as Stanislaus, minister plenipotentiary of Poland in France under Francis I, and Jaroslav (or Jerome), an eminent author, was taken to the palace of Cracow, by his uncle, who also bore the name of John Laski. The older man was then archbishop of Gniezno, capital of Great Poland, primate of that great country, and one of the most distinguished men of his day. He supervised the boy's education, and three years later took John, who he apparently intended should succeed him, and his older brother with him, to the Lateran Council in Rome.

For about four years John attended the University of Bologna. His uncle also guided his entrance into priestly orders, and obtained for him some benefices. Laski became successively canon of Leczyca, coadjutor to the dean of Gniezno, custodian of Leczyca, canon of Cracow and Plock, and dean of the metropolitan church in Gniezno, all by 1521, the year he was ordained a priest.

In 1523 he and his brothers went on a tour to visit foreign courts and universities. In Zurich he met Zwingli, who was the first to suggest to him that he study the Sacred Writings. At the close of the following year, at the invitation of Erasmus at Basel, he became a guest in the house of that great scholar, but with Laski bearing the expenses not only for his own share but providing handsomely for the entertainment of his host. In return Erasmus willed him his library.

From Europe's greatest Humanist Laski received his impetus to study the Scriptures. Erasmus told him it was one thing to aim at occupying the principal ecclesiastical post of a nation, but an altogether different affair to be prepared and fit for it. And with that the young Laski began to study the Hebrew of the Old Testament. Here he also met the Reformers Hardenberg; Konrad Pellicanus, who became his instructor in Hebrew; Glareanus, who likewise taught him Greek and Latin; and Oecolampadius, who guided him in doctrine.

Erasmus, the foremost thinker of his age, was so favorably impressed by the young man that he wrote of him in highest praise, "We have here John Alasco, a Pole. He is a man of illustrious family, and will soon occupy the highest rank. His morals are pure as the snow. He has all the brilliancy of gems and gold." He also described him as of "a glorious ancestry, high rank, prospects the most brilliant, a mind of wonderful richness, uncommon extent of knowledge, . . . and with all this there is about him not the faintest taint of pride. The sweetness of his disposition puts him in harmony with everyone. He has at the same time the steadfastness of a grown man and the solid judgment of an old man."

His friends in Poland became alarmed at his association with the Reformers, and King Sigismund I asked him to return. This he did, after visiting Paris. There he may have met Margaret, Protestant sister of Francis I, for he later corresponded with her; and perhaps he also went to Italy. His contact with the Reformers thoroughly shook his old faith, but at the moment his was merely an intellectual adoption of, rather than a spiritual conversion to, the new doctrines.

Once back in Poland, his rank, travel, family connections, and handsome bearing made him a social lion at the court. He declared himself an Erasmian, and had in mind to accomplish a renovation within the church in all Poland. He even asked Erasmus to write a letter to Sigismund urging him to liberate his country from the Romish yoke. Erasmus complied, but without results. The king had shortly before ordered the destruction of Luther's writings, and the seizure of all persons suspected of bringing them into the country.

Laski's old friends ridiculed him, even circulating the rumor that he had married a heretic and secretly brought her back with him. His uncle, the primate, greatly disapproved of his nephew's turn of mind in religious beliefs. The pressure exerted upon him from all sides proved too great, and when faced with an examination in 1526 he reversed his position and signed a statement declaring he believed only what the Catholic Church taught.

But this renunciation seemed merely a way out of an emergency, and did not in reality depict his true religious views. The spark of reform remained alive, and in 1531, when his uncle died, he was freed to throw off Catholic restrictions. His desires for reform, now fanned into a living flame through the writings of, and correspondence with, Melanchthon and others, took tangible shape as he attempted to introduce his new doctrines into Poland.

Indicative, however, of his confused thinking, is the fact that at the same time he sided with Protestantism he maintained and added to his benefices in the Catholic Church. In 1536 his brother Jaroslav, influential in Hungarian circles, obtained for him the bishopric of Wesprim in that country, and in 1538 he became the archdeacon of Warsaw and the bishop of Cujavia.

About this time Laski is supposed to have made a hurried trip to Germany, and upon his return he told the king of his convictions, and said that he intended to leave the country to go where he would have greater freedom to preach the gospel. "Brought to my right mind by the goodness of God," he asserted, "I will now serve, with what little strength I possess, that church of Christ which I hated in the time of my ignorance and my pharisaism."

Hoping at a more opportune time to return to unite all Poland under Protestantism, he left, probably about 1538, for Frankfort, Germany, and resided for a time in Hardenberg's house.

From there he went to the Netherlands, first by way of Metz, then Louvain, and finally to Emden in Friesland, a territory called "the battleground of Anabaptists, Roman Catholics, Zwinglians, and Mennonites." Here he settled in 1540, poverty stricken, and suffering from ill-health because of climatic conditions. At Louvain he married a poor but pious peasant girl, thus burning the last bridge between himself and the riches, honor, and chances for future glory he had left behind.

At Emden he became a pastor in 1542, and the same year Countess Anna of Oldenburg, regent of the country, made him the superintendent of all the churches in her territory. Laski accepted the position on the condition that he would be permitted to return to Poland in case his country called him to help with the Reformation. He wrote to Poland signifying his willingness to return if they needed him. But misunderstanding that he would return for any reason, the king wrote him that he might have a great bishopric.

This incensed Laski, leading him to remark, "It is asking me to return to my vomit." To the king he replied, "I will have no apostleship invested with the bishop's tiara or the monk's cowl. My return is not to be thought of, except it be for some legitimate vocation."

Beset by language difficulties, civil interference in affairs of church, antagonistic monks, grave errors among the members, and strife and contention in general, Laski aimed at accomplishing the stupendous task of uniting the diverging sects into one evangelical group. He was successful to the extent that he established the Reformed Church in Friesland, and Emden became known as the "Northern Geneva."

As he worked he assailed the monks and monasteries, the images and pictures in the churches; and gradually Romish rites gave way to Christian practices. He organized a Presbyterian form of church government, and appointed four elders to look after the discipline of the church. He organized a *Coetus*, a school for the cultural, pastoral, and doctrinal edification of the preachers, where many said they "learned more in it than at the university." He also prepared a catechism, or creed, for his members. The *Heidelberg Catechism*, the most outstanding of reformed creeds, was later partially based upon it. So well did he do his work that when the monks, through their spokesman Count John of Austria, asked

Countess Anna to get rid of him, she replied, "I cannot do without Alasco."

Among the most advanced in his doctrinal views, Laski differed considerably from Luther and Calvin on predestination. "God," he said, "so far as it rests with Him, shuts out no one from His mercy. Christ, by His holy death, has expiated the sins of the whole world. If a man be lost, it is not because God created him for the purpose of suffering everlasting punishment, but because he has voluntarily despised the grace of God in Jesus Christ. . . . God is the Saviour of us all, the most loving Father of all, most merciful to all, most pitiful for all. Let us then implore His mercy through Him to whom nothing can be refused, to wit, Jesus Christ."

A moderate, temperate man, he sought to reform by gentleness and kindness, rather than by force and ruthlessness. Contrary to the actions of some of his fellow Reformers, he defended the right of the various sects to live side by side. "An error of the understanding does not render a man liable to punishment; but guilty intentions alone," he maintained. But one sect he felt he could not fellowship, namely the one led by Menno Simons, although he entertained the utmost respect for the man personally; he thought him truly pious. For a period of days they debated, at Laski's invitation, upon the topics of the incarnation of the Son of God, baptism, and the ministry.

Among the many trials that came to Laski during this period were partial loss of eyesight, fever, death of his son Paul, and unjust accusations. For a time he retreated to a farm for rest and rehabilitation. "He was busied about his house, and also a little about his fields. . . . His wife managed the house affairs, milked the cows, and made the butter."

The report of Laski's work soon spread to other lands, and rulers and divines alike asked his counsel on church polity. He corresponded with Bucer, Bullinger, Melanchthon, and others, as they exchanged ideas on doctrine and policy. The duke of Prussia sought his assistance to supervise the churches in his territory, but Laski's insistence upon the withdrawal of civil interference in church matters and the abolition of Lutheran rites similar to those in the Catholic Church led the duke to cease pressing the matter. Needless to say, the Lutherans became Laski's violent enemies.

Laski spent his next period of service in England, driven there by the persecutions growing out of the Interim in 1548. In that country he made a favorable impression as he formed friendships among the leading bishops, such as Hooper, whom he supported in the vestment controversy. He discussed at length with Bucer the question of the real presence in the eucharist. For six months he lived with Cranmer at Lambeth, and Latimer praised him for a sermon he preached before the king and called him "a great learned man." It is said that he exerted a great influence at court.

The king asked him to organize all foreign Protestants in London, a group of about 3,000, into a church, to be acknowledged separate from the control of the Church of England. For its government Laski followed the Presbyterian organization he had used in Friesland, the first Presbyterian order used on English soil. He discarded the English liturgy and taught that Christ's body and blood were symbolized in the Lord's Supper. Besides, he exerted some influence on the English *Prayer Book*, he inspected the schools of his church, and sat on the commission to revise ecclesiastical laws. He wrote a decisive work on the sacraments and a confession to counteract the sectarian tendencies among his members. He used the catechism he had compiled in Emden for the instruction of the people. For his services he received a gift from the crown.

While in England his wife died, and he remarried shortly after. Altogether he had nine children.

With the accession of Mary, Laski's work disintegrated. The queen dissolved his congregation, and all had to leave the country. On September 15, 1553, he and 175 of his members embarked at Gravesend, hoping to find refuge somewhere among their Protestant brethren on the Continent The historian Charles Beard describes their plight as they encountered animosities and prejudices born of religious bigotry.

"Upon the accession of Mary, Lasco, with a large part of his congregation in London, fled beyond the sea. They embarked for Denmark in two small Danish ships which they found lying in the Thames, and to that zealously Lutheran country confidently looked for refuge and welcome. Late in the autumn they arrived, but were warned that they might not so much as land unless they would repeat the Lutheran shibboleths. It did not matter that they were flying from Catholic intolerance: Lutheran hearts were shut against Calvinist sufferers. All appeals were fruitless. The people in Copenhagen were friendly enough; it was the king and the preachers who would have none of them. So during almost the whole of a stormy northern winter, these poor creatures, among whom were many women and children, were driven from port to port: Rostock expelled them; Wismar allowed them a brief respite; Lübeck turned them out; Hamburg raged against them with special bitterness; at last in Emden they found a little rest. The very seas and storms were kinder to them than those who ought to have been their brethren. Calvin, who was at this very moment burning Servetus, raised a loud voice of protest, for the sufferers were his fellow believers; but I cannot find that any word of remonstrance came from Wittenberg."—*The Reformation of the Sixteenth Century*, pages 182, 183.

For almost a year Laski remained in Emden under the protection of Countess Anna. Later he went to Frankfort, where he was reported seriously ill for a time. But wherever he went he defended the faith and alleviated the suffering of the fugitives. At Frankfort he superintended the churches and sought to establish an agreement between the Lutheran and the reformed churches on the doctrine of the Lord's Supper.

Eventually, in 1556, after many years of sorrow and distress, he received the long-looked-for invitation from his king to return to his native land to preach the gospel. The king welcomed him warmly, despite the dire predictions of Laski's enemies that he was "a dangerous person, an outlawed heretic," and that he would "excite troubles and commotions." The king made him his secretary, and placed him in charge of the Reformed Churches in Little Poland, a most difficult undertaking.

Laski had finally come into his own, but probably too late to accomplish the mission he had set for himself and longed for during all the years of his exile. Calvin at this time wrote him that "the only danger was that he might fail through too great an austerity."

During his eighteen years' absence the Reformation had made great progress among all classes in Poland, because the people were as dissatisfied there as elsewhere in Europe with the dissolute lives of the clergy and the wealth and indolence of the Catholic Church.

The unpopularity of Romanism made the acceptance of the new doctrines easy. "Seeing in the Reformation a weapon for humiliating and plundering the church, as well as a key to a higher spiritual life, from one motive or another, they flocked to its standard, and under the leadership of their greatest Reformer, John Laski, organized a powerful church."—Preserved Smith, *The Age of the Reformation,* page 141.

Poland, like Friesland, had become the battleground for many persecuted and disaffected groups, or sects. The Bohemian brethren, followers of John Huss, had priority among the Protestants, by virtue of their seniority. They, with the Lutherans, Anabaptists, Catholics, Zwinglians, and Unitarians, were jealous for their rights, each hoping to gain the ascendancy. The Lutherans remained a dissident element, "a persistent obstacle to union," and the Unitarians, whom Socinus had developed into a strong faction, counteracted by their "fifth column" activities the work of the Reformed Church.

For the herculean task of bringing a semblance of order and unaniminity of religious opinion among these groups, Laski, with his gentle nature and moderate views, was considered the ideal mediator; his work as a co-ordinator and organizer in Friesland and England had not gone unnoticed. Melanchthon, helpful as usual, had sent along a modified copy of the Augsburg Confession.

By preaching, conferences, and synods he sought to secure harmony among the Protestant confessions. He broke the union between the reformed group and the Bohemian brethren to establish a pure evangelical body of believers. He wrote many treatises on Scriptural subjects, and with seventeen other ministers he helped prepare a Polish version of the Bible.

To the very end of his life he struggled against almost insurmountable difficulties, both from enemies within and from without the church; but death came before he achieved his goal. Nonetheless "his vigor, activity, and practical ability left a deep and abiding impress on the development of the Polish Reformation."—McClintock and Strong, *Cyclopedia of Biblical, Theological, and Ecclesiastical Literature,* article, "Lasko." He succeeded in laying the groundwork for a subsequent compromise. He died January 13, 1560, at Pinczow, Poland.

HANS TAUSEN

"The Luther of Denmark"

THE Protestant Reformation reached Denmark and Sweden simultaneously from Germany, the only European nation with which the inhabitants of the Scandinavian countries associated frequently. In Denmark, as in Sweden, the Reformation was accomplished largely by governmental decree supported by strong Protestant Reformers to instruct the people. As the Protestant church organization became effective in Denmark, it included its vassals Norway and Iceland.

"The Luther of Denmark" was Hans Tausen, son of a farmer and born in 1494 at Birkende on the island of Fyn. He attended schools in Odense on Fyn, and Stagelse in Zeeland. At the former he made his living by singing from door to door before the homes of the rich, after the fashion of poor schoolboys of his day.

Ambitious to become a priest, he entered the rich Johannite monastery at Antvorskov. He was certain of his call to preach, and frequently practiced upon his fellow monks, who recognized the pith and cogency of his remarks, then already directed against the abuses of the church.

He also attended the University of Rostock and lectured there for a time. He likewise studied at Louvain and Cologne, where he came in touch with Luther's writings and read them avidly. Drawn to Wittenberg, he probably came under the personal influence of Luther and Melanchthon sometime between 1521 and 1525. He returned to his native country firm in the resolution that he would preach the gospel of Jesus Christ.

Prior to this, Christian II, then king of Denmark and already influenced toward Lutheranism, had attempted to introduce the Reformation into the country. When he conquered Sweden in

1520, he asked his uncle, Frederick, elector of Saxony, to send him some Lutheran preachers. Martin Reinhard and Andrew Bodenstein of Carlstadt were sent, but neither knew the Danish language, and the latter was discredited by Luther.

Christian broke with the pope without further attempt at evangelizing the people; but his revolutionary changes, such as forbidding appeals to Rome, permitting the priests to marry, reforming the monasteries, and limiting the power of the clergy, brought upon his head the wrath of the nation, and he had to flee in 1523. His successor, Frederick I, former duke of Schleswig-Holstein, was forced to promise conformity to the old faith.

At this time Hans Tausen had been recalled from Wittenberg because of his prior's alarm over his Lutheran tendencies. For several years he was kept at the monastery, where the prior attempted to lead him back to the Catholic fold. But one day, as Tausen preached on justification by faith, he was imprisoned. Later he was placed under the supervision of the learned Peder Jensen in a Johannite house in Viborg.

Here after a time Tausen was put in a dungeon beneath the tower of the town. The prison was provided with a small air vent which filtered in a bit of light and looked out on a stretch of waste land behind the tower. To this spot came his associates, whom he had taught to love the gospel, in order that he might tell them more. "They called to him in low tones; he answered these friendly voices, and the conversation of the cloisters began again at the foot of the isolated tower."

Others came as they heard about these conferences, among them some of the burgesses of the city. "The pious Johannite approached the aperture and joyfully proclaimed the gospel to this modest audience. . . . Tausen declared from the depths of his dungeon that . . . a living faith in the Saviour alone justifies the sinner. His hearers increased in number from day to day; and this dungeon, in which it was intended to bury Tausen's discourse as in a tomb, was transformed into a pulpit. . . . They [his disciples] went about from house to house."—J. H. Merle d'Aubigné, *History of the Reformation in Europe in the Time of Calvin*, vol. 7, pp. 154, 155.

As his teaching gained more adherents and the prejudice and

persecution of the Romish clergy grew stronger, Tausen determined to strike for freedom. He asked the support of the citizens of the town, and Peder Trane, the burgomaster of Viborg, opened his home to him, and Jakob Skjonning, rector of the school and priest of the church of St. John, granted him his pulpit.

The townsmen welcomed him enthusiastically, and he kept on preaching, with the assistance of the Lutheran Jorgen Sadolin, whose sister Tausen later married.

When the crowds increased so that the church would not hold them, Tausen preached to them in the open air, even in the cemetery, where he used a tombstone as a pulpit. The townspeople, incensed at the opposition of the clergy, broke open the large Grey Friar's church, and there the Reformer spoke twice every Sunday, at the same time leading his congregation in singing hymns in the Danish tongue.

One day in the midst of Tausen's sermon the governor of the bishop's castle demanded that the Reformer accompany him to the bishop. Tausen replied, "Here I am standing in a greater Master's service, but when I have finished I shall gladly call upon the bishop."—Quoted by Jens Christian Kjaer in *History of the Church of Denmark*, page 43.

Tausen finished his sermon, but he and his congregation realized that his life was in peril. While the men protected Tausen's person with their presence, "the women hurried home for weapons." The governor was forced to leave, but a state of feud existed between the clergy and the Protestant citizens.

The bishop fortified his residence and sent foot soldiers and horsemen to prevent the people from going to hear Tausen preach; the townsmen, in defense, barricaded with iron chains the streets along which the soldiers needed to advance. A few persons were left to guard the barricades, and the rest, securely armed, went to church.

About this time, perhaps in 1526, Frederick I arrived in the vicinity, gave Tausen a letter of protection, and an invitation to become the royal chaplain. The king assigned the citizens to the Dominican and Franciscan churches in the town and left Tausen there for a while longer to preach the gospel.

The bishops continued to molest him, so much so that at times "the church rang with the sounds of horses' hoofs and Tausen's singing." Nonetheless, the Reformation made progress. Viborg soon became a Protestant city. Tausen was given the pastorate of one of the churches, and he also began to ordain men to the gospel ministry.

Although no longer subordinate to the Johannites, he continued to live in their house and wear their dress, as he took the gospel to other parts of Jutland. So thoroughly did the people begin to despise the old faith that when the begging friars with their wallets on their backs came around asking for "handouts" of butter and eggs, the people greeted them with words of disrespect and slammed the doors in their faces. Even the representatives of the bishops in their rounds of collecting tithes were repulsed.

Frederick, too, forgetting his promise to stay true to the old faith, sidestepped Rome and himself filled the vacancy of the arch bishopric of Lund and diverted for his own use the confirmation fees formerly given the pope.

The Diet of Odense, in 1527, confirmed his actions, the king stating in his defense that although he had promised to maintain the Catholic religion, "he had no intentions of shielding the worthless fables, the tricks and impositions of the priests, and the papal superstitions which had crept in." The next year, when the bishops demanded proceedings against Lutheran heresies, the king refused, leaving the Reformers free to preach as they pleased.

A further aid to reform, and doubtless its principal one, was the translation of the Bible into the Danish language. The first to accomplish this was probably Hans Mikkelsen, a fugitive with Christian II. His translation was printed in 1524 and imported in large quantities into Denmark. Five years later a much better version came from the hands of the Lutheran Christian Pedersen, called "the father of Danish literature." Gifted as a poet and a linguist, Tausen, too, helped with the literary work of the Reformation as he wrote many hymns, postils, and pamphlets.

It is said, "The Reformation rose like a tide," as the gospel in Danish was preached everywhere. The people read the Bible in their own tongue, the monks left the monasteries, and their buildings were used for hospitals, schools, and other useful purposes.

In 1529 Tausen proceeded to Copenhagen to take his office as chaplain to the king, who also appointed him pastor of the church of St. Nicholas. On his way to that city he converted Count Gyldenstern, a senator of Denmark.

At Copenhagen, as at Viborg, immense crowds listened to him, for he had the ability to clothe the dramatic story of the Christ in glowing, eloquent language. Soon many were converted to Protestantism, but not without some demonstrations of violence. Opposed to the iconoclasm which attended the Reformation in other parts of Europe, Tausen disapproved when the citizens broke into the Church of Our Lady and destroyed relics, altars, images, and pictures.

The most important event of Tausen's life, the one having the most far-reaching influence, occurred about a year after he arrived in Copenhagen. He was included among the twenty-two Lutheran ministers cited to appear before the diet on the charge of heresy. For this conference the Catholic bishops had called in as debaters some of their eminent colleagues, including the noted Dr. Stagefuhr from Cologne.

For eight days the Catholics argued their side, and at the end of that time Tausen delivered to the king forty-three articles, representing an independent confession of faith, a counterpart of the Augsburg Confession. These articles the Protestants distributed among themselves, "and every day the twenty-two ministers delivered in turn two sermons on the doctrines which they professed in it."—Merle d'Aubigné, *op. cit.*, p. 173. And great masses of people streamed into the church to hear them. This bold stroke greatly enraged the bishops, but Frederick refused to interfere.

This confession did not possess the polish of Melanchthon's, "but it had more clearness and force." It did not intend "to soften the statement of their doctrines, or to spare the Romish party."—*Ibid.*, p. 174. Some of the items included were: The Bible alone sufficient for salvation, righteousness by faith, the Holy Spirit the Third Person of the Godhead, the church the communion of those of the same faith, marriage honorable in all, the Lord's Supper the commemoration of the passion and death of Christ, all Christians are priests in Christ. It opposed indulgences, brotherhoods, invocation of saints, the mass, vigils for the dead, ornaments, cowls, the tonsure, monastic life, pretended good works, purgatory, the med-

dling of priests in business matters, images, sacraments not instituted in Scripture, and excommunication of those whom God
does not excommunicate.

The Lutherans wished to present their defense of these articles
orally in the Danish tongue so the people could understand, but
the bishops insisted that Latin be used. The people accused the
bishops of being afraid to argue the matter in a language the man
of the street could understand, and at this point the conference
broke down. But Frederick gave the Lutherans permission to continue preaching God's word, and Tausen published a learned
defense of his doctrines some months later.

In 1537, seven years later, his confession was set aside and the
Augsburg one adopted, along with Luther's *Small Catechism*, to
make of Denmark a thoroughly Lutheran nation.

But before that time the Romish party once more gained the
upper hand. In 1533, after the death of Frederick on April 10 of
that year, they determined to get rid of Tausen, whom they considered their archenemy. They accused him of calling the bishops
"tyrants" and writing a book against them, of usurping most of the
churches in Copenhagen, and of renouncing the mass. Tausen was
condemned to death, a sentence which the senators and magistrates
later commuted to banishment. But the authorities feared the
people, and Tausen ultimately went free.

For several years civil war ensued over the succession, but in
1536, Frederick's son, Christian III, ascended the throne. He,
too, was a Lutheran, and Tausen entered upon a period more or
less calm.

Determined to put an end to ecclesiastical authority in the
government, Christian asked Luther to send him help in religious
matters. This he did, and Bugenhagen from Germany took the
official ecclesiastical position in crowning the king the following
year. The king appointed seven bishops or superintendents over his
realm, somewhat after the manner of Sweden, and a constitution
for the Protestant church was promulgated. This treated, among
other things, with the evangelical doctrines, education, church
customs, duties of officials, revenues, and libraries for pastors.

Tausen shared in the construction of this constitution, and,
according to the historian Kjaer, he was one of those appointed as

new superintendents. He was also advanced to the post of professor of Hebrew at the University of Copenhagen, and he taught the pastors near Roskilde.

In 1542 he was made bishop of Ribe, where he continued to preach the Protestant faith until he died, in 1561. He had already some time previously translated the Pentateuch into Danish, and Christian granted him the privilege for a twenty-year period, beginning with 1543, to translate the rest of the Old Testament; but Tausen was unable to carry out this work.

Tausen has been called the "greatest of Danish Reformers. It has been fittingly said that his memory will linger in the hearts of the Danish people as long as a single church bell is calling them to worship."—Kjaer, *op. cit.*, p. 47.

GUSTAVUS VASA

Sweden's Reformer-King

I N SWEDEN the Reformation came
by governmental decree, rather than by a revolt of the people. The
process of reform was bound up with the country's struggle for
independence, and found its hero in the person of Gustavus Vasa,
its first Protestant king.

Sweden, Denmark, and Norway, existing as separate monarchies for four hundred years, were brought together in 1397 by the
Union of Kalmar. This was a rather loosely knit alliance, with
Denmark the dominating power. No king succeeded in holding
complete sway over all the territory, and Sweden in particular had
attempted repeatedly to establish her own independence.

After Christian II came to the throne in 1513, he attempted as
champion of Pope Leo X to break the power of the Swedish nobles
led by Sten Sture, and thereby extend his own rulership more
fully over that nation.

Following the Battle of Brakyrka in 1518, when Christian was
defeated, he asked Sture that six hostages be given him for personal
safety. These he traitorously sent to Copenhagen to be imprisoned.

In 1520 he returned and captured Stockholm, and on November 4 of that year he had himself crowned, amidst much pomp and
ceremony. Four days later he assassinated ninety of the high-rank-
ing Swedish nobility who had been especially invited to attend the
coronation, murdering them under pretext that they were excommunicated heretics and therefore enemies of the pope.

This Massacre of Stockholm, called its Bath of Blood, led, a
few years later, to a complete break between Sweden and Denmark, and created a root of indescribable bitterness which has not
been eradicated to this day.

Among the six hostages Christian imprisoned in Copenhagen was a handsome youth of the nobility named Gustavus Ericksson, born in Lindholmen in 1496. He was the son of Eric Johansson, who belonged to the Sture party. He later added the surname of Vasa, supposedly after a sheaf or bundle of flax, called "wase," which he bore on his coat of arms.

Indignant at his country's disgrace, young Vasa escaped from prison in 1519 and succeeded in making his way to Dalecarlia in central Sweden the following year. He learned about the massacre which had wiped out his whole family—his father and brother-in-law had been killed, his mother and sisters sent into exile, and a price put upon his own head. And the steel of resolution entered his soul.

He attempted to arouse the humble farmers of the Dalecarlia area to throw off the tyrant's yoke, but they eyed him coolly and forced him to seek a living as a field laborer, disguised in a peasant's jerkin, often a jump ahead of the sheriff. But he went from place to place telling his story, and people began to rally to his cause. "Similar stories are told of him during the time of preparation to those of King Alfred when in a like situation; how he gave vent to his grief in old national songs, discovered people's opinions by cunning questions, tried to gain them by burning words, wandered from farm to farm, gaining adherents everywhere, but particularly in Dalecarlia."—Ludwig Hauser, *The Period of the Reformation,* pages 154, 155.

When fugitives from Stockholm verified Vasa's story of the massacre, the peasants of Dalecarlia made him the head of their army. As he gained his first victories, more recruits joined. After he defeated the Danes at Västeras and at Uppsala, the Swedes, in 1521, declared him their regent; and in 1523, at the Diet of Strengnäs, they made him their king and declared the union with Denmark dissolved.

But he was king in name only, for the clergy possessed two-thirds of the land, and the most of the remaining third belonged to the nobility. The nobles supported the clergy, and the down-trodden peasants, still Catholics, had no knowledge of the rights and duties of citizenship. The land was poor, the country's resources were undeveloped, the expenditures of the crown were more than twice its income, and there was a huge war debt. The Danes still held the south of Sweden with its harbors, commerce, and coastal trade in their hands. Furthermore, he lacked good counselors; through long submission to Denmark, the Swedes had lost their power to govern. Vasa was the only one among them who could speak German, and he even had to do his own stenographic work.

But he was a shrewd-headed, practical businessman, as well as a first-rate statesman. He knew how to sway the people. He is said to have possessed "the most seductive power of speech" and prudent foresight. Singularly prepossessing, with an imposing presence and powerful physique, he appeared like the embodiment of a Paul Bunyan and an Apollo. With extreme good judgment and commendable patience he set himself to the task of constructing a well-organized and fairly administered nation, and he refused to be crowned king until he saw a semblance of his plans take shape.

Prior to this time he had made the acquaintance of the Petri brothers, students at Wittenberg, who had returned to Sweden to preach Lutheran doctrines. He had heard Olavus preach at the Diet of Strengnäs on the theme that the temporal power of the church was not substantiated by Scriptural authority, and had come away impressed. And apparently Laurentius Andreae, whom he had called to Stockholm as his chancellor, had instructed him about Luther and Luther's success in opposing the popes and the power of the church.

Some historians make much of what they consider Vasa's acceptance of Lutheranism because of his wish to get the possessions of the church under his control. They consider that he saw in Protestantism a way to strip Rome of its wealth and apply it to purposes of state. Others give him credit for being a true convert to the new doctrine, but likewise astute enough to see the political value of Protestantism in casting off the shackles of Rome and thereby reconstructing Sweden into a unified independent state.

For five years the king permitted his chancellor to guide him in making Sweden the nation of his dreams. One of Vasa's first acts was to break with Rome over tithes and the confirmation of the bishops. The tithes he diverted into the coffers of the crown, and the bishops he had sanctioned in Sweden, rather than at Rome. He also forced a loan from the bishops, maintaining that the church was the property of the people; he confiscated the monasteries and billeted horses and soldiers in them; and he reclaimed much church land for private ownership. He seemed to take particular delight in dispossessing the rich ecclesiastics, especially the aged Bishop Brask of Linköping. He banished those charged with conspiracy, and ordered the evangels to preach from the Scriptures.

He denied that a new doctrine was being taught, and asserted that the best remedy against false teachings was "the preaching of the gospel and the word of God alone." He also wanted the monks to study Luther's writings and "condemn them according to the Scriptures."—Conrad Bergendoff, *Olavus Petri and the Ecclesiastical Transformation in Sweden,* pages 11, 12.

But since there existed so much religious controversy, the people needed to have the Bible in their own tongue, that they might know the truth of the matter. Consequently he urged the translation of the Bible into Swedish. The New Testament in that tongue was published in 1526, probably as the joint work of Laurentius Petri, Olavus Petri, and Laurentius Andreae. *An Useful Teaching,* the first Protestant book to come off the press in Sweden, and thought to be the work of Olavus Petri, preceded it by a few months.

The greatest struggle ensued over the authority of the bishops. Vasa did not intend to take orders from them, and they had no intention of relinquishing their long-enjoyed primacy in spiritual matters. They bitterly opposed the king's efforts at taking from their hands the regulation of the property of the church.

The clashes between the king and Brask, then the only remaining bishop appointed by Rome, at times grew sharp and pointed. In 1525 Brask published on his printing press an attack on Vasa's policy and made a declaration against Lutheran heresy, which he called "Luciferan." Vasa replied that he suspected his policy displeased the church officials, whom he addressed as, "you and several others who do not know or do not want to know otherwise than that the office of bishop was instituted as some great lordship, forgetting the Scriptural teaching that the bishops are the servants of the people. . . . True bishops lived (in early Christendom) by suffering . . . who would rather receive blows for the sake of God's word, than they would give any. If you or others are dissaffected it is a sign that you do not, or do not want to, know what is the character of a true bishop." Vasa shut down Brask's printing plant and prohibited him from publishing any further religious propaganda, unless censored by the king.

With the marriage of Olavus Petri, whom Vasa had brought to Stockholm as secretary of the town and preacher at St. Nicholas Church, Brask complained to Vasa that such a marriage was unlawful. The king replied, "In our humble judgment it seems strange that one should be banned for the sake of marriage which God has not forbidden. Whereas among you ecclesiastics one is not banned according to papal law for whoredom, rape, and many other such crimes which God has forbidden."

But as the Reformation progressed, in no case was anyone in Sweden sent to the stake for his beliefs. Even though the clergy were deprived, the majority to a large degree lived in comparative security, many of them marrying their former housekeepers or mistresses to legitimatize the children.

The climax arrived in 1527 at the Diet of Västeras, which was attended by representatives of the clergy, nobility, citizenry, and peasantry, the last two finding seats in the diet for the first time in Swedish history. It was also the first time the bishops were deprived of their seats next to the king and placed below the senators.

The king presented to the diet the need for more revenue with which to wipe out the enormous war debt, to foster trade, and improve the state of the kingdom in general. He suggested the church as the only source from which to obtain the necessary funds.

The clergy asserted they had orders from Rome to maintain their holdings, and they were ready at the point of arms, if necessary, to defend their position; and the nobles sided with them.

With that the king, with all the eloquence, personal charm, and histrionic ability at his command, addressed the assembly, stating that "he had wished to make a final experiment, whether it were possible to reign there as a king." He proceeded to tell them of his difficulties and his resolution. "Rain and sunshine, famine and pestilence, all were laid to his charge, and every priest was allowed to sit in judgment on him; yet it was not from ambitious motives

that he had ascended the throne, but that he might save Sweden; he had sacrificed his patrimony for the public good, and he was repaid with ingratitude. Sweden was not yet ripe for a king, and in a voice choked with tears, he said, 'I must lay down this crown.' "
—Hauser, *op. cit.*, p. 159.

He asked them to return to him the personal means he had expended to help develop the kingdom and made this vow: "I will never return to this degenerate and thankless native land of mine."
—*The Cambridge Modern History*, vol. 2, p. 626.

Pandemonium reigned for three days after the king's abdication, as the members of the diet wrangled among themselves. At the end of that time they asked Vasa to return, and promised to do everything he wanted them to. What had happened was that the nobles had split, and part of them had joined the other parties; and the clergy had been completely routed from their position of arrogant self-sufficiency, as they were forced to submit to the will of the majority. This gave the king all the power he wished over the church.

The diet presented the king with an oath of allegiance, and proceeded to pass ordinances which embodied the legal aspects of the Reformation, which in turn laid the groundwork for Sweden's future greatness. Twenty-two of these ordinances were on the subject of religion, providing for the confiscation of church property, the appointment of the parish clergy at the hands of the bishops, the approval of the king on matters of appointment of dignitaries and decisions of the diet, the union of smaller parishes if desired, the teaching of the gospel in every school, the abolition of auricular confession, permission to preach the Lutheran doctrines, and the right of the nobles to repossess property they had given the church since 1454.

The king was now ready to be crowned. This event took place in January, 1528, "with great pomp" in the Cathedral of Uppsala, at the hands of bishops who had been consecrated by the bishop of Västeras "by command of the king," and not at the behest of the pope at Rome.

A national council in 1529, at Orebro, brought further advances in reform. The regulations there instituted included the daily reading of the Swedish Bible in the cathedral and in schools, "with a good and right-minded interpretation." The ministers were admonished to refrain from haranguing each other from the pulpit, but to preach the pure word of God, stressing every so often the Lord's Prayer and the Ten Commandments. Many church holidays were abolished, and the use of holy water, images, candles, palms, and church bells was discouraged.

Sweden was now "no longer a church above the state, nor even a church beside the state, but a church within the state."—Bergendoff, *op. cit.*, p. 48. In 1530 Vasa formally joined the Lutheran Church.

As to church organization, the king retained the episcopal order, but into it he introduced a semblance of Presbyterianism. Over the church he appointed twelve bishops, or superintendents, and one archbishop. Under the bishops were the elders, who administered in church affairs and visited the districts. In 1540 the king assumed for himself the office of supreme bishop, and no change could be made, or even proposed, in ecclesiastical procedure except by his consent.

Besides divesting the church of remaining elements of popery, he began a foreign missions program. Missionaries were sent to Lapland, and in Finland he enjoined a religious policy similar to Sweden's. In 1540, at the Diet of Västeras, Vasa declared the crown descendent by heredity to his sons.

Vasa has been rated as "one of the best and wisest princes of his time. He had found Sweden a wilderness, devoid of all cultivation, and a prey to the turbulence of the people and the rapacity of the nobles; and, after forty years' rule, he left it a peaceful and civilized realm, with a full exchequer, and a well-organized army of 15,000 men, and a good fleet, which were both his creations. . . . Gustavus was methodical, just, moral, and abstemious in his mode of life; an able administrator; and, with the exception of a tendency to avarice, possessed few qualities that are unworthy of esteem.' "—McClintock and Strong, *Cyclopedia of Biblical, Theological and Ecclesiastical Literature,* article, "Gustavus I, Vasa."

He refused the services of a priest, stating that he forgave all his enemies and asked all those whom he might have wronged to forgive him. He said he believed in Jesus Christ and partook of the Lord's Supper. He died September 29, 1560.

OLAVUS PETRI

He Brought a New Spirit to Sweden

OLAVUS PETRI, the first to preach the doctrines of the Reformation in Sweden, was born in Orebro, in the diocese of Strengnas, January 6, 1493. He attended school in the Carmelite monastery in Orebro, and also at Uppsala. His father, an ironmaster in Orebro, sent him to study in Germany along with his mild-mannered brother, Laurentius, who later was called "the Melanchthon of Sweden."

At first the brothers studied at Leipzig, but Luther's fame drew them to Wittenberg for two years. Here they saw Luther nail his ninety-five theses to the church door, and Olavus is said to have accompanied the Reformer on his visits to the convents of his order in Misnia and Thuringia.

Shortly after Olavus obtained his baccalaureate degree in 1518, he and his brother returned to Sweden, and Olavus was appointed master of the cathedral school at Strengnas, probably by the archdeacon, Laurentius Andreae. A cordial relationship sprang up between the master and the archdeacon, which resulted in the latter's conversion to the tenets of the Lutheran Church.

Olavus's teachings soon attracted attention, as he declared the falsity of the doctrines concerning the Virgin Mary, the saints, and the mass. He called monastic life, and chiefly the mendicants, "a devil's business," and said, "God has let the world be plagued with toads and grasshoppers."—Conrad Bergendoff, *Olavus Petri and the Ecclesiastical Transformation in Sweden*, page 80.

The fame of the young preacher spread, and students from outlying districts came to hear him. He also made preaching tours, stating that he taught the same gospel which "Ansgar, the apostle of the North, had preached seven hundred years before in Sweden."

Merle d'Aubigné tells that the Petri brothers were eyewitnesses to the Massacre of Stockholm, in 1520, and only by a miracle succeeded in escaping with their lives. The bishop of Strengnas had taken the young men with him at the time of the coronation of Christian II. When the brothers heard of the massacre, they rushed to the spot, and found corpses strewn over the place. They searched for the bishop and found his body in a pool of blood with his head lying at his feet. The young men were dragged to the executioner. Just as he was about to cut off their heads someone shouted that they were Germans, not Swedes, and they were released.

Of lofty stature and eloquent speech, Olavus had a powerful effect upon his audiences wherever he preached the Lutheran doctrines. At the Diet of Strengnas, in 1523, when Gustavus Vasa was elected king, Vasa was so greatly impressed that he wrote to Martin Luther, asking his opinion about both the Petri brothers. Luther replied, "I entreat you, Sirs, put your trust in God, and accomplish the Reformation. For this purpose I wish you the blessing of the Lord. You will not be able to find for this good work men more competent or more worthy than the two brothers of whom you speak."—J. H. Merle d'Aubigné, *History of the Reformation in Europe in the Time of Calvin*, vol. 7, pp. 259, 260.

Thereupon Olavus was invited to Stockholm the next year, to become secretary of the city and preacher in the St. Nicholas Cathedral. The King sent Olavus's brother Laurentius to Uppsala as professor of theology. He had already selected the archdeacon Laurentius Andreae for his chancellor. These three became his most trusted friends and counselors.

In Stockholm Olavus entered upon the great service of his life as he continued preaching the Reformation doctrines. The people referred to him as "Master Olaf in the basket"—the basket being the little round pulpit high above the people—as he preached, "We have Christ for a Master, Him we shall heed, in His name we are baptized, what He commands that we shall do."—Bergendoff, *op. cit.*, p. 207.

But the papists were watching, and Olavus could not long escape being accused of heresy. To harass him "the priests, the monks . . . threw stones at him, and held up their staves threateningly, and even made attempts on his life. One day, bent on putting an end to the evangelical preaching, these furious men made a dash at the pulpit and smashed it to pieces." Bishop Brask asked Vasa for Olavus's life, but the king gave his support to the new preachers. He maintained, however, that he merely desired a reform within, and not the downfall of, the church.

A disputation held in the king's palace in Stockholm in the middle 1520's resulted from the bishop's demands to silence the Reformers. Olavus was pitted against Dr. Galle, the papist, and the victory for the Protestants greatly strengthened the Reformation in Sweden.

To define the terms of the debate Vasa had presented twelve questions to which he wished an answer, and it is possible that Olavus formulated these questions for the king. Olavus's replies, which were later published, became one of the most important documents of the Reformation in Sweden, "the first *official* attack on the Roman Church to appear in print."—Bergendoff, *op. cit.*, p. 207.

In it Olavus maintained that only those teachings of the church which could be proved from the Bible were valid; the pope and the bishops could not be greater than their master, Christ; mass was not Scripturally celebrated; the Bible contained all that was necessary for salvation, and no other revelation was needed; and the soul did not lose direct communion with God as the result of excommunication.

Concerning the temporal power of the pope, Olavus remarked, "The important thing is not how old a thing is but how right it is. The devil is old, but not on that account any the better." He also stated that obedience came as the result of one's love for God, and not because the church commanded it. Furthermore, since salvation came by the free grace of God, indulgences, masses, and ecclesiastical orders were useless; through belief in Christ the sinner obtained forgiveness; and it was not the office of the Holy Spirit to withhold the wine and to make a sacrifice out of the Lord's Supper. He declared purgatory to be unscriptural, and maintained that adoration of saints had its basis in the church's desire for money.

Along with his preaching and his disputations Olavus did much writing. The first hymnbook in Swedish he translated, largely from the German. The translation of the New Testament into

Swedish in 1526 has been variously attributed to Olavus, to his brother Laurentius, and to Andreae. Probably all three had a part in it, as well as in the translating of the Old Testament, which was published in 1541.

Olavus also wrote a manual of service, or *Handbook,* said to have "the distinction of being the first of its kind to appear in any Protestant church." By providing for the form of service and Biblical instruction given in the churches, he did for Sweden what Luther did for Germany. He also wrote many homiletical treatises, sermons, and postils, or catechistical works. Three catechisms came from his pen within a comparatively short time. He likewise wrote the first Swedish lawbook and its first critical history.

When in 1525 Olavus married, in defiance of the laws of the church, Brask again shouted heresy; but the king's protecting arm remained around the Reformer. When Vasa was crowned king, in 1528, it was Olavus who preached the coronation sermon, in which he instructed the people concerning their responsibilities to the law and the crown.

As the Reformation progressed and Vasa succeeded in making sweeping political changes to circumvent the old church, he appropriated more and more authority to himself—far too much, in the opinion of the Reformers—and a break ensued between the king and his two advisers, Olavus Petri and Laurentius Andreae.

They saw in the king's rapaciousness a danger to the Protestant church, that its freedom would be destroyed. They had hoped that he would use the Catholic churches he had confiscated to establish schools, but instead he diverted them for the benefit of the crown, and "evangelical Christians were asking one another whether they had cast off the yoke of the pope in order to take up that of the king." The Reformers opposed him vigorously.

Never one to mince words, Olavus publicly reprimanded Vasa from the pulpit for his pet sin, namely, that of profanity, and friends stirred up further strife between the two by carrying tales. It was a case of two great men who, not being able to endure contradiction, washed off each other's faults and threw their scrub water on the public's front lawn.

The king sought counsel from Olavus's brother, the archdeacon at Uppsala, stating that a just cause for complaint against him should first be brought to him in private rather than be broadcast before a whole audience.

As the controversy enlarged, Olavus went to ridiculous lengths in making his point. He even had a canvas painted of seven or eight mock suns then appearing over Stockholm, and he interpreted the suns as pretenders to Vasa's throne, that someone else would soon take his place.

Naturally the king was angry, and he resolved to get revenge. He charged that Olavus had preached seditious sermons and had failed to reveal his knowledge of a conspiracy against the crown, information which he had gained by a confession.

Andreae was brought to trial with Olavus, and Olavus's brother, as archbishop of Uppsala, had to sit in judgment. In the spring of 1540 the two were sentenced to death, but this was later commuted to a heavy fine of fifty Hungarian florins each. Olavus's friends and church members paid his, but Andreae had to pay his own. The latter withdrew to Strengnas and remained in solitude until he died of a broken heart shortly after.

But Olavus returned to his church in Stockholm, realizing that opposition to the king was a futile business, that Vasa was the supreme ruler over both the government and the church. But Olavus seemingly regained his fearlessness in the presence of new dangers to the Protestant church. In 1544 he received a reprimand from Vasa for "beating on the authorities." When the king in 1548 wanted the opinion of his council as to what attitude the country should take on the actions of the Council of Trent in 1545, Olavus remarked that the council's actions would first have to be judged by the Bible before they could be sanctioned. He also opposed the Interim, which he called a "return to papistry."

Olavus's influence upon Sweden's Reformation was without an equal. He died April 19, 1552, at the age of fifty-nine years, and was buried in St. Nicholas Cathedral.

FRANCISCO DE ENZINAS

Spain's Greatest Reformer

RULED by Ferdinand and Isabella, Spain at the opening of the sixteenth century was approaching the zenith of her glory. Columbus's discovery of America had not only added to her national luster, but had led to many exploitations of foreign lands, with resultant enrichment of the mother country. Militant Catholicism had ejected the Moors who refused to subscribe to the Romish faith, and more than a hundred thousand Jews had been driven outside Spanish borders. Spain had established the Inquisition about 1478 to remove all traces of heretical thinking. In her zeal to reform and be reformed, Spain had become the ideal Catholic state, the most fit to prevent the encroachments of Protestantism.

However, the new doctrines succeeded in breaking through. Lutheran ideas gained momentum, and their adherents numbered in the thousands as they met secretly in small groups all over Spain. Seville and Valladolid were the most important centers, but later the adherents there were completely exterminated. Of Reformers Spain also had her share. Of the Valdés brothers connected with the imperial court, Juan soon transferred his allegiance to Italy, probably because of the Inquisition. Others accomplished much in Spain until the Inquisition, too, forced them to quit, either by death or by escape to another country. No Protestantism could flourish in its devastating presence.

Among those determined souls who remained for a season to work valiantly for the gospel and then escape to fairer lands when they could no longer work in their own was Francisco de Enzinas, belonging to a wealthy, noble family in Burgos, Spain.

His name has been variously translated as Dryander in Greek,

Eichman in German, Duchesne in France, and Van Eyck in Dutch, all meaning "oak man."

He was the second of three sons, all of whom accepted the Protestant faith. Juan, the youngest, chose medicine as his career, and escaped persecution by settling in Germany, where he became professor at the University of Marburg.

Jaime, the eldest, wrote a catechism in Spanish to help people understand the Bible. He had scarcely succeeded in getting it printed, when his father, who knew nothing of his Protestant leanings, ordered him to Rome with the hope that he might there find preferment.

But in place of the pope's approbation, he won a martyr's crown in 1547, probably at the age of twenty-seven. He spent some two or three years in Rome, when the Inquisition sucked him into its maw. He made the best use he could of his last opportunity to witness for his Master, as, before " 'a great assembly of the Romans,' . . . cardinals, bishops, and all Spaniards of eminence then at Rome, and of several members of the Roman clergy," he gave an account of the faith within him. It is recorded that "he forthwith condemned the impieties and diabolical impositions of the great Roman antichrist." When he refused to recant he was burned at the stake, the first Protestant in Italy during this period to die for his religion.

Of the three brothers it probably fell to Francisco's lot to bring the most lasting benefit to the Reformation in Spain. He was born about 1520 and attended the Universities of Louvain and Paris. At the latter his uncle, the great scholar Pedro de Lerma, had served for thirty years as dean of the faculty of theology. Here Francisco associated with George Cassander, who was perhaps the first to introduce him to Protestant ideas. At Louvain, Francisco came in touch with John Laski, the Polish Reformer, for whom he entertained a great admiration and affection, so much so that he presented him with an antique and costly sword. He asked Laski for letters of introduction to Luther, Melanchthon, and other Reformers.

His uncle, too, had Protestant leanings, which supposedly he had acquired at Paris. For his Erasmian views, and particularly for his belief in justification by faith, he was cited to appear before the Inquisition. This alarmed Francisco's parents so much that they recalled their son to Burgos and begged him to give up his studies in order to avoid all appearance of heresy. They, along with other inhabitants in Burgos who had sons in Paris, feared the contaminating influence of the great universities and the persecution of the Inquisition.

But Francisco did not abide by his parents' request, and as a result endured the suspicions of many influential people, who believed him already affected by heresy. He accompanied his uncle, then Abbot of Compludo in Spain, back to Louvain. His uncle died shortly after, and his nephew made his way to Germany to enroll in the Wittenberg university.

Enzinas's soul was fired with enthusiasm to accomplish two things: one, to see Spain converted to Protestantism, the other, to study under Melanchthon. The fulfillment of the latter desire was granted him in 1541, and although he was unable to bring about the former, he probably did more than any other individual in Spain to enlighten the people with the gospel. To this task he set himself as soon as he arrived in Wittenberg.

A student could hardly have been more fortunate. Not only did young Enzinas sit in Melanchthon's classroom, but he sat at his table and slept in his bed all the while he was in Wittenberg. A great affection sprang up between the two. The relationship between them must have been very close, for people called Enzinas "Melanchthon's soul." Here, at the suggestion and under the guidance of the great Reformer, he translated the Greek New Testament into excellent Spanish, as great a contribution to the Reformation in Spain as Luther's German translation was to the Reformation in Germany.

After completing the manuscript Enzinas conferred with a number of persons concerning the advisability of having it printed. All whom he consulted agreed that it would be a good thing. Some monks said, "Since the birth of Jesus Christ so great a benefit has never been offered to the Spanish people." But the attitude of the church toward such a translation may best be summed up by a statement made by the archbishop of Compostella: "To publish the New Testament in Spanish is a crime worthy of death."

When first printed, the title page of Enzinas's New Testament bore the words, "*The New Testament, that is, the New Covenant of our Redeemer and only Saviour Jesus Christ."* Friends advised him to change *covenant* to *testament,* as *covenant* sounded too Lutheran, and to omit the word *only* altogether. Enzinas had used it to help eliminate the idea, so prevalent in Spain, that other saviors existed. The sheet had to be reprinted.

In all guilelessness and naïveté Enzinas dedicated his New Testament to Charles V, a patron of some kinds of learning, but scarcely an exponent of the new religion. "Most sacred majesty, owing to the versions of the Holy Scriptures, all men can now hear Jesus Christ and His apostles speak in their own languages of the mysteries of our redemption, on which the salvation and the consolation of our souls depend. New versions are now continually being published in every kingdom of Christendom, in Italy, in Flanders, and in Germany, which is flooded with them. Spain alone remains isolated in her corner at the extremity of Europe. My desire is to be useful, according to my abilities, to my country. I hope that your majesty will approve of my work and protect it with your royal authority."—Quoted by J. H. Merle d'Aubigné in *History of the Reformation in Europe in the Time of Calvin,* vol. 8, pp. 67, 68.

Not wishing to offer his New Testament to the public until the emperor had seen it, the young Reformer made a trip to Brussels to present it to him. After he had been introduced to his presence by the bishop of Jaen, Enzinas, now twenty-three years of age, stood before the ruler of the Holy Roman Empire and asked him to approve his book and recommend it to Spain. This conference between the youthful Spaniard and Charles V bore at least some resemblance to the more dramatic and highly publicized meeting between Martin Luther and the emperor some twenty years before at Worms.

Charles said he would assent provided it contained nothing unsatisfactory. With that he turned to the bishop of Jaen and requested him to give the book to Fray Pedro de Soto, Charles's confessor, for review and judgment.

Although seemingly kindly disposed toward Enzinas, De Soto called him for an interview the following day and pointed out the dangers attending the wholesale reading of the Scriptures. He also accused him of disobeying the law by printing the Scriptures without a license, of associating with the Wittenberg heretics, and publishing a heretical book based upon one of Luther's works.

Enzinas defended himself by stating there was no law in Flanders against the printing of the Bible, that he had never published anything but the New Testament (the veracity of this statement is doubted by some), and that as for consorting with the Wittenberg doctors, Charles and others were as much to blame as he was.

De Soto had him committed to a Brussels prison, probably, it is thought, to prevent him from falling into the hands of the Inquisition. The real cause for his offense was the passage, printed in capital letters, "Where is boasting then? It is excluded. By what law? of works? Nay: but by the law of faith." Romans 3:27.

Here he remained for fourteen months in easy confinement. While so restrained he received visits from many people—more than four hundred from the city of Brussels alone, including many from the higher classes, as well as hundreds from the surrounding towns and countryside. These asked to hear the gospel story, and many believed. Enzinas was told that more than 7,000 people in Brussels alone had Protestant leanings.

But he was not a contented prisoner; he had all kinds of dire forebodings of torture and death. His friends and relatives sought, unsuccessfully, to effect his release. Money poured in, but this he refused.

Finally one day a friend informed him of the escape of the queen's preacher. This gave Enzinas courage, and he literally walked out of the prison, possibly because of the jailer's neglect, but more probably because of their connivance in getting rid of him.

From prison he went to the house of a friend, who helped him over the city wall. He made his way back to Wittenberg. There he wrote *The History of the State of the Netherlands and of the Religion of Spain,* his most important work next to his translation of the New Testament. From there he went to Strasbourg, Basel, and elsewhere.

Disgusted with the dissensions among the Protestants, he entertained serious ideas of going as a missionary to Constantinople.

Enzinas is said to have died at Augsburg, December 30, 1550, barely thirty years of age.

THEODORE BEZA

Man of Talent

THEODORE BEZA had noble birth, erudition, wealth, good looks, impressive oratory, a facile pen, courtly manners, diplomacy. As a Protestant he was more welcome in Catholic aristocratic circles of France than was any other Reformer. What an accession to the already long list of renowned propagandists for the evangelical faith! Small wonder that Calvin took to his bosom this brilliant young Beza and chose him as a successor to carry on the work in Geneva!

Last of the great sixteenth-century Protestant Reformers, Beza was born June 24, 1519, in the castle at Vezelai, in the duchy of Burgundy. Beza was three years old when his mother died. His uncle Nicholas, a distinguished lawyer and councilor in the Parliament of Paris, adopted him and supervised his education, giving him everything that money and influence could obtain. At the age of nine he was placed in the home of a famous Greek teacher at Orleans, Melchior Wolmar, who was "tainted" with Lutheran ideas. John Calvin also studied under this teacher. Thus early in life the future Reformer came in contact with ideas concerning justification by faith, and the shortcomings of the church.

When Beza was thirteen, his lawyer uncle died and left him to the care of another uncle, Claudius, abbot of a Cistercian monastery. Beza attended the University of Orleans, where he attained the degree of licentiate of laws in 1539. Contrary to the wishes of his father, however, he did not want to be a lawyer; he wanted to study the liberal arts. This he now did, with his father's consent, at the University of Paris.

Beza left Paris for Geneva, arriving there October 23, 1548. Here he adopted the name of Thibaud de May. Assuming aliases was common practice among religious fugitives of his day. Because he left France a Protestant, the Parliament of Paris confiscated all his property and pronounced the death penalty upon him. (The property was restored to him in 1564.)

After arriving in Geneva he became married to Claudine Denosse, and their marriage was blessed with happiness for forty-one years. Here he immediately gained Calvin's respect and affection. Looking about for a means of support, he was invited to teach Greek at the academy of Lausanne, in 1549. It is said that here he "entered upon a course of great usefulness and influence."

Beza gave his life unstintingly to teaching, preaching, mediating, and administrating; he was a man equally at home in the classroom, in the pulpit, at the council table, and at the court. Repeatedly he was called upon to make long journeys in order to gain the support of influential persons who could help advance the cause of the Reformation or retard the onslaughts of persecution.

Beza succeeded rapidly in winning a secure place in the hearts of the people in Lausanne. Indication of this is found in a letter Calvin wrote to Farel in 1551 at the time Beza was stricken by the plague: "I would not be a man if I did not return his love who loves me more than a brother and reveres me as a father: but I am still more concerned at the loss the church would suffer if in the midst of his career he should be suddenly removed by death, for I saw in him a man whose lovely spirit, noble, pure manners, and open-mindedness endeared him to all the righteous. I hope, however, that he will be given back to us in answer to our prayers." —Quoted by Philip Schaff in *A History of the Christian Church,* vol. 7, p. 852.

Particularly suited for the job of public relations, he entered with alacrity in 1557 upon the task of gaining the support of the Swiss cantons and the German princes to help stay the rigorous persecutions of the Waldenses in France.

At the age of forty, in 1559, Beza became the first rector of the University of Geneva, which had been founded by Calvin. Both in Lausanne and at Geneva many young men educated in Calvinistic doctrine under Beza became zealous preachers of the gospel. Beza also became the pastor of one of the churches in the city. From thenceforth the lives of the two great Reformers were closely associated, each reinforcing the other until death parted them. Time after time, Beza was sent forth on diplomatic missions. Once he asked Elector Frederick III to invite a new Protestant recruit, Anne du Bourg, president of the Parliament of Paris, to a professorship at the University of Heidelberg, in an attempt to save du Bourg's life. At another time he went to the court of Antoine, king of Navarre, in an attempt to win the king to the ranks of Protestantism. Repeatedly his life was in danger as he pursued his hazardous journeys, and long weeks were frequently consumed in taking devious routes to escape detection.

At this time the French Huguenots, followers of Calvinistic doctrine, had become a formidable body, to the extent of a fourth of the kingdom, an estimated 1,500,000. Besides being a religious group, they also formed a strong political faction. Beza, by virtue of his many services, became their religious head and repeatedly represented them in their attempts to achieve political and religious status.

When the nonreligious queen mother Catherine of France decided to hold a consultation, to be known as the Colloquy of Poissy, between the most prominent Catholic bishops and Protestant ministers, to iron out, if possible, the difficulties between the two parties, Beza was asked to assume the leadership of the Protestant group. Consequently he returned in 1561 to Paris, the first time since his departure in 1548. The noted Italian Reformer Peter Martyr, disciple of Juan de Valdés, was also present.

The historian George Fisher presents a graphic description of the scene: "In the great refectory of the Benedictines at Poissy, the young king sat in the midst of the aristocracy of France—Catherine de' Medici, the king of Navarre, and the prince of Condé, the great lords and ladies of the court, cardinals, bishops, and abbots, doctors of the Sorbonne, and a numerous company of lesser nobles, with their wives and daughters. In this brilliant concourse Theodore Beza appeared at the head of the preachers and elders deputed by the Huguenots to represent their cause, and eloquently set forth the doctrines of the party of reform. Beza was a man of high birth, of prepossessing appearance, of graceful and polished manners, who was at his ease in the society of the court, and, prior to the public conference, won the respect and favor of many of his auditors by his attractiveness in social intercourse." He was God's man of the hour.

There was no question about the verdict, for all the judges were Catholics. When Beza asserted, "The body of Christ was as far removed from the bread of the eucharist as the heavens are from the earth" (Schaff, vol. 7, p. 857), the prelates called him a blasphemer, and a near riot ensued. Although attempts were made to continue discussion and to arrive at a solution, the situation became worse instead of better. The colloquy had become "the watershed from which the two religions parted."—Edward Maslin Hulme, *The Renaissance and Reformation,* page 491.

Beza was called back to Paris to assist the Huguenots in obtaining some religious concessions. As the result of the Edict of Saint-Germain in January, 1562, the Huguenots were given the right to worship outside the cities.

Barely had the ink dried on this decree, when the duke of Guise, on March 1, massacred hundreds of French Protestants as they worshiped in a barn at Vassy. Beza immediately asked for redress. When told that the Protestants were to blame for the assault because of having thrown stones at the duke, Beza replied, "Well, then, he should have punished only those who did the throwing. Sire, it is in truth the lot of the church of God, in whose name I am speaking, to endure blows, and not to strike them. But also may it please you to remember that it is an anvil that has worn out many hammers."

After attending the third national synod of the reformed churches, Beza, at the behest of the prince of Condé, a Protestant sympathizer, went to Strasbourg and Basel to enlist the aid of Germany and Switzerland for the Protestant cause in France. He then returned to Geneva, and was about ready to resume his teaching, when an urgent request came for him to return to the aid of the Huguenot troops.

Unwilling to go, yet impelled by Calvin, he spent the next seven months with the Huguenot army, playing a role similar to that of John Knox in Scotland's Reformation, as he rode at the front of battle, serving as the almoner and treasurer.

The Pacification Edict of March 12, 1563, ended warfare for the time, and again Beza returned to Geneva, heavyhearted that so little had been accomplished.

As Beza again set foot in Geneva, Calvin's time was running out, and the mantle of the master was about to fall upon the disciple. When Calvin died in 1564, the affairs of the city and the church came to rest upon Beza; yet he continued preaching and teaching, giving counsel and advice to all comers, carrying on a vast correspondence, and entertaining large numbers of fugitives, including notable scholars, from other countries. It is said that the homes of the Reformers became hostels for the Protestant refugees.

Under him the theological school of the University flourished, and he made of Geneva "the virtual capital of Continental Protestantism." He gave it a milder, more conciliatory regime, but he brought a rigidity into the doctrines which later made it possible for a reaction to Calvinistic authority to set in.

Beza's duties at home did not, however, prevent him from responding to calls from abroad. In 1571 he attended as its moderator the seventh national synod of the Reformed Church in France. Here he assisted in drawing up a revised Confession of Faith, and on his return he attended the Synod of Nimes.

When the fugitives from the St. Bartholomew Massacre, August 24, 1572, in which an estimated 20,000 to 50,000 Huguenots were killed, began arriving in Geneva, that city, under Beza's leadership, made a wholehearted effort to aid the suffering. In 1574 he negotiated with Henry of Condé to get an army to help the French Protestants, and he sanctioned a military errand to France, thereby endangering his own city by inviting reprisals.

Beza retired from public life in 1600 and died October 13, 1605. He wanted to be buried beside Calvin, but because of a threat to transport his body to Rome, possibly for after-death reprisals, he was buried in St. Peter's at Geneva.

Among Beza's literary works are his *Life of Calvin* and a translation of the Psalms begun by Clement Marot. Doubtless Beza collected the materials for *Histoire Ecclesiastique des Eglises Reformees,* but he did not claim authorship. He was also an eminent editor of the Greek New Testament; both his Greek and Latin texts influenced the Authorized Version. He likewise performed a great service to Biblical scholars when he presented to the Cambridge University in 1581 the famous Codex D, one of the uncial manuscripts dating from the sixth century.

HEINRICH BULLINGER

A Spiritual Force in Switzerland

H‌EINRICH BULLINGER, successor to
Zwingli in Zurich and "the second founder of the German Reformed Church," has been variously described as a man of "an
admirable mixture of dignity and tenderness," a deep thinker with
"a spirit essentially unifying and sympathetic, in an age when these
qualities won little sympathy." He embodied the characteristics
of integrity and moderation, as well as hospitality, being "a generous
friend and patron of fugitives." He was greatly beloved by his
parishioners, and he tenderly cared for his flock in time of plague.

The son of a priest who manfully accepted the responsibility
of rearing and educating his child, Bullinger was born in 1504,
at Bremgarten, in the canton of Aargau, where he received his
grammar-school training. At the age of twelve he entered the school
of the Brethren of the Common Life at Emmerich on the lower
Rhine, where he followed the boyhood example of Luther at
Eisenach and engaged in street singing to supplement funds for
his education.

Both at Emmerich and later at Cologne, the focal point of
opposition to the Reformation, where he entered the university
in 1519 to take his degree the next year, he developed an abiding
interest in personal study of the Bible. Doubtless this tendency
received considerable stimulus from his acquaintance with the
Sentences of Peter Lombard, a twelfth-century professor at the
University of Paris, as well as from his knowledge of the writings
of other medieval churchmen. At Cologne he also came in possession of ideas gleaned from Luther's and Melanchthon's pamphlets.
About this time a New Testament, which raised further doubts
concerning Roman Catholic doctrine, fell into his hands. Conse-

quently, in 1522, although greatly troubled by the need for making the necessary adjustments, he had become a Protestant at heart. Since his theological views denied him access to an ecclesiastical career, he obtained a teaching appointment that year in the Kappel cloister school attached to the Cistercian monastery near Zurich, a post he filled until 1529. Here he taught the classics and also presented interpretations on the Bible. Although at times in physical danger from incensed priests, he also lectured on theological topics before the school dignitaries and townsmen, thus establishing Protestant ideas among the people.

In 1527 the monastery at Kappel came under the direction of the city of Zurich. Its church became the community church and Bullinger the pastor. In this pastor-teacher status he, with the collaboration of his associates, undertook the preparation of several tracts designed to spread the doctrines of the Reformation throughout central Switzerland.

Shortly after his arrival at Kappel he met Zwingli, who later became his father-in-law. With him he soon found himself in fullest accord and later became his "zealous lieutenant." In 1525 Zwingli invited him to a conference with the Anabaptists, a meeting called ostensibly to show those so-called fanatics the error of their ways. Bullinger regarded this sect as untrustworthy and faulty in doctrine, and he wrote a number of books against them. "God opened the eyes of the governments by the revolt at Münster," he wrote after that debacle in the middle thirties, "and thereafter no one would trust even those Anabaptists who claimed to be innocent."—Quoted by Preserved Smith in *The Age of the Reformation,* page 102.

At the disputation at Bern, in 1528, to which Bullinger also accompanied Zwingli, he met the leading figures in Protestant ecclesiastical circles of south Germany and Switzerland; and the following year he succeeded his father as pastor at Bremgarten, where his impassioned sermons led the entire congregation to participate in the burning of the images in the church. In his ministry he demonstrated great energy, preaching usually from six to eight sermons a week.

Bullinger's status was precarious, made thus by the perpetual threat of civil war growing out of religious differences in the cantons. In 1531, shortly after the death of Zwingli at the Battle of Kappel, Bullinger was banished from Bremgarten. He fled to Zurich, where in December the city fathers selected him as a successor to Zwingli. This position included the pastorate of Great Minster, the principal church in the city, and here he remained the rest of his life.

The aftermath of the Battle of Kappel, in which the forces of the Catholic cantons had inflicted an almost annihilating defeat upon the Protestants, and the fulfilling of the terms of the Second Peace of Kappel, in November of the same year, tested Bullinger's leadership sorely. Zwingli's lifework was endangered, and the advance of the whole Reformation in Switzerland had suffered a serious reverse. In the task of reconstruction, reorganization, and maintenance Bullinger displayed able generalship. "It was chiefly due to him that the disaster of Kappel had no worse results."— *The New Schaff-Herzog Encyclopedia of Religious Knowledge,* article, "Bullinger."

Prior to his death, Zwingli had attempted to make Zurich "the political head of the evangelical cause" in Switzerland, and had by means of an embargo on food tried to enforce Protestant preaching upon Catholic cantons. The Second Peace of Kappel provided for each canton the privilege of selecting and managing its own religion, and any alliance with powers outside the confederacy was prohibited, thus strengthening the Catholic cantons in their allegiance to Rome.

Bullinger advised humiliated Zurich to adjust herself to her changed status, as he proceeded to draw the Zwinglian churches into closer unity. Within the city he organized the schools so that they attained an excellent status in scholarship and efficiency. He established scholarships for ministerial students and instituted teacher-pupil plans. He also prepared a set of regulations for preachers and synods, the latter meeting twice a year to review the activities, qualifications, and deportment of every minister within their jurisdiction.

He also participated actively in developing church polity outside Zurich through co-operation with Calvin, Bucer, and others. So far as Zurich itself was concerned, its power to mingle in international affairs had ceased.

Out of the readjustment Zurich needed to make came a clearer understanding of the function of the state and that of the church. The spheres of the two became distinct but not opposed, nor was one subservient to the other. The duty of the church was to preach the word, unrestricted and unimpeded. The state, on the other hand, administered the property of the church and also carried out ecclesiastical sentences of punishment. In other words, the state reinforced and supplemented the church's pronouncements upon heretics.

At first rather tolerant in his views, Bullinger, in 1532, doubted that the power to excommunicate belonged to either the church or the state; but later he became more conservative, even counseling the execution of Servetus and the banishment of Ochino.

In spite of the renewed strength of the Catholic factions within the several cantons and the general Catholic reaction among the people, Bullinger's efforts at consolidation and expansion continued. The First Helvetic Confession, which he, as the chief representative of German-Swiss doctrine, assisted in formulating in 1534, and which did not reach Luther until late 1536, aimed at accomplishing a *media via* in the perennially mooted question of the eucharist. Bullinger attempted to maintain a middle ground between the views of Zwingli and Luther. He disliked Luther's "semipopery," but Luther, after Zwingli's death, found himself entertaining friendly feelings toward Bullinger. At first the Wittenberg Reformer appeared conciliatory, but later he broke forth again in violent attacks upon the symbolic interpretation of the Lord's Supper. Nonetheless, a worth-while indirect result of this overture at reconciliation came some years later in the closer union among the French and German portions of the Swiss church.

The repeated efforts to produce conformity of opinion were naturally accompanied by some degree of compromise, but the citizens of Zurich refused to make any concessions. At a conference in that city in 1538 they decided to permit no modification of their views.

Undaunted, Bullinger the following year put forth yet another experiment in the form of a document called *Consensus Tigerinus*, written jointly by himself and Calvin, to unite Protestant Switzerland. Anti-Lutheran in outlook, it made possible an accord between the Zwinglian and Calvinistic doctrines on the Lord's Supper. It emphasized the divine work of grace to the recipient, but only if received by faith. By this time hopes for an understanding with the Lutherans had wholly vanished.

As one of his self-imposed tasks, Bullinger wrote constantly, and produced many books, pamphlets, tracts, and sermons, estimated at more than one hundred separate works, still uncollected and unpublished. He also carried on a vast correspondence with persons in every land, including the crowned heads of England, France, Denmark, and Germany. His most important writing, still a valuable work, is *A History of the Reformation,* characterized by "excellent composition but with a studied moderation of phrase." These writings, and particularly his sermons, called *Decades,* were read eagerly wherever distributed, and especially in England. By order of convocation as late as 1586 every clergyman in England was commanded to obtain a copy of his sermons "and read one of them once a week."

During the Marian persecution (1553-58) he became acquainted with numerous leading English divines, many of whom he sheltered as they found refuge on the Continent. For this act of hospitality he received a silver cup with Queen Elizabeth's thanks.

Upon these bishops, such as Hooper and others, he exerted a profound influence, surpassing that of any other Continental Reformer, in achieving for England a uniform body of Protestant doctrine, and to restore the English church to what it had been in the days of Edward VI. "A better example of a purely spiritual power could hardly be found than the influence that was exercised in England by Zwingli's successor, Henry Bullinger. Bishops and Puritans argue their causes before him as if he were the judge. . . . And then when the bad day came and the pope hurled his thunderbolt, it was to Bullinger that the English bishops looked for a learned defense of their queen and their creed."—*The Cambridge Modern History,* vol. 1, p. 597. "Beza spoke of him as 'the common shepherd of all Christian churches.' "—Albert H. Newman, *A Manual of Church History,* vol. 2, p. 147.

Bullinger's last great labor consisted in the drawing up of the Second Helvetic Confession. This statement of faith consists of thirty lucid, effectively and shrewdly worded chapters of varying

lengths, and includes all phases of the beliefs of the Swiss Reformed
Church. He wrote the original draft in 1562. Two years later he
revised it, after which it came to the notice of Frederick III, the
elector palatine, who ordered it translated into German and published.

Barely had it come off the press when it received wide and
instant acclaim, first among the Swiss churches, with Basel ex-
cepted; and eventually, after a period of years, it also became the
authoritative confession among Reformed Churches in Scotland,
Hungary, France, Poland, Bohemia, and other countries. "It was,
strictly speaking, the bond uniting the scattered members of the
evangelical reformed churches."—*The New Schaff-Herzog Encyclopedia of Religious Knowledge,* article, "Bullinger." Next to the
Heidelberg Catechism, the creed of the Reformed Churches in Germany, it stands paramount among the Reformed Church confessions.

Bullinger's arduous labors as pastor, preacher, author, and
counselor doubtless contributed to the depletion of his physical
powers and made him an easy victim of the plague. He recovered
partially, but its ravages led to the development of calculus, with
its debilitating suffering. During his last hours he repeated the
Lord's Prayer, some psalms, and the creed. He died in Zurich
September 17, 1575, and Simler, his son-in-law, officiated at the
funeral.

JOHN CALVIN

Reformer From Geneva

FRANCE, the homeland of John Calvin, had a smoothly functioning, well-integrated governmental organization during the sixteenth century, and stood at that time among the strongest in Europe's sisterhood of nations. The University of Paris, which during the preceding century had been wholly given over to scholasticism, began, under King Francis I, a devotee of sound scholarship, to introduce the study of Greek into its curriculum. The theological faculty, though thoroughly loyal to the Roman Catholic Church, found the New Learning more or less acceptable because of the attitude of the king. Yet it must have been obvious to the university officials that wherever the Renaissance gained ground, there criticism of the church made its inevitable entrance.

In France the Catholic Church by the Concordat of 1516, to state it briefly, received additional funds but relinquished some of its hold on the people. Hence the people of France had less ill will toward the church than did the populace in Germany, where the Catholic Church had kept on fleecing the people by governmental consent without yielding any control.

This attitude in France also led to a less enthusiastic and vehement reformatory spirit than in other European areas. Many French Catholics were sufficiently dissatisfied with the church to complain, but comparatively few had sufficient impetus to break away from the fold completely. The ability of the church to track down heretics and bring them to court was perhaps also a deterring factor in lessening, at least in postponing, the revolt.

Into this governmental and religious situation, John Cauvin, later anglicized to Calvin, was born at Noyon in Picardy, July 10,

1509. His father, Gerard Cauvin, a middle-class gentleman, influential in both state and church affairs, provided his children with a good education. From the fragmentary records concerning John Calvin's childhood, it seems that his early days had a setting of comfort and a degree of prosperity.

At the age of fourteen he entered the University of Paris, and at nineteen he had completed the course in the arts. He also studied law at Bourges and Orleans, important centers for legal studies, where he also found time to study Greek, doubtless as a result of his humanistic leanings. His zeal for learning at Orleans led him into irregularity of rest and nourishment, with the result that he suffered from ill-health the remainder of his life.

The events leading to his full separation from the church and to his conversion are vague, or at least disputed. Apparently when a friend of his found himself under arrest in 1531 for heresy, Calvin deemed it advisable to leave Paris. In 1533 he returned for a short time, but by the following year it became dangerous for one of Protestant leanings to remain in France. And by this time he had reached the stage where his general attitude placed him in the ranks of the Protestants. He had read the New Testaments of Erasmus and Luther, and of his conversion he wrote: "God by a sudden conversion tamed and made teachable my mind." —Quoted by James Mackinnon in *Calvin and the Reformation,* page 44.

Upon this decision to cast his lot with the Reformation, he, with a companion, fled by way of Lorraine and Strasbourg to Basel, where he arrived in 1535 under the name of Martinus Lucanius. After a short stay in Basel he went to Italy for a brief visit. Then he began his return to Switzerland by way of Paris to settle some business matter and to bring his sister and brother to Switzerland. Leaving Paris, he planned to spend but a night in Geneva, which, except for a short interruption, became his home until his death.

Before recounting some of his activities in Geneva, it may be well to present some of his views on theology and government. He was never ordained either by Catholics or Protestants; he felt that his call came directly from God, and consequently believed that he did not need formal ordination. Although he is classified as a "second generation Reformer," having received most of his

Protestant views from Luther, Zwingli, and Melanchthon, he, nonetheless, demonstrated much freshness and originality in his formulation of the Christian doctrine.

In his view of the Lord's Supper he differed from Luther and had little in common with Zwingli, leaning more toward Melanchthon's views. To him the Lord's Supper had a strictly spiritual significance. Children were not allowed to partake of this sacrament until they had made a profession of faith based upon Calvin's *Catechism*. He permitted both infants and adults to be baptized, and used either sprinkling or immersion for the occasion.

According to his theology, church and state were separate instruments in God's hands to carry out His will. That he was unable to carry out his theory in Genevan practice was perhaps more a fault of the time than of Calvin. Salvation, he averred, came through faith in Christ. Man in himself was wholly bad and could not help himself. Teachers in religious schools he classed with the ministers of the gospel.

The doctrine by which Calvin is commonly known is that of "predestination," a belief that God directs the fate of specific persons.

All through his teachings he asserted that a strong measure of discipline over all individuals was necessary in order to bring them to God. He held more clearly, perhaps, than the other Reformers to a belief in the absolute and exclusive divine authority of the Scriptures.

He opposed the marginal sects, particularly the Anabaptists, the forerunners of the present-day Baptists, in their belief that civil authority should have no jurisdiction over spiritual matters, that the dead know not anything until the resurrection, and that baptism by immersion of persons after they had reached the age of accountability was the only valid one. He was in harmony with the other Reformers of his age in using civil authority to bring about spiritual advancement, particularly when their own doctrines were in danger of being destroyed.

On the question of original sin he differed from Luther, believing that man has a tendency to sin but is not possessed with original sin. He advocated the abolition of the mass, clerical celibacy, belief in purgatory, and Lenten observance. On those four points all Reformers were quite well in accord.

With this summary of Calvin's beliefs, it is fitting that attention be directed to his work in Geneva.

When he arrived there in 1536, the city in all its turbulent past had never witnessed a clash of more varied interests than at that particular time. The contending forces had developed into a mixture of politics and religion which only a determined leader could make tractable. William Farel, a former acquaintance and fellow countryman, as well as an admirer of Calvin, had attempted to give spiritual leadership to the city. When he knew of Calvin's presence that night, he persuaded Calvin to remain. At first Calvin refused, stating that he wanted to study in peace and quiet at Strasbourg. Farel said: "May God curse your studies if now in her hour of necessity you refuse to lend your aid to the church." —E. M. Hulme, *Renaissance and Reformation*, page 292.

Calvin soon stepped into public view and began to prepare an outline for church government, a confession of faith, and a catechism. He had prior to his coming to Geneva prepared his *Institutes,* a handbook of Christian belief, and this doubtless furnished the basis for his church constitution and a regulation of the moral life of the community.

By the opening of 1537 it appeared certain that Calvin and his associates were assured of the city government's support in making Geneva a place after Calvin's own heart. But his harsh, undeviating ways and a misunderstanding between the cities of Bern and Geneva led to Calvin's banishment in the spring of 1538.

This time his wanderings led him to the city of Strasbourg, where he became the minister to a congregation of French Protestant refugees. Here he continued writing and studying to further develop the doctrines for which he became famous.

But his exile from Geneva did not settle the difficulties there, and erelong the city officials voted to invite Calvin to return. This he declined to do unless certain stipulations were met. When these were promised, he returned September 13, 1541.

Although he held no office and received none of the powers of government, nonetheless from thenceforward until his death he was the guiding hand that determined the destinies of Geneva. That he actually ruled the city few would deny; that God had called him back to Geneva he had no doubt. His three years' absence had brought no change in his original plan, which was to make Geneva the standard for a Christian community.

Immediately upon his return he requested the city government for the assistance of a committee of six to help him and the other ministers to draw up an over-all plan. His work moved along smoothly, for many of his former opponents had died or left the city. The ministers who did not co-operate fully he gradually (he had gained some control of his former youthful rashness) replaced with men who gave him unquestioning support.

The plan drawn up stipulated that the city be divided into three parts with sufficient ministers in each area so that no one would lack the opportunity of hearing sermons. The lives of the people were regulated in strictest detail, and punishment fell on high and low alike if what they did failed to meet with Calvin's approval. The city government gave final decisions on all matters, items of conduct as well as disputes on doctrines; and as a rule its judgments were unsparing.

Again Calvin stood in danger of losing ground because of his censoriousness. In the city elections of 1547 several of his enemies rose to positions of responsibility, and in the following year the city council felt itself forced to ask Calvin to be less harsh in his criticism of officials. For several years he found it difficult to maintain his position of leadership.

His standing was further tested in 1553 by the famous trial of Servetus. This liberal-minded Spanish intellectual, versed in law and medicine, and with a penchant for theological wrangling, had as early as 1531 published his *De Trinitatis Erroribus,* in which he opposed the prevalent doctrine of the trinity. In 1553 he published another work, *Christianismi Restitutio,* virulently antagonistic to the Trinitarian tenets of the Nicene Creed.

Early in 1553 Servetus had been imprisoned in France awaiting the Inquisition's findings on his heretical utterances. In June of that year the court sentenced him to be "roasted to death on a slow fire," but the fire consumed merely his effigy, for he had escaped to Geneva.

He must have known the dangers attending his arrival, for he appeared incognito in August, but he straightway tempted the fates by attending one of Calvin's sermons. Upon hearing of his presence the reformer ordered his arrest, and at the trial Calvin the prosecutor soon had Servetus hopelessly enmeshed in incriminating and acrimonious statements. As the case progressed, it became evident that Protestant leaders favored the death of Servetus, for they honestly believed the souls of many were endangered by letting him live.

On October 26, 1553, the council sentenced him to be burned alive the next day. At the stake he reiterated his contention that Jesus had no eternal equality with God, as in his death throes he cried out, "Jesus, Thou son of the eternal God, have pity on me." The Nicene Trinitarian doctrine demanded that he confess Jesus as the eternal son of the eternal God.

That Calvin lent his active influence to Servetus's execution is undeniable, but to make him out a bloodthirsty ogre is to ignore the temper and attitude of the age. The meaning of the term *toleration* in its present sense was unknown. The Catholic Church, the Inquisition, and the Protestants considered themselves international benefactors as they eradicated heretics. Calvin, for all his zeal in spiritual matters, was a product of the sixteenth century with all its overwhelming medieval tendencies. For his conspicuous service in ending the disturbing controversial thrusts of Servetus, he received the thanks and approbation of his fellow Reformers in and outside of Switzerland.

The condemnation and execution of Servetus for daring to be different from the currently accepted norms stands as a crime of giant proportions, but it was no greater, in fact not a small fraction as great, as the wholesale execution of the Anabaptists, the burning of scores of worthy men by Catholics and Protestants alike, or the hideous massacre of St. Bartholomew. The arraignment of Servetus has received attention far beyond its significance in relation to other events of the times; it did not constitute the only example of miscarriage of justice. Lamentable, yes, but the acts of the sixteenth century cannot be measured by the mores of the twentieth.

Calvin's triumph over Servetus greatly strengthened his position in Geneva, and by 1555 he felt reasonably secure of his status. Calvin's despotic, domineering attitude toward all who did not fully agree with him led to the statement that more wept under him than over him.

During all the years of his close personal supervision of Genevan affairs, and even before, he wrote and published a great deal. His first book, *A Commentary on Seneca's Treatise on Clemency,* made its appearance when he was twenty-three years old. This placed Calvin in immediate favor among the learned men of his day, in the ranks of mature scholars with deep understanding of human problems. Four years later he produced his *Institutes,* which gave an explanation of doctrinal points as he understood them and also contained a letter to the French king defending the French Protestants.

This letter placed Calvin at the head of French reformers, for no one prior to this had clarified the Protestant position to the nation's leaders. Later came his *Catechism,* with its subsequent revisions. And then his *Ordinances,* which dealt with the respective fields of activity of the church and the state and how they were to be helpful mutually in guiding the people. Still later he published several psalms and some verses to be sung in the French tongue. In all, he wrote enough to fill fifty-nine volumes.

Interspersed among all this activity were his travels. At least once he went upon the invitation of Charles V, the emperor, to discuss the possibility of arriving at some common ground for Catholic and Protestant understanding. As a result of his attendance and advice at many religious councils he was considered one of the foremost leaders of the Protestant Reformation.

Calvin soon realized that if the work to which he had set his heart and soul was to have proper fruitage, he must have an educated ministry. To this end the government of Geneva agreed in January, 1558, that a college should be established. This institution soon attained a high reputation among the leading schools of the time and eventually became the University of Geneva.

Calvin never seemed to rest. His capacity to accomplish work was enormous. Letters to many of Europe's men of distinction both in church and government flowed from his pen constantly. It was said that he preached nearly three hundred sermons a year, besides delivering nearly two hundred lectures, not to speak of his attendance at secular functions and his private visitations.

Calvin's influence on Protestant thought was literally stupendous, due largely to his transcendent ability as a theologian. He stands as one of the most conspicuous religious leaders of the six-teenth century, perhaps second only to Luther. Intellectually he ranked among the best scholars of his period. His legal training and lucid explanation gave him the ability to bend logic to his opinions and placed him in the vanguard among reasoners. His inflexible spirit and keen mind made it difficult to oppose him successfully.

His writings stand today as a most worth-while contribution to the world's religious thought, and his ability as a unifying power among Protestants who did not espouse the faith of Luther assures him a place in the hall of famous religious leaders. His influence reached far beyond the boundaries of Geneva, Switzerland, and France to Germany, the Netherlands, England, Scotland, Poland, and, in later centuries, to America. It is possible that he selected the proper title for himself, the one by which he wished to be known, namely, "The Only International Reformer."

He fell asleep peacefully May 27, 1564, and was buried the next day without ceremony or pomp. Since no marker designates his final resting place, the exact spot remains unknown.

ERASMUS

Translator of the New Testament

AMONG the Reformers, and yet not a Reformer in the truest sense of the term, may be named Desiderius Erasmus Roterodamus, the high-sounding appellation apparently having been chosen by Erasmus himself. Sired by an unmarried priest and mothered by the daughter of a physician, he was born near Rotterdam in the autumn of 1466. It can be said to the father's credit that he carried the responsibilities of the child's care and education.

He attended school for the first time at Gouda, and at the age of nine he began high school at Deventer, a first-rate school of its type, where the Renaissance first reached Northern Europe. It was also at Deventer that he first learned to love the study of literature, a devotion which became the guiding force of his life. For nine years he remained at Deventer, where for a time it seems that he was a chorister at Utrecht under the famous cathedral organist Jacob Obrecht.

When Erasmus was in his teens, both his parents died, possibly from the plague, and the funds arranged by his father for educational purposes were diverted to the personal use of the appointed guardian. Erasmus was sent to a monastery at Hertogenbosch to get him out of the way.

Erasmus had hoped to attend a university, but the death of his parents and the subsequent loss of his funds through his guardian's dishonesty left him little choice but to prepare for the life of a monk. The strict discipline encountered in the monastery did not quench his spirit, but it did develop a hatred for the kind of teaching he received there. The three years spent at this school he considered wholly wasted. The tragedy of extreme poverty, harsh treatment, and delayed realization of ambition which clouded his boyhood undoubtedly influenced his entire life.

In 1492 he was ordained to the priesthood, and soon after this he began his studies in Paris through the friendship of the bishop of Cambray, whose secretary he became in 1494. In 1498 he received his degree of bachelor of theology, and in 1499 he was found in England, where Colet and More influenced him to take up the study of Greek in order to obtain a better insight into the Holy Scriptures. It appears he attended Oxford, but for a short time only, for January of 1500 found him back in Paris. In the fall of 1505 he was back in England upon the invitation of Lord Mountjoy, his patron, and at this time he met the archbishop of Canterbury and other notables. During the years he spent in England he joined with John Colet and Sir Thomas More to become one of the trio comprising the Oxford Reformers.

In 1506 he reached Italy, thereby realizing a long-desired ambition, and here he attained the doctorate in theology. In 1511 he was back in England as an instructor at Cambridge. In 1514 he was in Switzerland, where he superintended the printing of his books and where by 1521 he had settled permanently in Basel as general editor and literary adviser of the famous Froben Press.

From the foregoing it may readily be construed that Erasmus was by nature a wanderer, for he never lived more than eight consecutive years of his adult life in any one place. His life showed no particularly dramatic periods, but moved along with few startling developments, although he was highly honored by rulers and the papacy alike. Sometime before his death he was freed from his monastic vows by papal intercession.

In spite of the fact that he suffered from ill health he was of a free and easy nature. Short of stature, blue-eyed, and fair complexioned, he was graceful in build and action, with affable and polished manners, all capped by a cheerful expression and a clear enunciation which overcame the deficiency of a weak voice. His brain was ever alert, as from early childhood he showed a marked interest in intellectual activity which astounded his teachers.

He has been designated by some writers as a man with a one-track mind. As had been stated, he traveled widely, but nowhere in his writings does one find a description of cities, landscapes, or

people. Among his contemporaries were such notables as Michelangelo, Titian, and Raphael, but he does not mention them or their
work. The discovery of America or the famous rounding of the
Cape of Good Hope did not call forth a single line from his able
pen. And the Spanish conquest of South America likewise left
him unmoved. His one all-pervasive activity was the study of the
literature of the ancients.

What was Erasmus's aim in life? From source material it seems
apparent that he hoped to accomplish a renaissance of Christendom,
for he worked incessantly for the advancement of knowledge both
spiritual and secular. In the midst of the growing storm of the
Reformation he attempted to ride the middle course. Only at times
did he deviate slightly. He mercilessly denounced the clergy and
the monks, and thereby made possible Luther's success. In fact,
his attacks on the corruptions in the church were even more pointed
than Luther's, but he accomplished them with a greater degree
of tact.

Repeatedly he called for a return to the source and simplicity
of Christianity; but it is possible that his position was weakened
by the fact that he did not condemn much of the mass of church
dogma, but merely called it irrelevant. Reason settled everything
with him. He stood with Luther in his indignation against the
moral laxity of the clergy, but he considered Luther's theology too
reactionary.

Because of his writings he earned the enmity of papal leaders,
but he never severed his connections with the church. He could
have had ecclesiastical preferment had he come out openly and
boldly against Luther, but he did not do this any more than he
contemplated a complete rupture with the church.

His first publication, *The Praise of Folly*, a satire written in
the house of Sir Thomas More in England, appeared in 1500. In
it, as in all his books and correspondence, he shows a liberal mind,
and there is little doubt that his writings hastened the Reformation.
The publication of his Greek New Testament, accompanied by a
Latin translation, shook the foundations of the church, it is said,
for it gave opportunity to the people to compare the acts of church
officials with the teachings of Christ. This work no doubt stands
as his most notable contribution to the Reformation. Some monks

were reported to have said that Erasmus laid the Reformation egg and Luther hatched it. In fact, Erasmus himself maintained that Luther, and also Zwingli, only taught what he had told them.

How is Erasmus to be classified? Was he a Reformer or a foe of the Reformation? Was he a man of principle or a weakling? Or was he, as one writer declared him to be, almost as a John the Baptist and a Judas in a single person? Actually in his expressed theology he was neither Protestant nor Catholic, but with more leanings toward the Catholic dogma than to the Protestant dogma. He was a distinct rationalist. He knew that a change was necessary, but he devoutly hoped that it might be accomplished within the framework of the church.

Up to the time of Luther's open challenge to the papacy, Erasmus is usually listed among the Reformers. He had said enough against the papal corruption that had he been a lesser light he would doubtless have been burned as a heretic. He had been tireless in exhibiting the ignorance and abuses found in the church. He was also the center of a company of men devoted to the New Learning and to criticism of existing religions. Among his devotees was Zwingli, one of the Swiss Reformers, whose life and work will be reviewed in a subsequent chapter. Zwingli praised Erasmus as a paragon of learning and the sum of all the virtues. He thought so much of Erasmus that he said he never went to sleep at night without reading a little of his works. But Erasmus was accustomed to being addressed in superlatives by those who courted his favor.

But a true reformer must be willing to be a martyr, and Erasmus was apparently not made of such material. He had a purpose and a mission, but he lacked courage. Or was it true conversion? At times he was willing to modify his policy or position, like that of a trimmer, for the sake of expediency. As evidence of such vacillation is his statement that he never read Luther, this in order to make life easier for himself with his friends among the Catholic princes and ecclesiastics.

It is possible that Erasmus might have broken with the church had his conception of the plan of salvation been clearer. To speak of Jesus, Socrates, and Paul without distinction in classification, as he did, does not necessarily betray a lack of intellectual power, but it does indicate a weak spiritual understanding.

It needs to be said to his credit, however, that in his writings he showed that an actual problem existed. He helped promote the Reformation, and for this contribution alone he deserves full appreciation. His fault lay in that he did little toward the solution of the problem other than to point it out. But in doing that he made, intentionally or otherwise, the papal organization shudder in all its parts.

Also, there were bounds beyond which he would not go, were he ever so anxious for praise and honor. After 1535 a final attempt appears to have been made to swing him openly against the Reformation. A cardinal's hat was swung temptingly near in order to secure his help to assure a unified church; but, to his credit, he declined it.

Erasmus's greatness lay primarily, however, in his intellect. He was the greatest of the Humanists. In 1903 Samuel Macauley Jackson, editor of the *Heroes of the Reformation* series and author of the book, *Huldreich Zwingli,* gave the following estimation of Erasmus as a Humanist, and this opinion is probably as worthy and as fair a one as may be found:

"The position of Erasmus among the young Humanists of the early part of the sixteenth century had many points of similarity to that of Matthew Arnold's among the college men of the United States thirty and perhaps twenty years ago. Like Arnold, he was read by the whole set and sworn to with all a young man's ardor. His skepticism, his cynicism, his wit, his learning, his versatility, were appreciated, but by no means implicitly approved by those who read him. There was a fascination about him even to those who knew how defective his character was. Those who came ultimately to quite different conclusions were grateful to Erasmus for having exposed the hollowness of mockery and the falsity of the medieval claim of finality for the scholastic methods."—Page 86.

During the winter of 1535-36 illness kept Erasmus constantly confined to his quarters. Often he was in bed for days at a time, but he continued writing to the end, which came July 11, 1536. In the disposition of his means nothing was left for any church purpose, and no priest or confessor was with him when he died. "Liever Gotté" (Dear God), spoken in his native Dutch tongue, were the last words he uttered.

WILLIAM FAREL

A Reformer of Courage

WILLIAM FAREL, the scourge of priests, the pioneer and apostle of Protestantism in western Switzerland, and the most courageous of the French and Swiss Reformers, sprang from a poor but noble family whose ancestral home lay in a village near Gap among the mountains of Southeastern France. Born in 1489, he was the eldest of seven children, and from his earliest years he displayed a singular honesty of character combined with a consuming devotion to spiritual values.

Notwithstanding his overcredulous obedience to all that the church taught, he manifested an intense desire for learning. Consequently he found his way to Paris, where it seems he began his study of ancient languages, including Hebrew, at the university before he reached his teens. Theology and philosophy also challenged his interest. In January of 1517 he attained his master of arts degree. In the same year he began to teach at the college of Cardinal Lemoine, which was equal in rank to the Sorbonne.

While attending the university he came under the influence of Jacques Lefèvre of Etaples, a reputable scholar, a doctor of divinity, and Farel's teacher at the University of Paris. Deeply attached to his master, Farel learned from him that salvation comes by faith in Jesus Christ, that the only formula for faith is found in the word of God, and that the traditions of the Roman Church are based, not on Scriptural foundations, but upon the ordinances and imaginations of men.

As early as 1512 Lefèvre said to Farel, "My son, God will renew the world, and you will witness it."—Quoted by Philip Schaff in *A History of the Christian Church*, vol. 7, p. 239. From the influence exerted upon him by Lefèvre, Farel, the zealous papist, became through great spiritual struggle an ardent, audacious Protestant who saw nothing in the Roman Church except moral corruption and clerical abuses. His persistent preoccupation centered on the idolatry of the mass, the comparison of pictures and relics of the church to heathen idolatry, and the status of the pope as antichrist.

In spite of a small, weak physique, pale features topped by a narrowing forehead, and a poorly kept beard which matched his temper, he drew people to himself and convinced them of the truthfulness of his cause by his masterful oratory, remarkably well-timed gestures, his expressive mouth, the intensity of the delivery of his improvised sermons, and a trumpeting voice which belied his size.

Little by little, he became the guiding star of an organized group of propagandists who pledged themselves to preach the gospel to French-speaking Switzerland.

No record of a regular ordination seems to be in evidence, unless it is a reference to his being set apart to the gospel ministry by John Oecolampadius, the Reformer of Basel. It is said that he felt himself called of God to uproot the idolatry of the Roman Church and to point all men to the worship of the Creator by spiritual means.

Soon after he began to accept the opinions of Lefèvre, he found that he had opened the door to oppression by the doctors at the Sorbonne, the leaders of theological thought in Paris. Because of their opposition he left for Meaux, where by 1521 he obtained permission to preach from Bishop Briconnet, who also felt the need of spiritual regeneration in the church; but after a few years his impetuous and vehement preaching had aroused so much opposition that even the bishop was powerless to protect him.

Then he fled to Switzerland, where he held public discourses, possibly as early as 1524, on such topics as Christian liberty, the doctrine of justification by faith, and the perfection of the Scriptures.

It was about this time, too, that he returned to his home, where his preaching won three of his brothers and several other persons to Protestant views; but his impetuousness soon banned him from France, whereupon he returned to Basel. Here Oecolampadius found pleasure in "the learning, piety, and courage of the young Frenchman," but Erasmus could not stomach what he considered Farel's impudence (Farel had failed to pay homage to Erasmus) and apparently lent his influence to have him expelled from Basel in 1524.

Strasbourg and other cities of the area were the scene of his activity for the next year. From Oecolampadius he received counsel to temper his aggressiveness and appear more lamblike so as to put to rout that old opponent, the devil.

During the winter of 1526-27 a schoolmaster who called him-self Ursinus entered the little town of Aigle in Switzerland. "He was a man of middle stature, with red beard and quick eyes, and who, to a voice of thunder (says Beza) united the feelings of a hero: his modest lessons were intermingled with new and strange doctrines."—J. H. Merle d'Aubigné, *History of the Reformation of the Sixteenth Century*, vol. 4, p. 289. For a time this schoolmaster taught ordinary lessons mingled with Bible teachings to the children in the daytime, but at night when he resorted to his humble abode he studied the Scriptures in the Greek and Hebrew. Here he read Zwingli's first publication to the Germans, and it fired the school-master with zeal to be up and doing.

Instead of limiting his activities to the teaching of children, he now drew the parents within his circle of instruction. To them he expounded concerning the fallacy of the doctrine of purgatory and the invocation of saints. As for the pope, according to Ursinus, he was nothing in those parts, and the priests merely provided material for Erasmus to turn into ridicule.

Imagine the consternation of the priests and magistrates when this schoolmaster ascended the pulpit, with the flock he had gath-ered around him, and announced that he was William Farel, minister of the word of God! To them the name of Farel was a sign of terror, a name to be reckoned with, a formidable antagonist.

Against their onslaughts to drive Farel from the town and to bring to nought his reformatory work, the Council of Bern, which had granted him a roving commission to preach the Holy Scriptures, stood as an effective bulwark. But as his work branched out into other French-speaking areas, he continued to meet opposition: Romish agents excited the people to resist, and the threat of death dogged his footsteps. But Farel was not discouraged.

In January of 1528 he attended the Synod of Bern, where the victory of the Reformation was decided. Permission to preach in all the districts under the control of Bern was granted him in March of that year. Whereupon, regardless of indignities, such as being spat upon, bodily injury, and threats of death, "he turned every stump and stone into a pulpit, every house, street, and market place into a church; provoked the wrath of monks, priests, and bigoted women."—Schaff, *op. cit.*, vol. 7, p. 242. Time after time during public disputations the proponents of the church were powerless against his arguments.

At Lausanne, Farel was repulsed twice, even though some of the people were conscious of the abuses of the church, which Ruchat described as follows: "The ministers of the Virgin were seen in public playing at games of chance, which they seasoned with mockery and blasphemy. They fought in the churches; disguised as soldiers, they descended by night from the cathedral hill, and roaming through the streets, sword in hand and in liquor, surprised, wounded, and sometimes even killed the worthy citizens; they debauched married women, seduced young girls, changed their residences into houses of ill fame, and heartlessly turned out their young children to beg their bread."—Quoted by Merle d'Aubigné, *op. cit.*, vol. 4, p. 293.

But at Morat his preaching won many converts. Thirsting for more conquests, he went to Neufchatel, preaching with such vigor that he gained many people. For his pains the monks threatened to drown him, and one of them carried a dagger in his hand. Farel, it is said, escaped with difficulty.

He went from town to town, from valley to valley, reforming as he went. In the Val de Ruz, probably at Boudevilliers, he and a companion, Boyves, were instrumental in interrupting the mass. Consequently they were stoned, beaten, and dragged to the river. This was perhaps the closest Farel came to a martyr's death, but friends from Neufchatel arrived in time to save him. Nonetheless, the two Reformers were covered with blood and filth. Nearly dead, they were put into a dungeon. Later his preaching at this place resulted in the wholesale destruction of images, idols, crucifixes, paintings, and statues, and plates which held the bread of the eucharist were thrown into the river.

When Farel arrived in Geneva in October, 1532, Protestantism had reached the status where the new doctrines were gaining favor throughout the whole Swiss confederation. His first visit to Geneva was of short duration, however, for the episcopal council ordered him to leave the next day. Undaunted, he returned to conduct the first public worship of the new order March 1, 1534. His hold on Geneva became so strong that nuns, monks, and priests gradually left the city. He soon won acclaim as the most capable theologian at the disputation in Bern.

Farel's popularity, frequently on the wane, received new impetus when in July, 1535, he seized the church of St. Madeleine, and in the following month the Cathedral of St. Pierre came under his control. At this time the principal churches of Geneva were also placed under his jurisdiction and that of his supporters.

It is not to be supposed, however, that all these quasi-political moves came solely from a spiritual awakening. Actually many municipal changes during these years were prompted as much by political consideration as by any religious feelings, for to many of that time the line of demarcation between religion and politics was nebulous at best. Yet by the end of 1535 the government of Geneva ordered the end of the mass, and by special governmental fiat the city committed itself to the Reformation.

The following year brought further evidence of Geneva's decision to break fully with Catholicism. By the end of May, 1536, Farel, under the general assembly, had completed control; and the older church system lagged to extinction. The great Council of Two Hundred issued an edict, the first official act of the Reformation, which, among other things, removed images and relics from the churches, established schools, ordered the preaching of daily sermons, stipulated the giving of communion four times a year, and instituted a Sunday closing law. The edict even specified certain garb for a bride.

More adept at fiery denunciation than at organization of religious institutions along Protestant lines, Farel recognized his limitations. Consequently when one night in July, 1536, a young French acquaintance passed through Geneva, Farel induced him to stay, under threat of ruin to his lifework if he failed to heed the injunction. And from that night on John Calvin became Geneva's guiding star.

For several years Farel continued in Geneva and seemed to

have reached an unassailable eminence in his career; yet before the close of 1538 he was expelled from the city by order of the government.

From Geneva he went to Neufchatel, where, with the exception of short trips to adjacent cities, he remained the rest of his life. His first work there, which took four years to perform, was to effect order in the reformed societies of that city. During this period he also visited the Waldenses at Piedmont, where it is said he turned many to Protestantism. In 1557 he made at least two fruitless visits to Germany with the hope of enlisting the aid of German princes in behalf of French Protestants and the Waldenses.

At the age of sixty-nine, in December, 1558, to the great annoyance of Calvin, and against the advice of his friends, he married a poor girl who had fled from France with her widowed mother. Six years later he became the father of a son who survived him three years.

The year following his marriage he encouraged the French refugees in Alsace and Lorraine. In 1560 and 1561 he was back in France for brief visits. Here his radical ways and bitter denunciations led to his expulsion. Approximately three months before his death he visited the Protestants at Metz, where it is said he preached with the vigor of youth.

He died peacefully at his home in Neufchatel September 13, 1565, at the age of seventy-six years. His last days were marked by the steadfastness of a hero. On May 4, 1876, a monument in his memory was erected in the city of his demise.

His literary contributions are composed of aggressive controversial materials and some tracts of a practical nature for the time. He left no written sermons. To his credit is also the founding of schools and hospitals.

His primary defects existed in his method, rather than in his intent. Seemingly he knew no moderation. Doubtless the times demanded all-out warfare against the evils of the church. Discretion went to the winds, and the willful development of opposition seemed to add zest to his life. His work brought him many gains, but seldom did he show much ability as an organizer.

No circumstances, however dangerous, stopped him from what he believed to be his duty. Amid all the planning of his enemies to scourge him, he used no violence, except the whiplash of his tongue. Persecutions seemed to strengthen his will and endurance. Schaff describes him a "man full of faith and fire, as bold and fearless as Luther and far more radical, but without his genius." —*Op. cit.*, vol. 7, p. 237. And Thomas M. Lindsay says that Farel always carried with him a perpetual spring and the effervescing recklessness of youth.

ULRICH ZWINGLI

Founder of Swiss Protestantism

IN ORDER to understand the place of Ulrich (or Huldreich) Zwingli in the scheme of the Protestant Reformation, one must first have an overview of the plan of the Swiss government at the time Zwingli came into the limelight. At the opening of the sixteenth century Switzerland had a federal organization called a "diet," composed of representatives from each of the cantons, or states, within the confederation. This diet, however, functioned primarily in international situations; the everyday governmental activities were carried on mainly within the jurisdiction of each separate canton.

Strategically situated as to commerce and politics, Switzerland was being courted by other powers, but without receiving the respect of any of them. To belittle herself still more in the eyes of foreign countries, there was the constant striving for ascendancy among the different cantons. The confederation was at times imperiled, because of jealousy over some purely local problem.

Into such a political and social organism Ulrich Zwingli, son of a farmer and stockman, was born in the village of Wildhaus in the Toggenburg Valley of Switzerland, January 1, 1484. His father reached the distinction of chief village magistrate, and of two uncles, one served as a priest and the other attained the status of abbot in a Benedictine monastery.

None of Zwingli's writings reveal that any great spiritual or inner urge led him to become a preacher. He arrived at such a decision apparently as the result of mental assent growing out of calm, dignified, scholarly pursuits along humanistic lines. He never passed through the inward struggle and soul searching brought on by an extreme sense of sin as preceded Luther's conversion. And once having reached the conclusion that he should give himself to the study of the Scriptures, he remained as true to the calling as if he had been impelled by pure religious enthusiasm.

Because of his father's hope that he would become a priest, he found himself under the direction of his uncle, already a priest. Since this uncle had aforetime tasted of the ways of the humanists who were interested, among other things, in studying the Scriptures for their original meaning, Zwingli early became a student of the Bible and of Greek.

When but a mere child of preschool age he began to live with his uncle and to attend the parish school at a place called Wesen, not far from his ancestral home. By the time he reached the age of ten he displayed marks of scholarship far beyond his years. Then he journeyed to Basel, where he found a competent instructor in the school of St. Theodore's church. The following two years he attended a school at Bern which had fully accepted the educational outlook and ideas of the Renaissance, or New Learning.

In a period of four years he mastered the courses offered there and showed himself an efficient scholar and debater. By 1504, at the age of twenty, he received the bachelor's degree, and two years later he attained the master's degree. While studying the Scriptures and ancient writers, he found time to become an accomplished performer on several musical instruments as the result of musical education offered by a Dominican monastery.

Zwingli greatly admired both Luther and Erasmus, but he broke with both—with the former over a point of doctrine, and with the latter for his extreme caution and apprehensiveness when some of his own ideas were carried out.

As was true of many other sixteenth-century reformers, Zwingli had no thought of separating from the Roman Catholic Church when he began to draw attention to its un-Biblical teachings and to the moral lapses and outright corruption of the clergy in high and in low places alike. He soon perceived that the medieval church concerned itself with money-making, with baseless theological discussions, with condoning a clergy of low intellectual standards and few, if any, moral ideals. He turned with disgust from such a noxious example and took the position that the doctrines of the Scriptures should suffice for the religious instruction of the laity.

One of the first practices Zwingli condemned in the church was that of selling indulgences, and when a dispenser of such came into his area, Zwingli roundly denounced him and his wares—so much so, in fact, that the man left those parts. Yet, despite this criticism of the church, Zwingli maintained his status with the pope, who supplied him with a yearly fee, which Zwingli in turn used to enlarge his library. Surprisingly enough, Zwingli retained both his position and his fee for many years, even after he became the Zurich Reformer.

His study of the Bible soon convinced him, as it had Luther, that one is saved by faith through Jesus Christ. Apparently he arrived at this doctrine independently and taught it to his members, but Luther holds the distinction among the Reformers of being its author, or discoverer.

Probably one of Zwingli's main contributions to religious thought consisted in the idea that the reorganization of community life on Scriptural foundations had as great importance as the spiritual needs of an individual.

The doctrine of the Lord's Supper, as held by the church, he renounced fully. To him this ordinance had a spiritual significance and concerned itself not at all with the actual body and blood of Christ, but rather with its symbolism. On this point he and Luther differed violently in a controversy which lasted at least five years and ended in a draw at the Colloquy of Marburg in 1529.

Much of his activity concerned itself with working for a political alliance which he hoped would safeguard the followers of Christ. He knew of the emperor's hatred of all that did not favor full accord with the Catholic Church. And the church itself constantly fought against anyone who differed from its doctrines or dared have an independent opinion. Closely allied to these two mighty anti-Scriptural forces stood the Swiss cantons which favored the papacy. With such an array of powers standing against Zwingli and his followers, his desire for political alliance for personal safety can well be understood, if not justified. In fact, it was the only procedure he knew of to effect the Reformation he desired.

Knowing only too well the ignorance of many of the priests, he put forth great efforts to develop an educated clergy. To this end he established a theological seminary in 1525. Yet in all his laudable endeavors he lost sight of an ideal which he frequently preached, namely, the liberty of the individual to determine his own spiritual course. Many times he used or arranged to have used the arm of governmental force to obtain obedience. This adamant attitude he revealed in his treatment of the monasteries, nunneries, and the Anabaptists. He lent his hand to their ruthless extermination, and this served as the one dark blot on his character. The same persecution the Catholic Church meted out to heretics, he in turn meted out to those who did not conform to his ideas when once he had the power to enforce these opinions. But, then, most of the Reformation heroes fell into the same pitfall of false reasoning.

A magnetic personality and a ready, pleasant, agreeable wit brought him followers as the result of sheer love for the man himself. Quite early in his career as a Reformer he began to display a great measure of deliberation. He worked toward the development of public sentiment in favor of his preaching, but he never moved overtly until he felt reasonably sure of winning his point both politically and religiously.

His professional status as a preacher and teacher grew with his influence. From 1502 to 1506 he taught the classics at St. Martin's School in Basel. At the close of this period he accepted the call as rector of a town called Glarus. At the time of this call he had not yet been ordained to the ministry. Here he remained until 1516. This position carried with it the post of army chaplain, which took him to Italy three times with the Glarus troops.

At the close of his service at Glarus he became people's priest at Einsiedeln, which post he accepted because of the ill will of certain prominent families against him at Glarus. According to his writings, the full impact of Christian truth came to him while he served at Einsiedeln.

His next important appointment called him to the Great Minster at Zurich, in 1519, where he continued his open opposition to the sale of indulgences as he had done while at Einsiedeln. At Zurich, when his opponents charged him with heresy, he called on the city council for its opinion. When this group decided that he did not classify as a heretic, it found itself forced to support him in order to save its own face.

Whenever Zwingli wished to institute a reform, he went before the city council and argued his case like a lawyer. If the members subscribed to his views, they voted the reforms for the citizens to follow. In 1520 the council granted full freedom to preach the gospel, and by 1523 Zwingli's views and doctrines were accepted as the religion of Zurich. His status in the city and the canton, it is said, even kept the pope from attacking him openly.

In harmony with his position against an unmarried priesthood, he publicly wed Anna Reinhard, a widow, in 1524. Since 1522 she had been his wife under what was then known as a clerical marriage and which had an acceptable social status. To this marriage four children were born.

His last position was that of rector of the Great Minster School at Zurich. This responsibility, which he accepted in 1526, carried with it an official residence. By 1529, the year made famous by the Diet of Spires and the application of the term *Protestants* to the Swiss and German opponents of the papacy and the empire, Zwingli stood at the zenith of his prestige. He had staunch followers over wide areas both in the southern part of Germany and in the northern cantons of Switzerland.

Concerning his doctrinal views it may be said that his beliefs about sin and grace closely paralleled those of Luther. During 1522 the works of Luther had a ready sale in Switzerland, and Zwingli did not seem averse to their distribution.

Contradicting the teachings of the church that it never changed its teachings, Zwingli discovered that whereas the church asserted that only the bread of the Lord's Supper had ever been given to lay members, in former times both the bread and the wine had been given them. He also discovered that other changes had been made in the services of the church. In his writings he showed no mercy in exposing the fallacy of many of the church's doctrines. For example, Zwingli soon denied the intercession of the saints, which the church considered of great importance. His further study convinced him that the guidance of the Holy Spirit also made the intercession of a priest or pope unnecessary.

Between 1523 and 1525 the Reformation became an established fact in Switzerland, and Zwingli had broken fully with the papacy. By April, 1525, everything that resembled the services of the Cath-

olic Church, including the mass, came to an end in Zurich, the
capital of the Swiss Reformation, and the Lord's Supper was celebrated by permitting the laity to partake of both the bread and
the wine.

In order to make the break with the papacy as complete as
possible, Zwingli ordered that the use of choir and instrumental
music cease, since both words and music were a constant reminder
of the Catholic Church. To make his demands still more binding,
he ordered the organ of his church dismantled. But "the churches
in Zurich," wrote S. M. Jackson in his *Huldreich Zwingli*, "rein-
troduced music in 1598."—Footnote, page 290.

Another contribution, perhaps little noticed, which Zwingli
made to Switzerland consisted of awakening the people to the
degrading effect of the custom of furnishing soldiers, called "merce-
naries," to other nations for hire. By 1522 the city of Zurich had
given up such practice, with the recommendation that other cantons, too, put an end to the mercenary business.

The closing scene of Zwingli's life centers in the civil war
engendered by his efforts to force the Catholic cantons, called
the Forest Cantons, to allow preachers of his doctrine to enter
their environs. When his request for admission brought a refusal,
the council at Zurich, situated as it was on routes of trade and
commerce, placed an embargo on food going to the Forest Cantons. They hoped thereby to force the Catholics to accept Zwingli's
doctrines.

Instead of quiet compliance, a war broke out. Zwingli, as
chaplain of the Zurich forces, accompanied the troops. He died
on the battlefield of Kappel, October 11, 1531. Here his enemies
found him, for the Zurich troops had retreated in a rout, and consequently, though dead, he received a traitor's punishment, which
meant that the official hangman quartered and burned his body.

Heinrich Bullinger became Zwingli's immediate successor. But
in reality Zwingli's work suffered a severe setback. Several of his
strong doctrinal points were soon forgotten, possibly because Calvin
began his preaching in Geneva some five years after Zwingli's death.

Zwingli's great service to Christendom lay in his fearless attacks
on the corruptness of the church and the falseness of its doctrines.

REFORMATION RESULTS

To ATTEMPT a fair and compact summation of the effects, or aftermath, of the sixteenth-century Reformation, characterized as "the greatest . . . emancipation that the world has yet seen, or perhaps will ever see," constitutes a somewhat ramified undertaking, because this period of transition from medieval to modern times presents an array of chain reactions, which covers the range of all human activities.

This revolution, easily consummated within the confines of a lifetime, produced a new universe of phenomenal span. Much in modern thinking, including regions outside the sphere of religion, has its roots in this interim.

Historians agree essentially that the phases which particularly felt the impact of the Reformation include the religious, intellectual, economic, social, and political. Within these fields changes affected Catholic and Protestant organizations alike and set direct and indirect forces in motion, the repercussions of which have not yet ended their reverberations.

In its spiritual aspects the Reformation ended the pre-eminence of the Roman Catholic hierarchy and divided Western Europe into at least two rival ecclesiastical organizations. The doctrine of justification by faith cut deeply into the theory of salvation by good works and made men acutely aware of a personal responsibility to their God. Auricular confession proved inadequate when a personal Saviour stood revealed.

The direct approach to the Scriptures, likewise, brought greater satisfaction than did whimsical reliance on superstition and tradition. In short, the search for truth now became the privilege and responsibility of the individual; and the church, so long the arbiter of Scriptural teachings, needed to adjust itself to the view that the Bible did not need the church as its mentor.

(282)

New forms of worship appeared, and a definite return to the simplicity and purity of the apostolic period became apparent, even though the Reformers retained some of the forms of Roman Catholic organization, as well as some of its doctrines. This simplicity and purity was, however, more apparent among sects like the Anabaptists, Huguenots, and Separatists than among the Lutherans, Calvinists, and Anglicans, who sought governmental support for their doctrines. The living standards and church government of the former conformed more nearly to Biblical standards.

The Catholics, too, resorted to a house cleaning. Realizing that the Reformation was more than a monk's quarrel, the Catholic Church soon discovered that she could not cope successfully with the situation through excommunication, interdict, or Inquisition; and the Council of Trent, 1545, came as the direct result of these conclusions. Out of this conference Pope Pius IV issued the Tridentine profession of faith, one of the received statements of faith of the church. As a consequence all Southern Europe was kept in the fold of the church, the power of the pope was increased, and the church was consolidated into a powerful unit for aggressive development and militant expansion, causing her to regain much of her lost status in Europe. Her missionary endeavors in the New World compensated for her European losses.

On the intellectual front the Reformation created a complete break with the church. Preceding the Reformation the church had controlled learning by making university courses contribute to the development of theology, and thereby perpetuated a type of thinking aimed at sustaining the prestige of ecclesiastical authority. The Humanists, the forerunners of the Reformers, weakened the scholastic approach, and learning soon reached into other spheres of intellectual pursuits.

As a result, university education, unhampered by the vested interests of the church, received its primary stimulus to find truth. Reason became a companion to faith, and undeviating submission to priestly authority gave way to intellectual liberty. New universities were established, and most of those founded in Germany since the Reformation are Protestant.

The founding of the public-school system is also credited to the Reformation. The work, for instance, of Colet, Luther, and

Melanchthon, in giving impetus to the ideal of compulsory education, places them high on the roster of public benefactors. Where-
ever reform made marked progress, there education attained a
secure status.

Another educational outcome became obvious when the exclusive use of Latin in religious services, and Greek and Hebrew in
scholarly circles, gave way to an ever-expanding use of the vernacular tongues. As in the days of Pentecost, the common man "heard
them speak in his own language." The Reformers lifted English,
French, German, and other modern languages to the pedestal of
literary merit. "The English Bible," T. H. Huxley said, "has been
woven into the life of all that is noblest and best in English history."
This is equally true of all other countries where the Bible in the
vernacular found acceptance.

The Reformation also made a worthy contribution to hymnol-
ogy and other forms of music. In Germany, Luther wrote songs
containing the doctrines of the period. The same was done in Denmark by Hans Tausen and in Sweden by Olavus Petri. In France,
where "the psalms, for a time, crowded out the ribald songs of the
street," thousands gathered in song fests as they were gripped by
evangelical fervor. It is said that "Clément Marot (the hymn writer
of France) did as great a work for Huguenoterie, in its infancy, as
Charles Wesley did 250 years afterwards for Methodism."—S. E.
Herrick, *Some Heretics of Yesterday,* page 241. Hymnbooks came
off the press in nearly every country. But in the field of religious
art, destruction and retrogression set in. The zeal for the building
of cathedrals and the painting of great pictures almost ceased.

Questions centering around the propriety of procuring wealth
inevitably became a part of this great upheaval. As the confiscation
of ecclesiastical holdings and the suppression of the monasteries
gave added power to the recipients of these riches, they in turn
introduced newer methods of agriculture to pyramid their incomes
to undreamed-of heights. This class ultimately became members
of lawmaking assemblies, where still greater opportunities arose to
popularize and legalize capitalistic tendencies. When frugality
became a virtue, poverty no longer symbolized piety; and the isolation
of monastic activity with no personal income gave way to the pursuit
of worldly vocations which provided a pay check.

The elimination of numerous church holidays also gave labor and industry an added opportunity to increase their income with honor; and the Calvinist Reformers, in particular, preached that finance and trade were on an equality with rents and wages, thereby lending respectability to merchant activities. Furthermore, their sanction on the use of usury, long subject to ecclesiastical restrictions, developed an interaction which assured growth to both capitalistic and Protestant principles alike. As the Calvinist and Puritan leaders supported the principles of capitalism as an acceptable part of fundamental Protestant polity, their ideas on economy gradually gained the ascendancy over the more reactionary opinions of Lutheranism.

One of the outstanding effects of the Reformation in the social sphere appeared in the elevation of family life to a new level of respectability. No longer did service to God demand the asceticism of the monastery and the rejection of home and family. All Protestant leaders looked askance at a celibate priesthood, and as a result a new emphasis was placed upon the desirability and stability of a home and family. Erelong there developed a cleaner, better, and more reliable clergy, actuated by high moral principles.

A greater respect for social order also became apparent as the individual learned new duties and welcomed new responsibilities. The masses began to recognize the obligation of tolerance; for as the compulsion of living in close proximity became apparent, the practice of forbearance became a necessity. Its antithesis could flourish only where a given group maintained a predominant status. The growth of numerous religious bodies consequently guaranteed at least a type of charitableness with others' foibles and beliefs.

Tremendous strides were likewise made within the scope of national development. Once having dispensed with the medieval theory of the supremacy of ecclesiastical power in world affairs, the evolution of states proceeded apace. As soon as the hitherto undisputed political power had been struck from the hands of the papacy, national governments rose above the fear of interdicts. Consequently there appeared a new conception of governmental organization and its responsibility to the individual in search of freedom.

As they became ambitious for national character, rulers and masses alike began to realize their hitherto-unknown duties; and they became willing to repulse all efforts at papal intervention in national affairs.

The mantle of absolutism, long a monopoly of the church, now fell upon the rising European dynasties. There developed or evolved a secularization of government which assumed the control of many of the activities and functions formerly regulated by the Catholic Church. "The great wide realms of human activity lying between purely personal religion on the one hand and politics, sociology, economics, and science on the other,—realms which, though often disputed by church and state, had usually been ruled ultimately by the former,—were now, in modern times, to be gradually lost to the church and appropriated by the state."—Carlton J. H. Hayes, *Political and Cultural History of Modern Europe,* vol. 1, p. 219. The universal church also lost its exalted status to the several growing national churches and to the numerous sects which had their origin in the doctrine that one may appeal directly to God.

After absolutism had run its course, political democracy, basically an awareness of a personal responsibility to God and man, eventually appeared out of the religious democracy sponsored by the Reformers. The people gradually recognized the rights of others, and kings began to regard their subjects as more than mere chattels. As popular assemblies came into existence, the widespread prevalence of high ecclesiastics in political posts came to an end.

The democratic principles born of the Reformation also caused the development of colonies in the New World. The Pilgrims, refugees from the Anglican Church, in the New England area; the Dutch with their love for freedom and their persistent opposition to Catholic Spain; the Germans, who were soon erecting churches and establishing schools to promote Lutheranism; the Swedes and Huguenots up and down the eastern seaboard; all joined their endeavors, though sometimes divergent, to produce a government eventually characterized by republicanism and religious freedom.

As the Reformation expanded some paradoxical results developed, among them the servile subservience of the Protestants to the several national governments. In some instances, as in Germany and England, the Reformers did nought but shift from the control of the papacy, a religio-political structure, to that of a secular government, a politico-religious entity.

Nowhere did Protestantism gain effective ends without recourse to the secular arm. In Germany, England, Switzerland, and in the Scandinavian countries it succeeded because of the support of civil authority. In France, though the Reformation under the Huguenots displayed remarkable strength, the opposition of Catherine de' Medici, culminating in the Massacre of St. Bartholomew, and later the opposition of Louis XIV, effectively silenced and crushed the Protestants or drove them from France. In Spain and Italy, although these countries produced able evangelists, teachers, writers, and organizers, the Reformation failed through lack of governmental support.

Even in those countries where Protestantism was supported by the civil arm, the total result was not all to the good. Deviations and detours—serious ones—became apparent, causing the enemies of reform to point the pen of scorn and criticism at the deeds of the Protestants. All was not pure and holy by any means. Controversies and schisms among the Protestants over questions of the eucharist, works versus faith, infants' versus "believers' " baptism, Trinitarianism versus anti-Trinitarianism, and the Lutheran Reformers' sanction of the bigamy of Philip of Hesse gave the Catholics enough ammunition to riddle the Protestant doctrinal armor with holes, had there not existed a God who overruled all for the good of mankind.

Then, too, the repeated and prolonged deplorable resort to armed might sowed seeds of mutual distrust and dissolution over much of Europe. Yet out of this era ultimately came a complete realization that no given government and no specific religious body would ever again dominate all. Civil liberty, and ultimately religious freedom, came out of these devastating clashes of mingled interests of religion, power politics, economics, and greed, all commonly called by the anomalous term of "religious wars."

As the long-unchallenged grip of the church suddenly lost its power, the masses in their more or less sudden emancipation became bewildered and did not know what to do with their new-found freedom. Once the full rupture from the Catholic Church had been effected and the individual freed from restrictions and thrown upon his own judgment to think through his own beliefs, strange conclusions and conditions developed.

The combined doctrines of justification by faith, which freed the individual from good works, and that of predestination, which included one among the elect and left him in a state of grace regardless of his evil deeds, could have but one outcome when carried to their logical conclusion; namely, immoderation and excesses which left even the Reformers at their wit's end to know how to stem the current of loose living combined with riotous drinking, lack of respect for life, law, and order, and a general state of moral laxity. There existed also a needless destruction of works of art and irreplaceable manuscripts, a shallowness in religious life, and pointless theological colloquies. People indulged in recriminations, name calling, criticism of church and state alike; and persecutions and executions indicated the lack of respect which persons entertained for one another's rights. All this was part of the interlude between their emancipation from spiritual slavery and their finding their freedom in Christ where faith without works is death in itself.

All this was more or less temporary. Gradually order emerged out of disorder, and people began to adjust themselves to the opportunities offered by a better condition in church and state. The good results of the Reformation ultimately came to fruition, and excesses yielded to respectability.

The Reformation gave the people ideas formerly reserved for the few. It gave a better opportunity for personal development, and it laid the foundation for separation of church and state. Wherever the Reformation raised its ensign, there political freedom and education flourished.

As a final verdict upon the benefits accruing from this era it may be said that "almost all the fruitful thoughts of Europe for the last four centuries, even in Roman Catholic countries, are direct or indirect results of the Reformation."

THUMBNAIL BIOGRAPHIES

LOUIS DE BERQUIN (1490-1529), royal counselor, nobleman, lay Reformer, and France's first Protestant martyr, was born near Artois. Introduced to Protestantism by Erasmus and Lefèvre, he taught the Bible at the court and by going from house to house near his childhood home. His greatest ambition was to make France a Protestant nation, but the churchmen became incensed at his translations of some of the writings of Erasmus and Luther, as well as at his own works. He had declared Christ the only way of salvation, and had ridiculed celibacy, the invocation of Mary, and monkish ignorance. Three times he was imprisoned, twice to be released at the intercession of Margaret, sister of Francis I; but the last time no one could save him. He was executed in Paris by strangulation and burning.

THEODORE BEZA (1519-1605), Reformer, educator, theologian, author, leader of the French Huguenots, and Calvin's friend, was born in Vezelai, France, of noble lineage. A French Protestant refugee, he taught Greek at the academy at Lausanne, Switzerland, and became the first rector of the university at Geneva. As the religious head of the Huguenots, he represented them at numerous councils, conclaves, and colloquies, and thereby procured soul liberty for the Reformed churches in France. He made a brilliant defense of the symbolic presence in the eucharist before the Colloquy of Poissy. As a poet and prose writer he ranked among the best. He is also known for having discovered the ancient Bible manuscript known as Codex D, which he presented to the University of Cambridge. As Calvin's successor he made Geneva the headquarters of Continental Protestantism and softened the rigorous discipline of his predecessor. He died in Geneva.

THOMAS BILNEY (ca. 1495-1531), priest, Reformer, devotee of the Bible and prayer, leader of the Protestants at Cambridge, and the father of the English Reformation, was born at Norwich, England. By personal appeals he convinced others that Christ saved from sin; many eminent scholars who later became Reformers owed their conversion to his tact and zeal. He denounced the worship of saints and relics and the profligacy of popes and priests. After arrest he recanted under pressure from his friends, but later he made amends for his weakness. He met death serenely at the stake in Norfolk, England.

ROBERT BROWNE (*ca.* 1550-1633), founder of the Brownists or Separatists, and "the first Englishman to express the Anabaptist doctrine of complete separation of church and state," was born near Stamford, England. Originally a Presbyterian, he later maintained that the power of the church resided in the membership rather than in the ministry. To him doctrine meant less than polity; he opposed Anglicanism and Presbyterianism alike. He established a church on democratic principles at Middelburg, in Zeeland, but with its disintegration he went to Scotland. He suffered many imprisonments, and finally excommunication. Discouraged and defeated, he returned to Anglicanism, and for forty years he served Achurch at Northampton, where he died.

HEINRICH BULLINGER (1504-75), successor to Zwingli in Zurich, the second founder of the German Reformed Church, and mediator between Zwinglians and Lutherans on the doctrine of the eucharist, was born at Bremgarten, Switzerland. After Zwingli's death he saved the Swiss Reformation from complete collapse. He influenced England's Reformation more than did any other Continental Reformer, and the Second Helvetic Confession, one of his more than one hundred separate works, became the bond uniting the scattered members of the evangelical Reformed Churches in all countries. It ranks among the foremost of Reformed Church confessions. Bullinger has been termed a "common shepherd of all Christian churches." Death came in Zurich as the result of calculus.

MARTIN BUCER (1491-1551), German theologian, Strasbourg Reformer, and author, was born at Schlettstadt, Germany. Noted for his untiring attempts at peacemaking and conciliating divergent Protestant theology, he took a position on the Lord's Supper midway between the consubstantiation of Luther and the symbolism of Zwingli. He, with his associate Capito, prepared the *Tetrapolitana*, a creed for four Protestant cities. In 1547 he took refuge in England, where he became regius divinity professor at Cambridge. The Anglican ritual owes much to his influence. He died in England. Under Queen Mary his body was exhumed, tried for heresy, and burned; but Queen Elizabeth ordered all honors reinstated to him.

MILES COVERDALE (1488-1568), priest, preacher, Reformer, and translator of the first complete Bible printed in the English language, was born in Yorkshire in the district of Cover-dale. Under Thomas Cromwell's patronage his version of the Bible, a translation of translations, came out in 1535, but it was not officially accepted by the English government. In 1539 he brought forth, with Grafton and Whitchurch the printers, the *Great Bible,* sometimes called the Cranmer Bible. He also translated many other works. His Puritan tendencies and his opposition to the wearing of vestments lost him the appointment to several bishoprics. He died in London.

JOHN CALVIN (1509-64), scholar, author, Reformer, and organizer, was born at Noyon, France. He fled to Switzerland as French persecution grew too strong, and eventually made his home in Geneva, where he became the real leader of the Genevan republic. As a theologian he stands pre-eminent; his tenets attained greater international significance and acceptance than did those of any other Reformer. His name became synonymous with the doctrine of predestination. He believed, among other things, in the symbolic meaning of the Lord's Supper, salvation by faith, and the absolute and exclusive divine authority of the Scriptures. His polity of church organization gave the laity a voice in its government and used the secular power to enforce the doctrines and laws of the church. He died in Geneva.

THOMAS CARTWRIGHT (1535-1603), Puritan leader, brilliant Latin, Greek, and Hebrew scholar, was born in Hertfordshire, England. An eloquent preacher and doctor of divinity, he opposed vestments, hierarchical titles, and all ceremonies which savored of Catholicism, and advocated the adoption of the presbyterian system of church government. He wrote the Second Admonition to Parliament, a request to adopt Puritan ideas in church government. Suspected of having a part in the Marprelate controversy, he was imprisoned for two years. He died at his home in Warwick, where the earl of Leicester had made him the master of the hospital.

JOHN COLET (*ca.* 1466-1519), one of the trio of Oxford Reformers, noted preacher, and leader of the English Renaissance, was born in London of noble stock. He founded the famous St. Paul's School, and the influence of his educational leadership still remains in England's secondary middle-class system. As dean of St. Paul's Cathedral, he exposed worldliness wherever he found it. He advocated personal religion, sincere piety, and the Bible as the ultimate rule of faith; and he considered church traditions and the teachings of scholastic divines as of minor importance. His high favor with Henry VIII protected him from condemnation under heresy charges, and made it possible for him to die peacefully in his home in London.

GASPARD DE COLIGNY (1519-72), nobleman, statesman, admiral of France, military expert, and Huguenot leader, was born at Chatillon-sur-Loing. He is noted as the pioneer in establishing colonies of Huguenots in the New World and as the defender of Saint-Quentin. He accepted Protestantism while in prison in the Netherlands, after which he repeatedly pleaded the Huguenot cause at assemblies, colloquies, and other national gatherings. To make France a Protestant nation he sought to win the confidence of Catherine de' Medici, but her jealousy of his power over her son, King Charles IX, led to his assassination in Paris as the first victim of the St. Bartholomew Massacre.

THOMAS CRANMER (1489-1556), educator, ambassador, author, and archbishop of Canterbury, was born in Aslacton, England. He gained international prominence by obtaining Henry VIII's divorce from Catherine. He promoted the translation and circulation of the Bible, opposed the Act of the Six Articles, won Edward VI to Protestantism, and invited Continental churchmen to aid England's Reformation. Upon him fell the responsibility of working out the details of ecclesiastical reform in England, and to this end he wrote and published numerous books dealing with dogma and ritual. His high status and able pen aided materially in freeing England from papal jurisdiction. Mary's accession led to his arrest, trial, and condemnation for heresy. He recanted, only to abjure his recantation before going to the stake at Oxford. There he faced death calmly, thereby further aiding the cause against papal reaction, to the end that England might become Protestant.

FRANCISCO DE ENZINAS (*ca.* 1520-50), scholar, Reformer, and brother of the first Protestant martyr in Italy, was born of a noble family in Burgos, Spain. He studied at Paris and later at Wittenberg, where Melanchthon inspired him to translate the Greek New Testament into Spanish. Imprisoned after he presented a copy for approval to Emperor Charles V, he escaped to Germany. Upon Cranmer's invitation he went to England and taught Greek two years at the University of Cambridge. He died in Augsburg shortly after he returned to the Continent.

DESIDERIUS ERASMUS (1466-1536), member of the Oxford Reformers, Humanist, rationalist, and priest, was born near Rotterdam in the Netherlands. He desired a reform within the church and opposed extremes of all kinds. Much of what the church sanctioned he denounced. He held the clergy up to ridicule, and considered many church practices irrelevant, rather than sinful. He also urged simplicity in Christian living, and a return to the sources for Scriptural study. His Greek New Testament translation constituted one of the greatest boons to Reformation progress; it was the ember which lighted the candle of reforming zeal. He died at Basel, Switzerland.

WILLIAM FAREL (1489-1565), professor, Reformer, and audacious apostle to Switzerland, was born near Gap in southeastern France. He preached under Bern's jurisdiction in many of the Swiss villages and laid the foundation for Calvin's reform at Geneva. Laudable in purpose, he was weak in method, moderation, and organizing ability. An impetuous evangelist who found happiness amidst danger, he denounced clerical abuses, moral laxity of the clergy, the mass, veneration of images and saints, and church tradition. He accepted the Bible as the rule of faith. He founded schools and hospitals. He died in his home in Neufchatel, Switzerland, where he served the Reformed societies.

JOHN FOXE (1517-87), Nonconformist preacher, author, and visionary, was born in Boston, in Lincolnshire, one hundred miles north of London. His chief claim to fame rests on his *Acts and Monuments,* a history of the Reformation popularly called *The Book of Martyrs,* which is unexcelled as religious propaganda. It went through many editions and was placed alongside the Great Bible in every college hall, university, and parish church in England to become the most popular reading of the day and for centuries after. Foxe was noted for his charitableness, tolerance, and his opposition to the wearing of the surplice. He died in London.

JOHN FRITH (1503-33), martyr, an associate with Tyndale in the translation of the Bible, and the first in England to expound the doctrine of the symbolic presence in the eucharist, was born at Westerham, Kent. He escaped prison at Oxford and went to Marburg, where he translated Hamilton's *Patrick's Places* from Latin to English, and later joined Tyndale in Holland. He returned to England without Henry VIII's permission, in 1532, and went to Reading, where he was put in stocks for vagabondage. In London he wrote a treatise on the sacraments which incensed Sir Thomas More, who had him captured and imprisoned. He was tried for his denial of purgatory and transubstantiation, and later he was burned at Smithfield.

PATRICK HAMILTON (*ca.* 1504-28), preacher, and first Reformer and martyr of the Scottish Reformation, was born of Scotland's royalty either at Stonehouse or at Kincavel. At the University of Paris he came under Erasmus's influence, and later his association with Luther and Melanchthon at Wittenberg, and with Francis Lambert at Marburg, increased his anti-Catholic tendencies. Back in Scotland he taught at the University of St. Andrews. His treatise, *Patrick's Places,* became the cornerstone of Protestant theology in Scotland and England. His reforming zeal brought him afoul of Archbishop Beaton, who connived at his apprehension and subsequent death, a lingering one, at the stake near St. Andrews. As a Scottish Reformer he was second in rank only to John Knox.

JOHN HOOPER (*ca.* 1500-55), Hebraist, leader of a reforming group, and bishop of Gloucester and Worcester, was born in Somerset, England. Puritanism, in its embryonic phase, claims him as its parent. His intense scruples, and implacable temperament made him the foremost opponent to the wearing of vestments and the observance of Catholic Church ritual as practiced by the evolving Church of England. His desire for a better-prepared clergy led him to institute a training course for the ministers of his diocese. He opposed the Act of the Six Articles. Because he married, denied papal authority and the bodily presence in the eucharist, and opposed the wearing of vestments, he was condemned to death at the stake in Gloucester, England.

JOHN HUSS (ca. 1373-1415), Reformer, educator, national hero, and beloved for his vernacular discourses in Bethlehem Chapel, was born in Bohemia. A tireless Bible student, he fearlessly supported Wycliffe's views. He decried the moral laxity of the clergy, denied Peter as the church's foundation, and declared the Scriptures to be the only rule of faith. Masses and indulgences he condemned as worthless, and he maintained that individual rights were not subject to church regulations. The Council of Constance convicted him as a heretic and sentenced him to death at the stake. He was executed in Constance.

JEROME OF PRAGUE (ca. 1365-1416), Humanist, patriot, and renowned lecturer at universities and churches, was born of noble parentage in Bohemia. A layman of international fame and wide learning, he opposed the sale of indulgences and stigmatized the clergy for its moral corruption. While at the Council of Constance, where he went to aid Huss, he was apprehended and tried for endorsing the teachings of Wycliffe, and condemned to death at the stake. He recanted from fear; but, later, regretting his irresolution, he calmly faced death at Constance.

JOHN KNOX (1505-72), Reformer, chaplain to the English king, and a Calvinist, was born near Edinburgh, Scotland. He preached effectively in England and Scotland, and on the Continent. He served on the commission that compiled the English *Book of Common Prayer*. Fearless in his denunciations, he opposed the pope, mass, the Lord's Supper in one kind, and other Catholic usages. His audacious interviews with Mary, Queen of Scots, made him a glamorous figure in Reformation history. As organizer of the church in Scotland, he is accorded by history the place of a great national hero who by his dynamic, courageous personality established a degree of unity in his country at a time of extreme religious and political chaos. He died tranquilly in Edinburgh.

JOHN LASKI (1499-1560), nobleman, scholar, Reformer, co-ordinator, and organizer, was born at Lask, near Warsaw, Poland. Intended for the primateship of his country, he renounced his wealth, rank, and prospects of advancement to preach the Protestant tenets in the Netherlands. There he organized the Reformed Church, and Emden became known as the "Northern Geneva." He preached that God's grace was free to all. Later in England he was the first to institute the presbyterian form of church government for the 3,000 foreign Protestant refugees in London. After an absence of eighteen years he returned to his home country to organize the Reformed Church in Poland, but he died in Pinczow before he achieved his goal.

HUGH LATIMER (ca. 1485-1555), bishop, Reformer, noted preacher, was born in Thurcaston, England. He fostered practical Christianity, upheld the authority of the Scriptures, and preached Jesus as a personal Saviour. He decried human traditions by opposing worship of saints and denying purgatory. In opposition to the Six Articles, he resigned the bishopric of Worcester. Several times he was imprisoned for his faith, and once he recanted. After Henry VIII's repudiation of papal authority, he became one of the king's principal counselors, whereupon he supposedly urged the monarch to provide English Bibles for the people. Mary imprisoned him for denying transubstantiation. Tied to the same stake with Ridley, he died a martyr's death at Oxford.

JACQUES LEFEVRE (ca. 1452-1536), Humanist, educator, brilliant leader of French intellectuals, translator of Scriptures, and one of the Meaux Reformers, was born at Etaples, France. One of the first Reformers to express belief in justification by faith and the supremacy of the Scriptures, he rebuked the dissolute lives of the clergy. He also denied the efficacy of works, indulgences, and pilgrimages as a means of salvation. By his love for Christ he exerted a powerful influence on future Reformers. During his declining years he became tutor to the French royal household, and king's librarian. He died at Nérac, France.

MARTIN LUTHER (1483-1546), Augustinian monk, university professor, eminent Reformer characterized by clear thinking, courage, originality, and a pioneering spirit, was born in Eisleben, Germany. By posting his ninety-five theses against indulgences on the Wittenberg church door he made his rupture with the papacy inevitable, and his determination to answer the summons to appear at the Diet of Worms to defend his position before the emperor made him a national hero. His translation of the Bible into the German language ranks him among the masters of German prose. The doctrine of justification by faith, made popular by him, became the battle cry of the Reformation. Failing in health for several years, he died in the town of his birth.

PETER MARTYR (1500-62), Augustinian prior and vicar-general of his order, public preacher, Reformer, and able disputant, was born of well-to-do parents in Florence, Italy. As a disciple of Valdés he preached the doctrine of salvation by faith, both at Naples and at Lucca. When cited for heresy by the Inquisition, he fled, later to become Bucer's close associate at Strasbourg. Upon the invitation of Edward VI and Cranmer he went to England to become regius divinity professor at Oxford, where by his moderation and skill he influenced English episcopacy. He believed that the real presence in the eucharist was determined not by an undeviating fiat but by the faith of the recipient. He ably defended the Protestant cause at the Colloquy of Poissy in 1561. He died of a fever at Zurich.

PHILIPP MELANCHTHON (1497-1560), intimate of Luther, Humanist, Reformer, scholar, theologian, linguist, and professor, was born at Bretten, Germany. He won the support of the learned by moderation and sincerity and by cogency of argument. He charmed even Erasmus by his consummate versatility. Famous as the author of the Augsburg Confession, he displayed exceptional ability in organizing German ecclesiastical polity. He was also the cofounder with Luther of the modern German educational system. Affirming supremacy of the Bible and justification by faith, he denounced

Communion in one kind, celibacy, and the mass. He died of a cold at his home in Wittenberg, Germany.

ANDREW MELVILLE (1545-1622), Reformer, educator, and archfoe of prelacy, was born in Montrose, Scotland. Endowed with intellectual insight, scholarly precision, and an intrepid nature, he reorganized Scotland's educational system to make the Scottish universities equal those on the Continent. His opposition to episcopacy and his organization of Presbyterian Church government, as exemplified in the *Second Book of Discipline*, led to personal clashes with the king, who expelled him as head of St. Andrews, and later sanctioned a prison term in England. The king refused permission to have him return to Scotland, and Melville died in France while occupying the chair of divinity at Sedan.

BERNARDINO OCHINO (1487-1564), Capuchin monk, Reformer, and ascetic, was born in Siena to become Italy's greatest evangelist of the Reformation. As Valdés's disciple, his influence extended throughout Italy as he preached salvation by faith, and ridiculed the foibles of the Catholic Church. The Inquisition cited him to appear at Rome in 1542, but instead he, with Peter Martyr, escaped to Switzerland. He preached to Italian congregations at Geneva, Augsburg, and London. He also wrote prolifically; and one of his works, interpreted as advocating polygamy and anti-Trinitarianism, forced him to flee from place to place. He died in exile and disgrace in Slavkov, Moravia.

AONIO PALEARIO (1500-70), philosopher, public orator, professor, author, and martyr, was born of noble parentage in Veroli, Italy. He, too, was a disciple of Valdés and taught justification by faith to his students in the universities at Siena, Lucca, and Milan. He is thought to be the author of *Benefits of Christ's Death,* the greatest piece of religious writing to come out of the Italian Reformation. Repeatedly cited for heresy, he at first escaped execution by his eloquent defense; but in 1568 the Inquisition arrested, imprisoned, and frequently tortured him. Two years later he was hanged and burned in Rome.

OLAVUS PETRI (1493-1552), "Sweden's Luther," trusted adviser to King Gustavus Vasa, preacher, educator, and author, was born in Orebro, Sweden. When he returned from the University at Wittenberg he opposed monastic life, the mass, purgatory, invocation of saints and the Virgin, and preached salvation by faith. While serving as secretary of the city of Stockholm and preacher at the St. Nicholas Cathedral, he made the first official attack on the Roman Catholic Church to appear in print. He also helped translate the New Testament into Swedish and wrote a manual of service, several catechisms, homiletical treatises, and the first hymnbook in Sweden. His influence upon Sweden's Reformation was unequaled. He died in Stockholm, and lies buried in the St. Nicholas Cathedral.

NICHOLAS RIDLEY (*ca.* 1500-55), educator, polemicist, bishop of Rochester, was born in Northumberland, England. He helped establish Protestantism at Cambridge, and assisted in the preparation of the first English prayer book. He was also instrumental in removing England from papal jurisdiction. Denouncing the theory that designated Peter as the rock, he opposed Communion in one kind, mass, pilgrimages, celibacy, and the Latin service. He opposed Mary's succession. While in prison he continued, by writing letters and treatises, to aid the establishment of Protestantism in England. With Latimer he died at the stake at Oxford.

JOHN ROGERS (*ca.* 1500-55), scholar, priest, Reformer, author, editor, martyr, was born near Birmingham, England. The first to write a Bible commentary and an English concordance, he was also the first to compile and edit an authorized version of the English Bible, known as the Thomas Matthew Bible, taken from Tyndale's unfinished manuscript. As a nonconformist he preached against the mass, the celibacy of the clergy, and the recognition of the pope or the monarch as head of the church. His sermon at Paul's Cross three days after Bloody Mary's accession resulted in his becoming the first Protestant martyr under her reign. He died at the stake at Smithfield, in London.

GIROLAMO SAVONAROLA (1452-98), Dominican monk, author, mystic, and great preacher, was born in Ferrara, Italy. Believing patriotism akin to Christianity, he attempted to achieve for Florence, the city in which he served as prior of the San Marco monastery, a democratic society in a pure church directed by an honorable clergy. A devoted student of the Bible, he applied the prophecies of the Scriptures to current events, and he predicted dire consequences upon Rome for its worldliness as he denounced popes, priests, princes, and paupers impartially. He maintained the supremacy of God's word over the word of the church. His constant diatribes brought excommunication, and a threat of interdict turned Florence against him. His attempt by intrigue to unseat the pope resulted in his being captured, tortured, and hanged in Florence. He founded schools and influenced the great artists of the Renaissance.

MENNO SIMONS (*ca.* 1500-60), priest, Reformer in the Netherlands, and strict disciplinarian, was born in Witmarsum, Friesland. For twenty-five years he preached and traveled incessantly, to gather the later group of Anabaptists, named Mennonites, together into one body. His key doctrine was "believers' " baptism, on the basis that infants were unable to express faith in Christ. He pioneered in the field of religious liberty as he advocated separation of church and state. He also opposed bearing arms, taking of oaths, and capital punishment. At the time of his death at Oldesloe, Holstein, he had assembled a large following and a considerable fortune.

HANS TAUSEN (1494-1561), priest, preacher, hymn writer, "the Luther of Denmark," and her greatest Reformer, was born at Birkende, on the island of Fyn. As royal chaplain he drew immense crowds in Copenhagen. In 1530 he presented an independent confession of faith, of forty-three articles, a counterpart of the Augsburg Confession. He stipulated the Bible alone as sufficient for salvation, the eucharist a commemoration of Christ's death, the Holy Spirit the Third Person of the Godhead; and purgatory, monastic life, indulgences, mass, and celibacy of priests he declared to be contrary to Scripture. He was named one of the seven superintendents over the realm; he shared in the construction of the ecclesiastical constitution; and he served for nearly twenty years as bishop of Ribe, until he died.

WILLIAM TYNDALE (*ca.* 1483-1536), Reformer and linguist, was born in England on the Welsh border. His translation of the

Scriptures into the English tongue placed him among the renowned in scholarship and literary ability. Because of religious persecution in England, he went to the Continent. As a guide to his work he used the translations of Luther and Erasmus. His Bible became the basis for the Authorized Version and served as the fulcrum on which the English Reformation balanced. He was captured and imprisoned on the charge of advocating justification by faith, opposing the doctrines of purgatory and the invocation of saints, and was executed by strangulation and burning near the castle of Vilvorde, in the Netherlands.

JUAN DE VALDES (*ca.* 1500-41), scion of royalty, mystic, Reformer, member of the courts of emperor and pope, and master of Castilian prose, was born in Cuenca, Spain. He fled the Spanish Inquisition, ultimately making his home in Naples, Italy, where he became the center of an aristocratic Protestant circle, drawing to himself the finest and most intellectual of Italy's noble men and women. He ridiculed the invocation of saints, pilgrimages, purgatory, and mass; and he censured the pope for his worldliness and for the greed of the church. He believed that knowledge of God could be obtained through prayer and meditation, that faith alone atoned for sins, and that the Bible constituted man's guide to salvation. He died in Naples before the Italian Inquisition dispersed his followers to spread his influence throughout the European Continent.

GUSTAVUS VASA (1496-1560), Protestant king of Sweden, was born of noble parentage in Lindholmen. Traitorously imprisoned as a hostage at the Battle of Brakyrka in 1518, he returned to Dalecarlia after the Massacre of Stockholm in 1520 and aroused the peasants to revolt against Denmark. When elected king in 1523 he made the Lutheran Petri brothers and Laurentius Andreae his counselors, and in 1527 succeeded by edict in establishing Protestantism as the religion of the country. He demoted the bishops, confiscated church property, and established a presbyterian form of church government, but with himself as supreme head. He was crowned in 1528 and became known as "one of the best and wisest princes." He died in Stockholm.

GEORGE WISHART (*ca.* 1513-46), Reformer, scholar, teacher, preacher, and forerunner of John Knox, was born near Montrose, Scotland. He was among the first to teach Greek in his native land. He also taught at Cambridge, where he was lauded for his piety and thoroughness of instruction. His chief claim to fame is his popularizing of Calvinistic Protestantism in the kirk. He affirmed that salvation comes only by faith in Christ. He opposed auricular confession, infant baptism, prayer to the saints, and celibacy. Purgatory he declared nonexistent. When driven from the churches, he preached wherever he could gather a crowd. He was arrested, tried, and condemned for heresy, and executed by hanging and burning near St. Andrews castle.

JOHN WYCLIFFE (*ca.* 1320-84), authority on canon and civil law, consultant to Parliament, king's chaplain, Reformer, and founder of the Lollards, was born in Yorkshire, England. He based his first opposition to the papacy on its political activities. To Parliament he recommended that the fines assessed by the pope against the realm under King John be abrogated. Later he attacked the doctrine of transubstantiation and the ecclesiastical supremacy claimed by the pope. He affirmed his belief in salvation by faith. His translation of the Bible gained him literary prominence. Papal pressure expelled him from his university position, but was unable to effect his excommunication. He died of a paralytic stroke in his parish at Lutterworth, England.

ULRICH ZWINGLI (1484-1531), Reformer, organizer, founder of Swiss Protestantism, was born in Wildhaus, Switzerland. Displeased with the unlettered state of the priesthood, he established a theological school to assure a better-trained clergy. He opposed the sale of indulgences and the doctrines of transubstantiation and celibacy. He accepted justification by faith and the authority of the Scriptures. At Zurich, where he was rector of Great Minster, he reorganized the community according to Scriptural ideas, with the assistance of civil law. His advocacy of political alliances to gain religious ends brought about his death. As the result of his efforts to force Protestantism upon the Catholic cantons in Switzerland, war broke out, with resultant victory to the Catholic forces; and he died in the battle of Kappel, in Switzerland.

BIBLIOGRAPHY

GENERAL REFERENCES

Americana, The Encyclopedia.
Britannica, The Encyclopedia, 11th edition.
Catholic Encyclopedia, The.
Cambridge Modern History, The.
Columbia Encyclopedia, The.
Dictionary of National Biography, The.
Encyclopedia of Religion and Ethics.
McClintock and Strong, *Cyclopedia of Biblical, Theological, and Ecclesiastical Literature.*
Schaff-Herzog Encyclopedia of Religious Knowledge, The New.

BOOKS

BAX, E. BELFORT. *Rise and Fall of the Anabaptists,* 1903.

BEARD, CHARLES. *The Reformation of the Sixteenth Century in Its Relation to Modern Thought and Knowledge,* 1885.

BENRATH, KARL. *Bernardino Ochino.* Translated from the German by Helen Zimmern, 1877.

BERGENDOFF, CONRAD. *Olavus Petri and the Ecclesiastical Transformation in Sweden* (1521-52), 1928.

BERSIER, EUGENE. *Coligny; The Earlier Life of the Great Huguenot,* 1884.

BEZOLD, FRIEDRICH VON. *Geschichte der Deutschen Reformation,* 1890.

BIGG, CHARLES. *Wayside Sketches in Ecclesiastical History,* 1906.

BLUNT, J. J. *A Sketch of the Reformation in England,* 1840.

BOEHMER, HEINRICH. *Luther and the Reformation in the Light of Modern Research,* 1906.

BROWN, G. K. *Italy and the Reformation to 1550,* 1933.

BROWN, JOHN. *The English Puritans,* 1910.

BROWNE, ROBERT. "A Treatise of the Reformation Without Tarrying for Any," in *Old South Leaflets,* No. 100.

BURLEIGH, LORD BALFOUR OF. *The Rise and Development of Presbyterianism in Scotland,* 1911.

BURNETT, GILBERT. *The History of the Reformation of the Church in England*, 7 vols., 1865.

BURRAGE, CHAMPLIN. *The Early English Dissenters*, 2 vols., 1912.

BUTTERWORTH, CHARLES C. *The Literary Lineage of the King James Bible*, 1941.

CHAMBERS, R. W. *Man's Unconquerable Mind*, 1939.

CHAPLIN, F. K. *The Effects of the Reformation on Ideals of Life and Conduct*, 1927.

CHESTER, JOSEPH LEMUEL. *John Rogers*, 1861.

CUNNINGHAM, WILLIAM. *The Reformers, and the Theology of the Reformation*, 1862.

CHURCH, C. FREDRIC. *The Italian Reformers* (1534-64), 1932.

D'AUBIGNE, J. H. MERLE. *History of the Reformation in Europe in the Time of Calvin*, 8 vols., (Translated by L. R. Cates), 1878; *History of the Reformation of the Sixteenth Century*, 5 vols., (Translated by Henry Beveridge), 1845.

DEXTER, HENRY MARTYN. *The Congregationalism of the Last Three Hundred Years, as Seen in Its Literature*, 1880.

DEXTER, HENRY MARTIN, and MORTON DEXTER. *The England and Holland of the Pilgrims*, 1905.

FARMER, JAMES EUGENE. *The Rise of the Reformation in France*, 1897.

FAWCETT, MRS. HENRY. *Five Famous French Women*, no date.

FEBVRE, LUCIEN. *Martin Luther: A Destiny*, 1929.

FISHER, GEORGE P. *The Reformation*, 1906.

FOXE, JOHN. *Acts and Monuments*, 8 vols., (edited by S. R. Cottley with introduction by Canon Townsend), 1837-41; also *Book of Martyrs*, a condensation of *Acts and Monuments*.

FOX, PAUL. *The Reformation in Poland*, 1924.

FULLER, THOMAS. *The Church History of Britain*, 6 vols., 1845.

FUNCK-BRENTANO, FRANTZ. *Luther*, 1936.

GARDINER, S. R. *The Puritan Revolution* (1603-60), 1928.

GRANT, A. J. *A History of Europe 1494-1610*, 1931.

GRAY, CHARLES M. *Hugh Latimer and the Sixteenth Century*, 1950.

GUPPY, HENRY. *Miles Coverdale and the English Bible* (1488-1568), 1935.

HAILE, MARTIN. *Life of Reginald Pole*, 1910.

HARE, CHRISTOPHER. *Men and Women of the Italian Reformation*, no date.

HAUSER, LUDWIG. *The Period of the Reformation* (1517-1648), 1868.

HAYES, CARLTON J. H. *A Political and Cultural History of Modern Europe*, 2 vols., 1936.

HERRICK, S. E. *Some Heretics of Yesterday*, 1885.

HODGIN, E. STANTON. *The Faith of the Reformers*, 1914.

HOWIE, JOHN. *The Scots Worthies*, 1870.

HULME, EDWARD MASLIN. *The Renaissance, the Protestant Revolution, and the Catholic Reformation*, 1915.

HURST, JOHN F. *A Short History of the Reformation*, 1884.

JACKSON, SAMUEL MACAULEY. *Huldreich Zwingli*, 1901.

JONES, RUFUS M. *Spiritual Reformers in the Sixteenth and Seventeenth Centuries*, 1914.

Kirchen-Gesangbuch für Evangelisch-Lutherische Gemeinden, 1886.

KJAER, JENS CHRISTIAN. *History of the Church of Denmark*, 1945.

KNIGHT, SAMUEL. *Life of Colet*, 1823.

LATIMER, HUGH. *Works.*

LINDSAY, THOMAS M. *A History of the Reformation*, 2 vols., 1908-09.

LORIMER, PETER. *Patrick Hamilton*, 1857.

LUCAS, HENRY S. *The Renaissance and the Reformation*, 1934.

MARTI, OSCAR ALBERT. *Economic Causes of the Reformation in England*, 1929.

MACKINNON, JAMES. *Calvin and the Reformation*, 1936.

McCRIE, THOMAS. *Life of Andrew Melville*, 2 vols., 1824; *Life of John Knox*, 1813.

McGIFFERT, A. C. *Martin Luther, the Man and His Work*, 1911.

MISCIATTELLI, PIERO. *Savonarola*, 1929.

MONROE, WILL S. *Bohemia and the Czechs*, 1910.

MOZLEY, J. F. *John Foxe and His Book*, 1940; *William Tyndale*, 1937.

NEWMAN, ALBERT HENRY. *A Manual of Church History*, 2 vols., 1932.

PENNIMAN, JOSIAH H. *A Book About the English Bible*, 1919.

Ploetz' Epitome of History, (translated by William H. Tillinghast), 1925.

PLUMMER, ALFRED. *The Continental Reformation,* 1912.

POLLARD, A. F. *Thomas Cranmer,* 1904.

POWICKE, FREDRICK H. *Robert Browne, Pioneer of Modern Congregationalism,* 1910.

PRICE, IRA MAURICE. *The Ancestry of Our English Bible,* 1911.

RICHARD, JAMES WILLIAM. *Philipp Melanchthon,* 1907.

ROBINSON, J. H. *Readings in European History,* 1906.

SAMPLE, ROBERT F. *Beacon Lights of the Reformation,* 1889.

SANFORD, ELIAS B. *A History of the Reformation,* 1917.

SCHAFF, DAVID S. *John Huss, His Life, Teachings, and Death, after 500 Years,* 1915.

SCHAFF, PHILIP. *A History of the Christian Church,* vols. 6, 7, 1892.

SEEBOHM, E. *The Era of the Protestant Reformation,* 1894.

SEEBOHM, FREDERIC. *The Oxford Reformers,* 1887.

SELLEY, W. T., and A. C. KREY. *Medieval Foundations of Western Civilization,* no date.

SERGEANT, LEWIS. *John Wycliffe,* 1893.

SHAW, W. HUDSON. *Oxford Reformers.*

SHORT, RUTH GORDON. *Stories of the Reformation in England and Scotland,* 1944; *Stories of the Reformation in the Netherlands,* 1948.

SIME, WILLIAM. *A History of the Inquisition,* 1834.

SMITH, PRESERVED. *The Age of the Reformation,* 1920.

SPALDING, M. J. *The History of the Protestant Reformation,* 1875.

STALKER, JAMES. *John Knox,* 1905.

STOKES, GEORGE. *Lives of the British Reformers,* 1841.

VAN DYKE, PAUL. *The Age of Renascence,* 1906.

VEDDER, HENRY C. *The Reformation in Germany,* 1914.

VILLARI, P. *Life and Times of Girolamo Savonarola,* 2 vols., 1888.

WALKER, WILLISTON. *A History of the Christian Church,* 1922; *The Reformation,* 1912 (in ten epochs of church history); *John Calvin,* 1906.

WALMSLEY, LUKE S. *Fighters and Martyrs for the Freedom of the Faith,* 1912.

WHITE, ELLEN G. *The Great Controversy,* 1907.

WHITING, C. E. *Studies in English Puritanism* (1660-88), 1931.

WHITEHEAD, A. W. *Gaspard de Coligny*, 1904.
WIFFIN, BENJAMIN B. *Life and Writings of Juan de Valdés*, 1865.
WILKENS, C. A. *Spanish Protestants in the Sixteenth Century*, 1897.
WILLSON, THOMAS B. *Church and State in Norway*, 1903.
WRATISLAW, A. H. *John Hus*, 1882.

MAGAZINES

The Converted Catholic Magazine, January, 1949.